GREGORY MARDON
ADRIFT

HUMANOIDS

GREGORY MARDON
Writer & Artist

MARK BENCE
Translator

•

JERRY FRISSEN
Book Designer

ALEX DONOGHUE
& TIM PILCHER
U.S. Edition Editors

FABRICE GIGER
Publisher

Rights & Licensing - licensing@humanoids.com
Press and Social Media - pr@humanoids.com

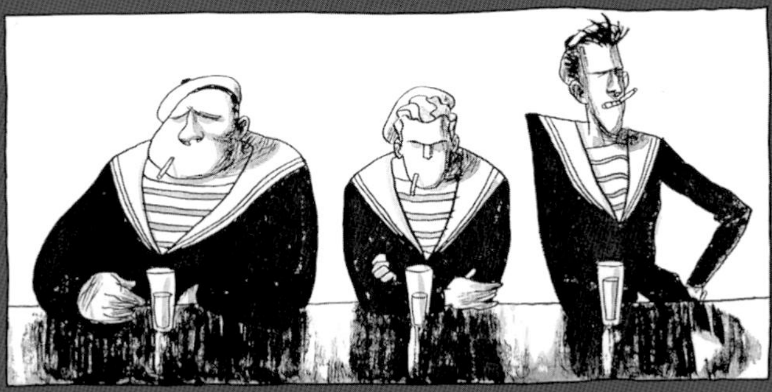

ADRIFT
This title is a publication of Humanoids, Inc. 8033 Sunset Blvd. #628, Los Angeles, CA 90046.

Originally published in French by Les Humanoïdes Associés (Paris, France).

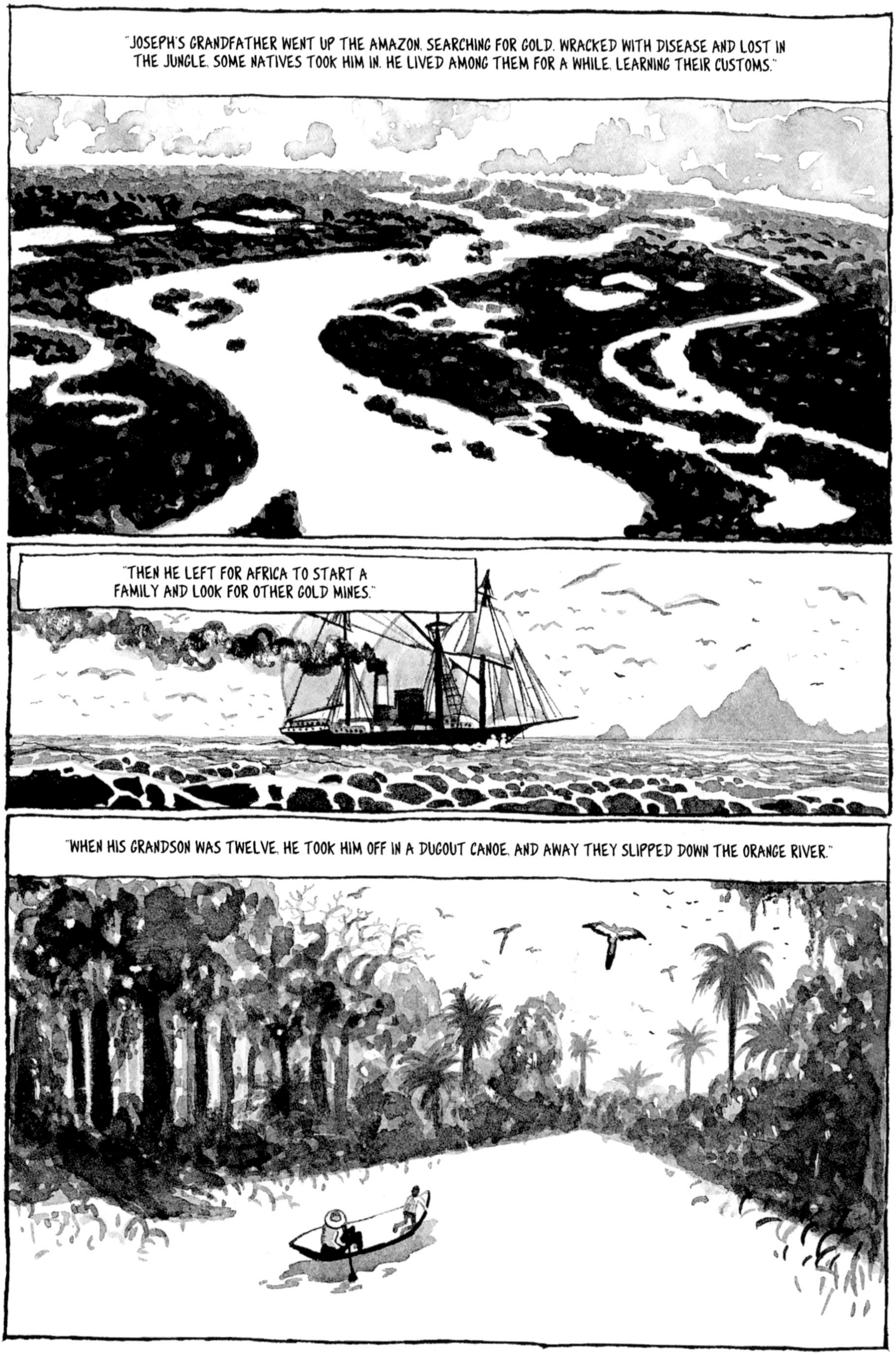
"JOSEPH'S GRANDFATHER WENT UP THE AMAZON, SEARCHING FOR GOLD. WRACKED WITH DISEASE AND LOST IN THE JUNGLE, SOME NATIVES TOOK HIM IN. HE LIVED AMONG THEM FOR A WHILE, LEARNING THEIR CUSTOMS."
"THEN HE LEFT FOR AFRICA TO START A FAMILY AND LOOK FOR OTHER GOLD MINES."
"WHEN HIS GRANDSON WAS TWELVE, HE TOOK HIM OFF IN A DUGOUT CANOE, AND AWAY THEY SLIPPED DOWN THE ORANGE RIVER."

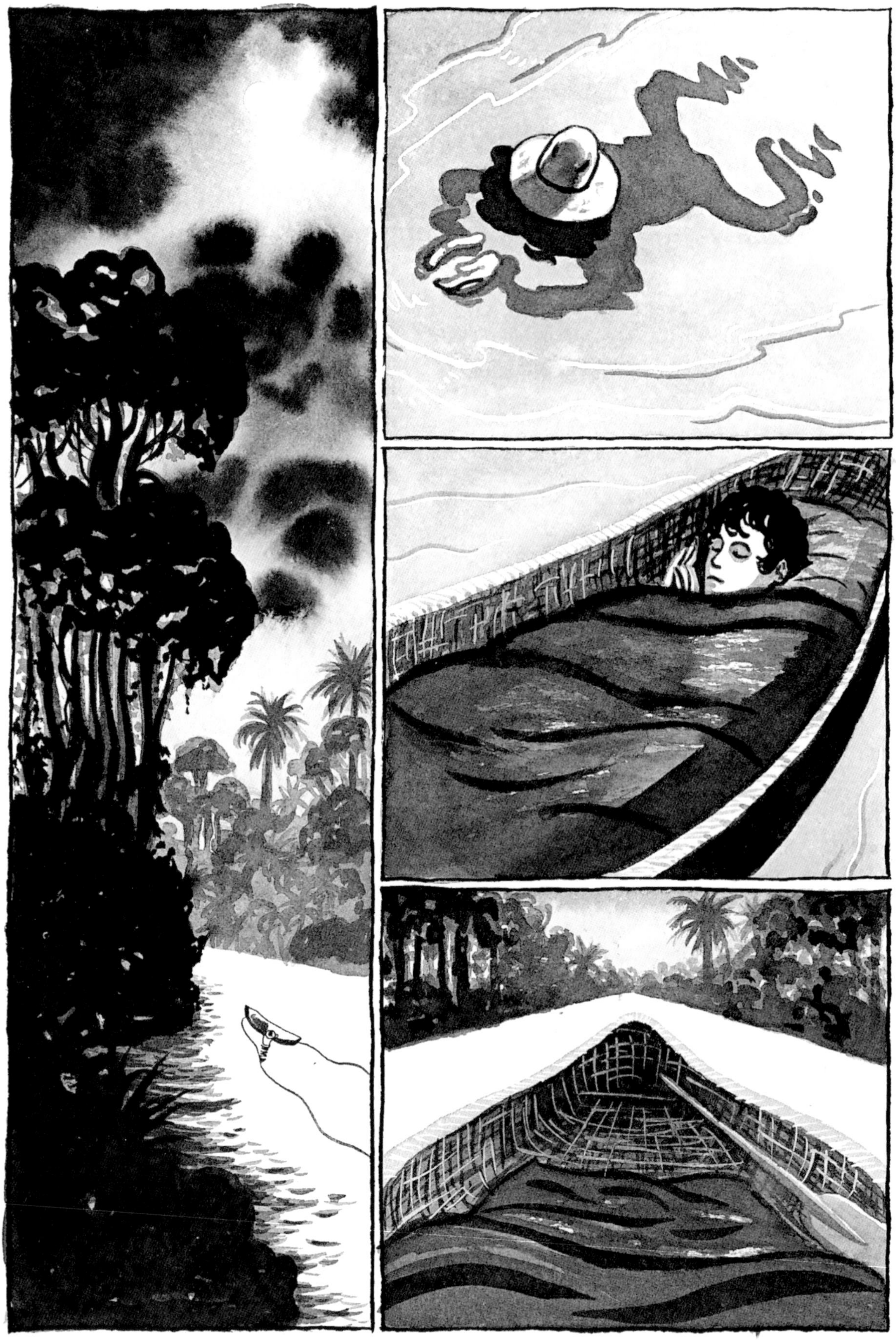

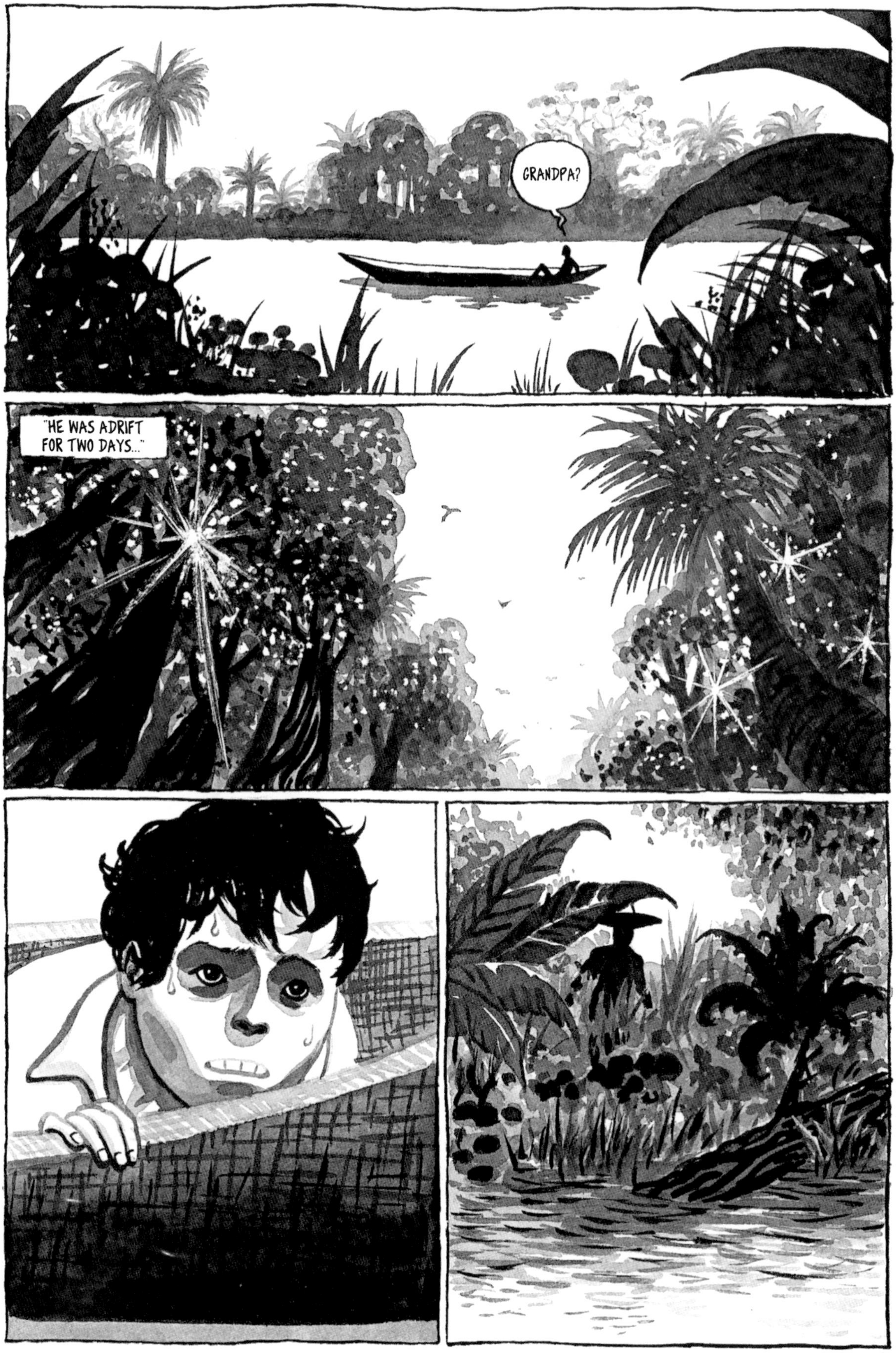
GRANDPA?
"HE WAS ADRIFT FOR TWO DAYS..."

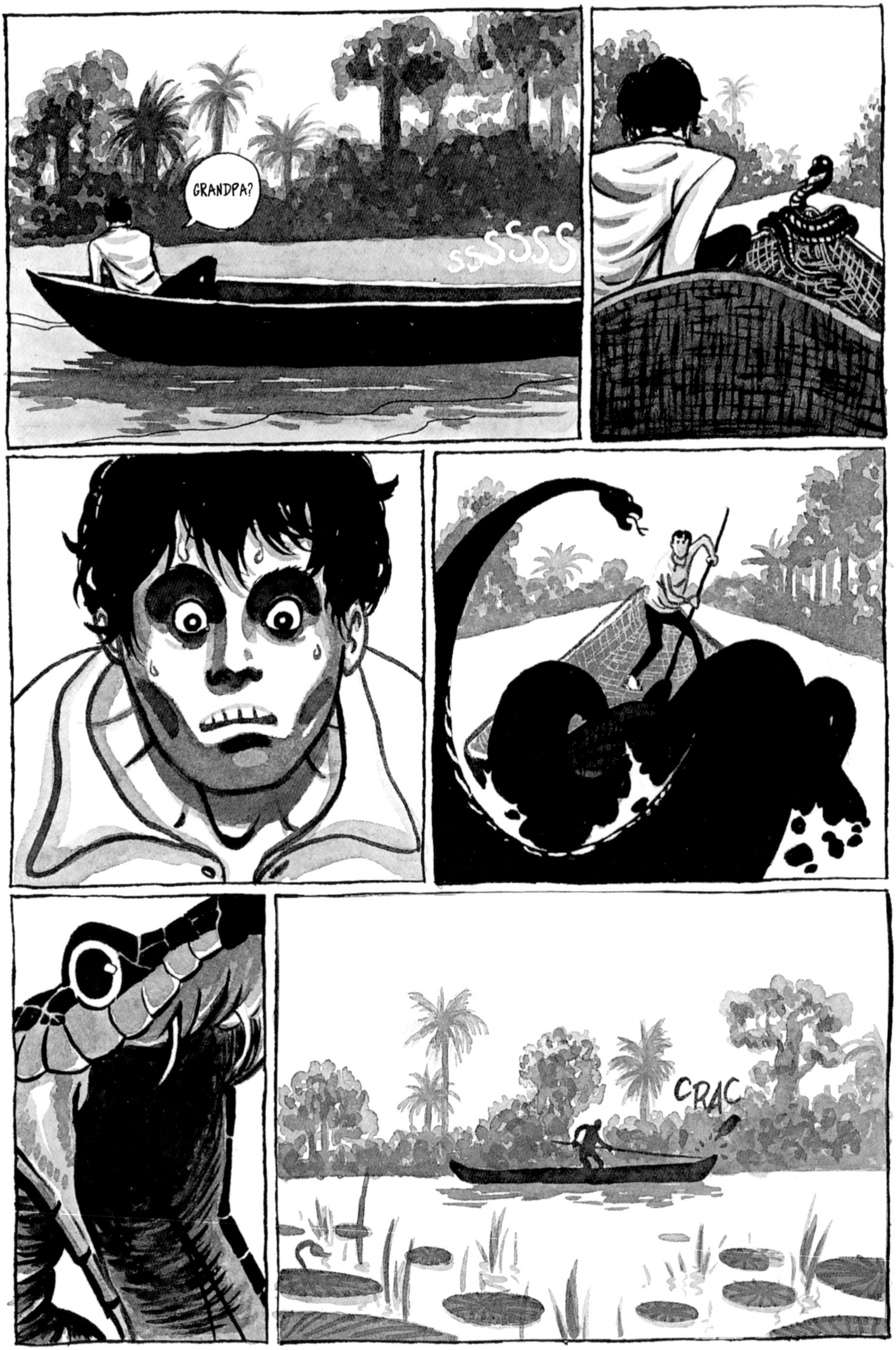
GRANDPA?
SSSSSS
CRAC

"THE HEAT, HUMIDITY, HUNGER, THIRST, AND FEAR QUICKLY DROVE HIM TO DELIRIUM. ATTACKED BY VARIOUS DEMONS, HE WAS PETRIFIED AT FIRST, THEN FOUGHT THEM OFF FIERCELY."

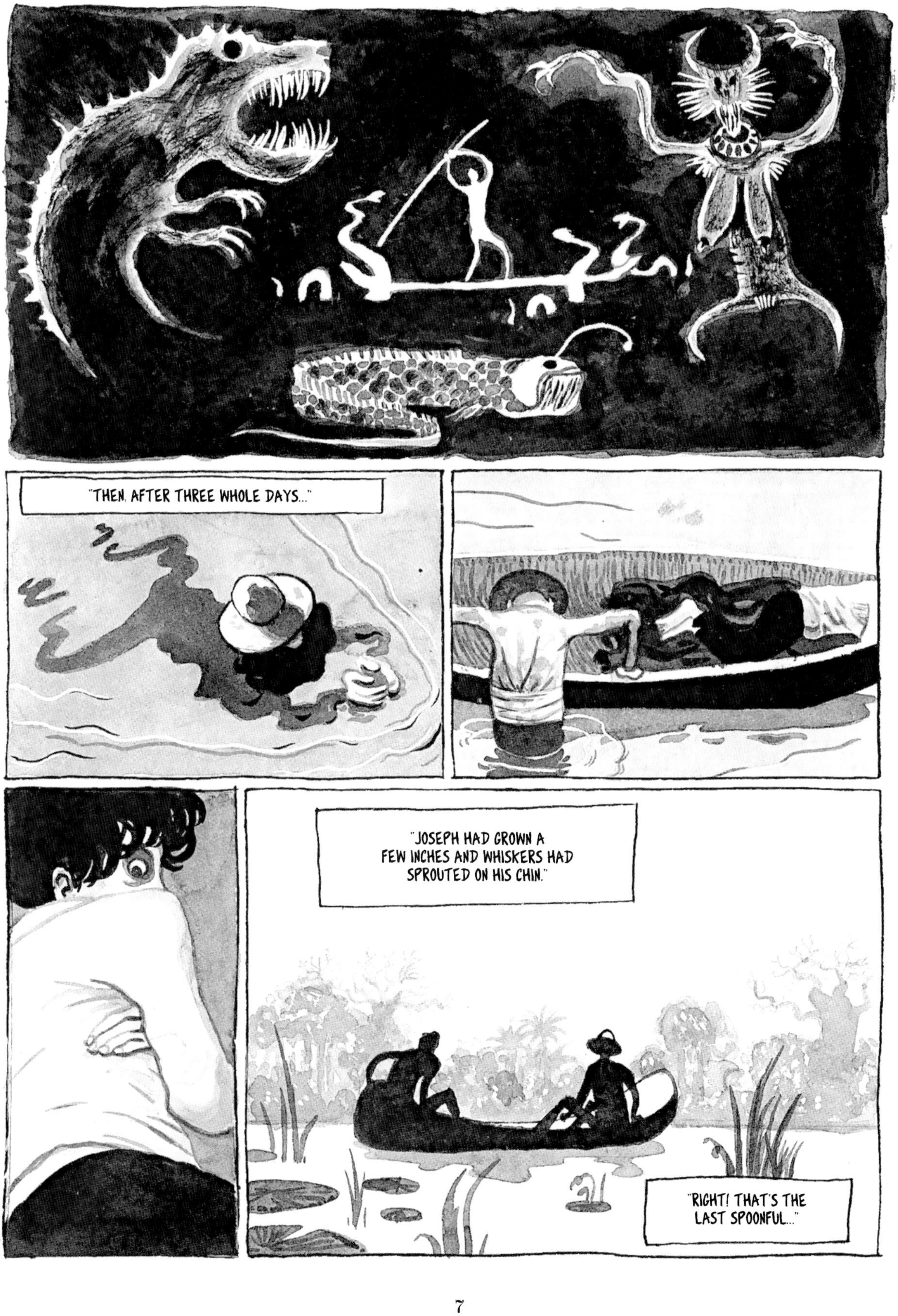
"THEN, AFTER THREE WHOLE DAYS..."
"JOSEPH HAD GROWN A FEW INCHES AND WHISKERS HAD SPROUTED ON HIS CHIN."
"RIGHT! THAT'S THE LAST SPOONFUL..."

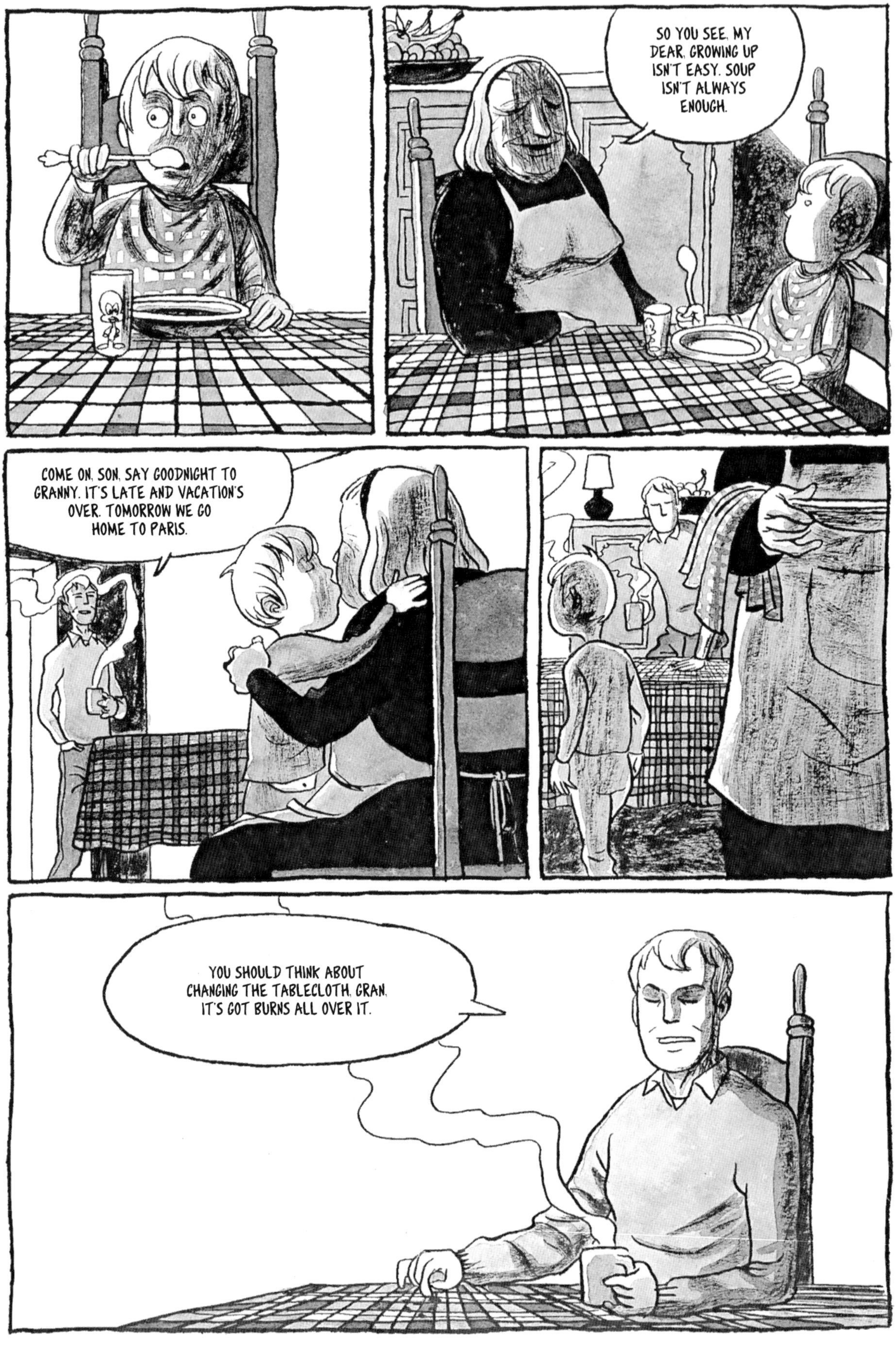

SO YOU SEE, MY DEAR, GROWING UP ISN'T EASY. SOUP ISN'T ALWAYS ENOUGH.
COME ON, SON, SAY GOODNIGHT TO GRANNY. IT'S LATE AND VACATION'S OVER. TOMORROW WE GO HOME TO PARIS.
YOU SHOULD THINK ABOUT CHANGING THE TABLECLOTH, GRAN. IT'S GOT BURNS ALL OVER IT.

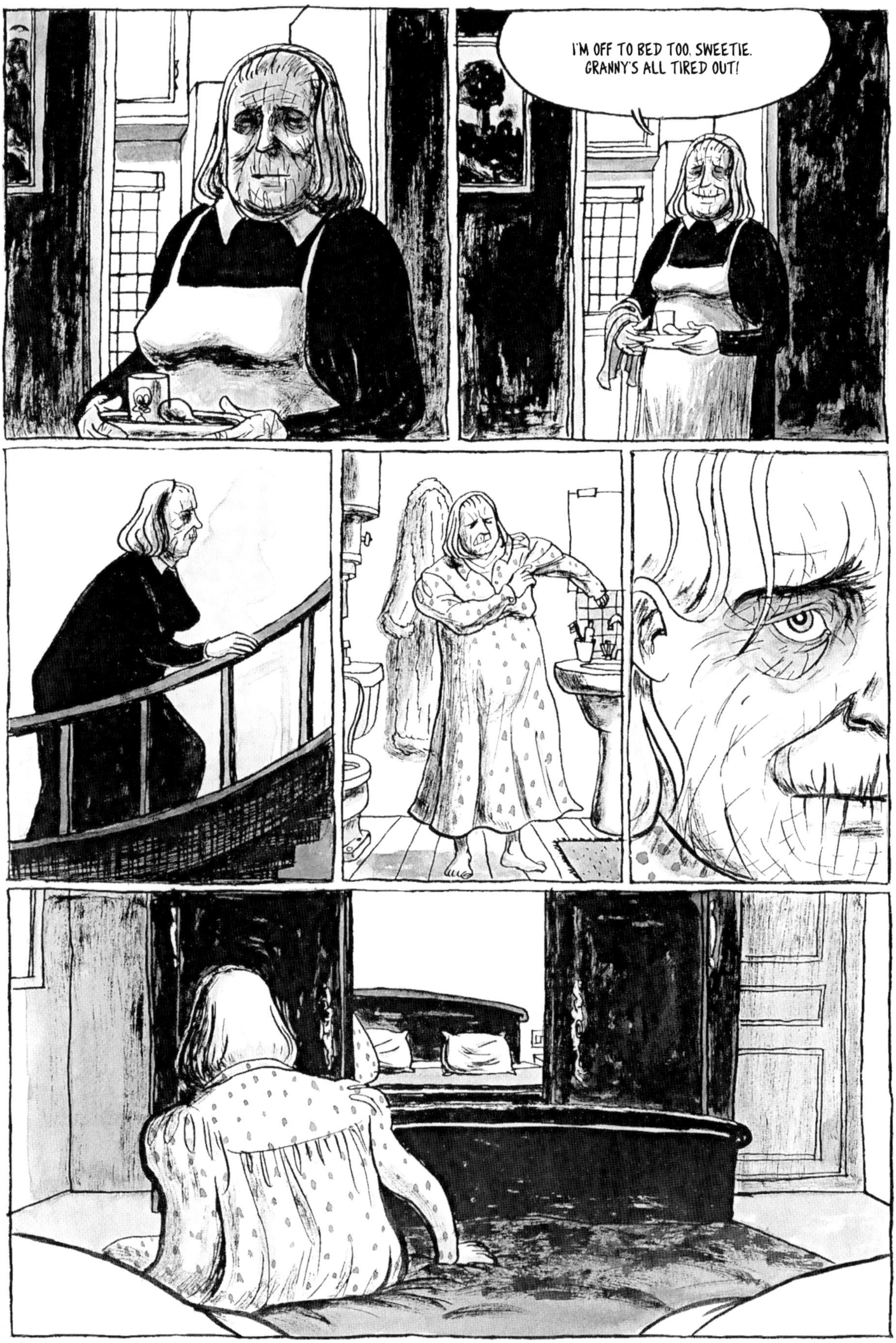
I'M OFF TO BED TOO, SWEETIE. GRANNY'S ALL TIRED OUT!

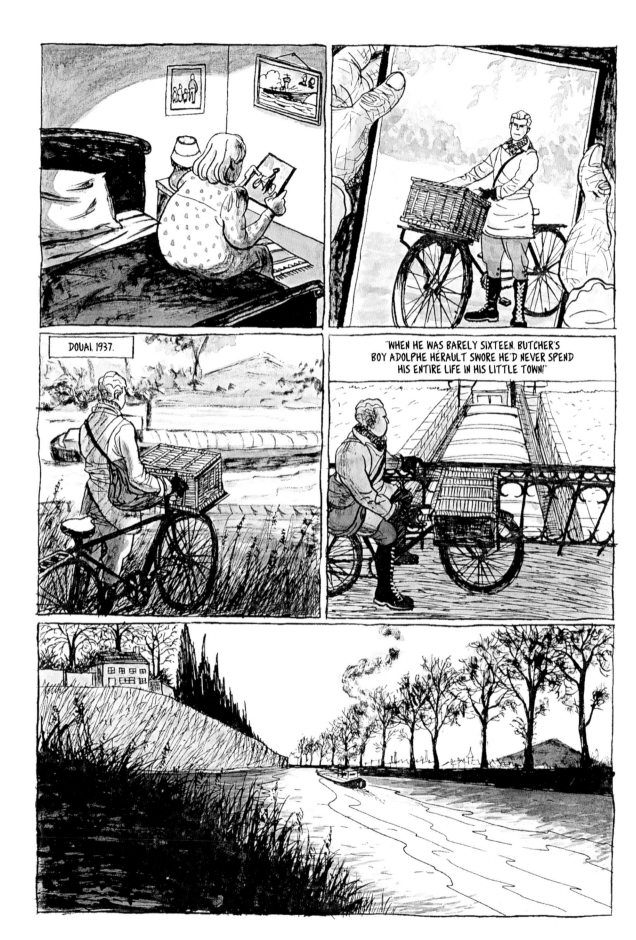

DOUAI, 1937.

"WHEN HE WAS BARELY SIXTEEN, BUTCHER'S BOY ADOLPHE HÉRAULT SWORE HE'D NEVER SPEND HIS ENTIRE LIFE IN HIS LITTLE TOWN!"

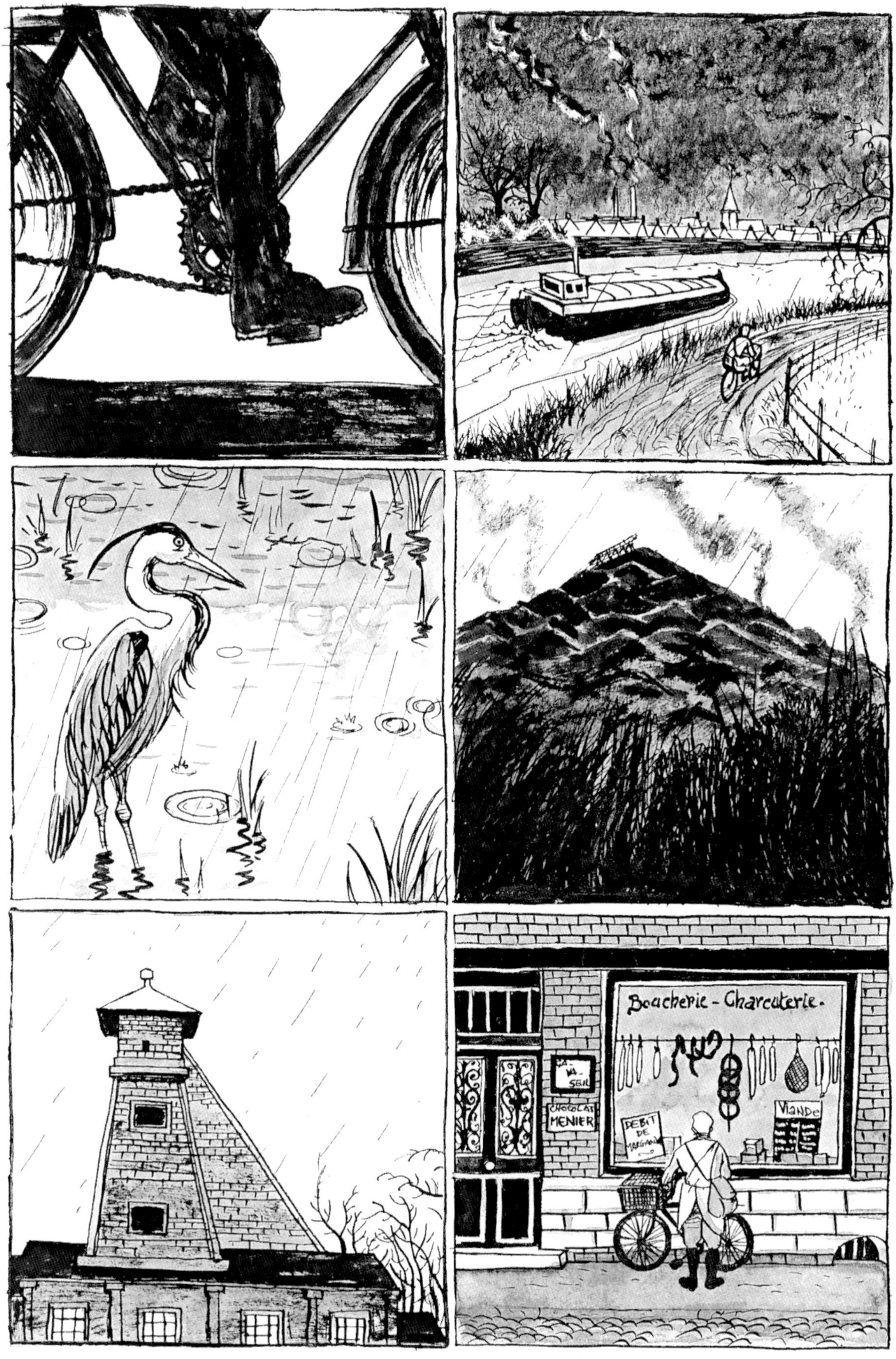
Boucherie - Charcuterie.
CHOCOLAT MENIER
DEBIT DE
Viande

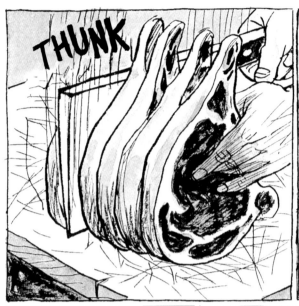

THUNK

CHOP
THWACK
HACK

RUB

RUB RUB

ALL FINISHED, MR. HALLARD.

SEE YOU BRIGHT AND EARLY TOMORROW, DODO.

"ADOLPHE HÉRAULT, BUT THEY ALL CALLED HIM DODO."

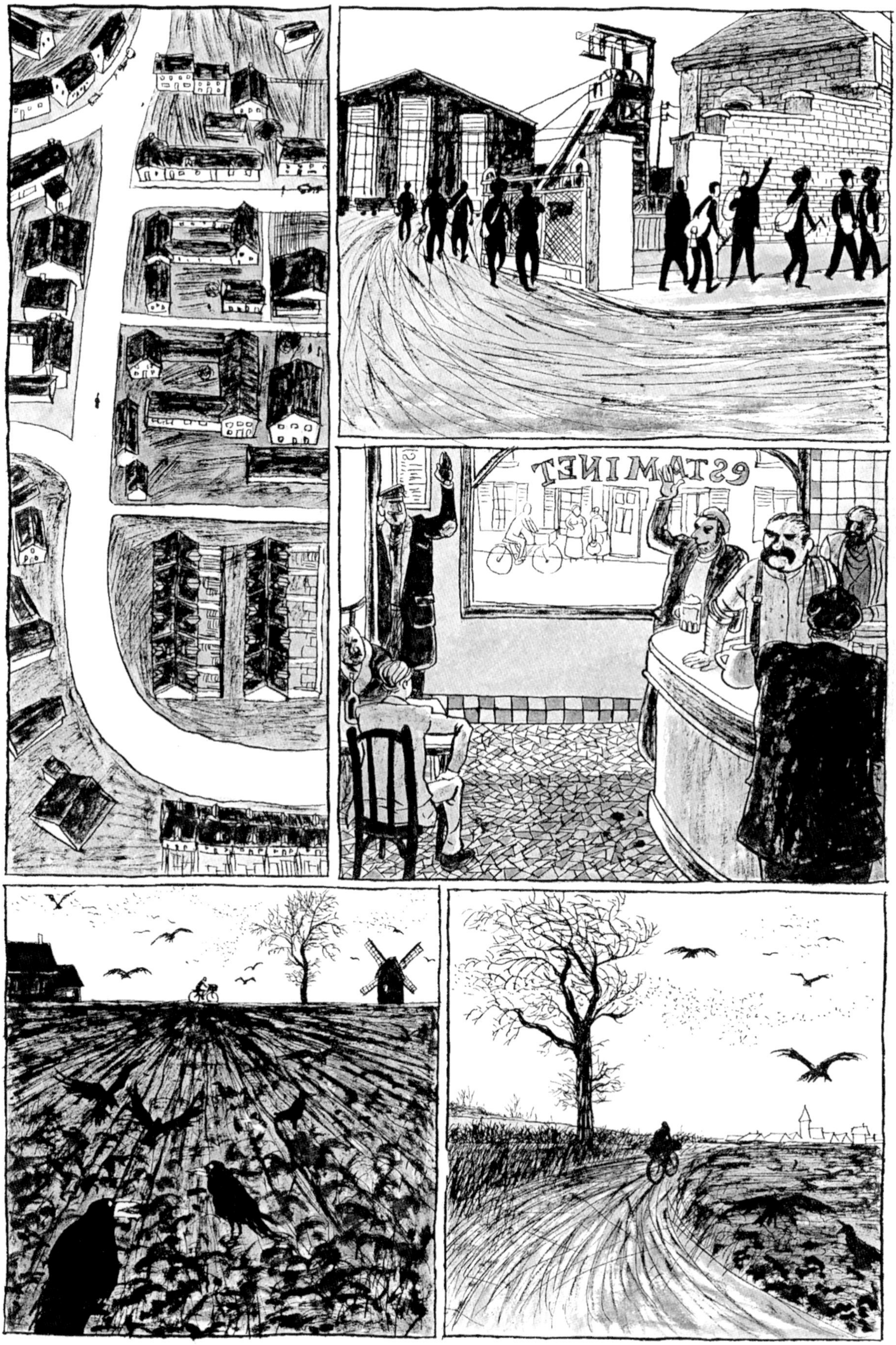
ESTAMINET

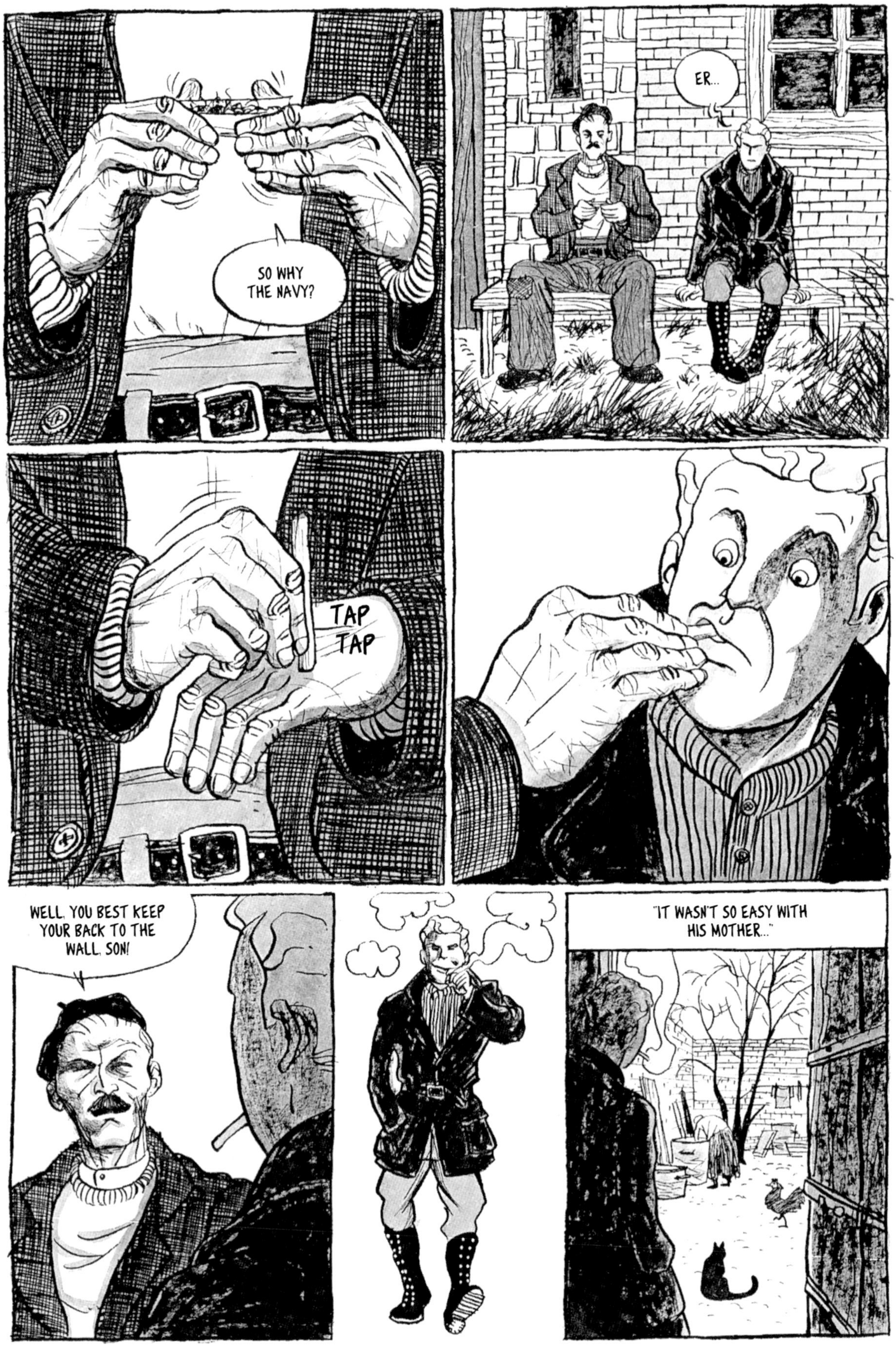
SO WHY THE NAVY?
ER...
TAP
TAP
WELL, YOU BEST KEEP YOUR BACK TO THE WALL, SON!
"IT WASN'T SO EASY WITH HIS MOTHER..."

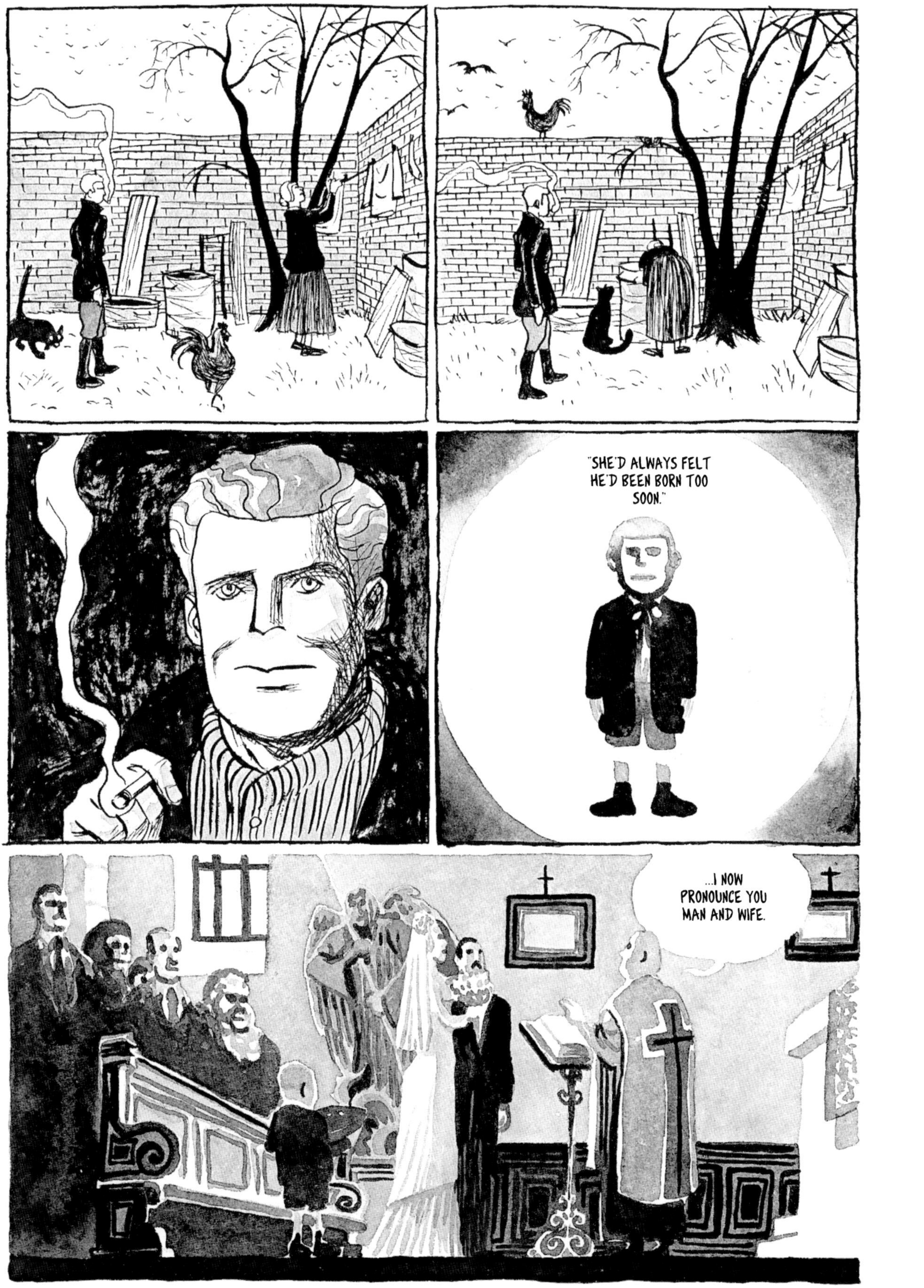
"SHE'D ALWAYS FELT HE'D BEEN BORN TOO SOON."
...I NOW PRONOUNCE YOU MAN AND WIFE.

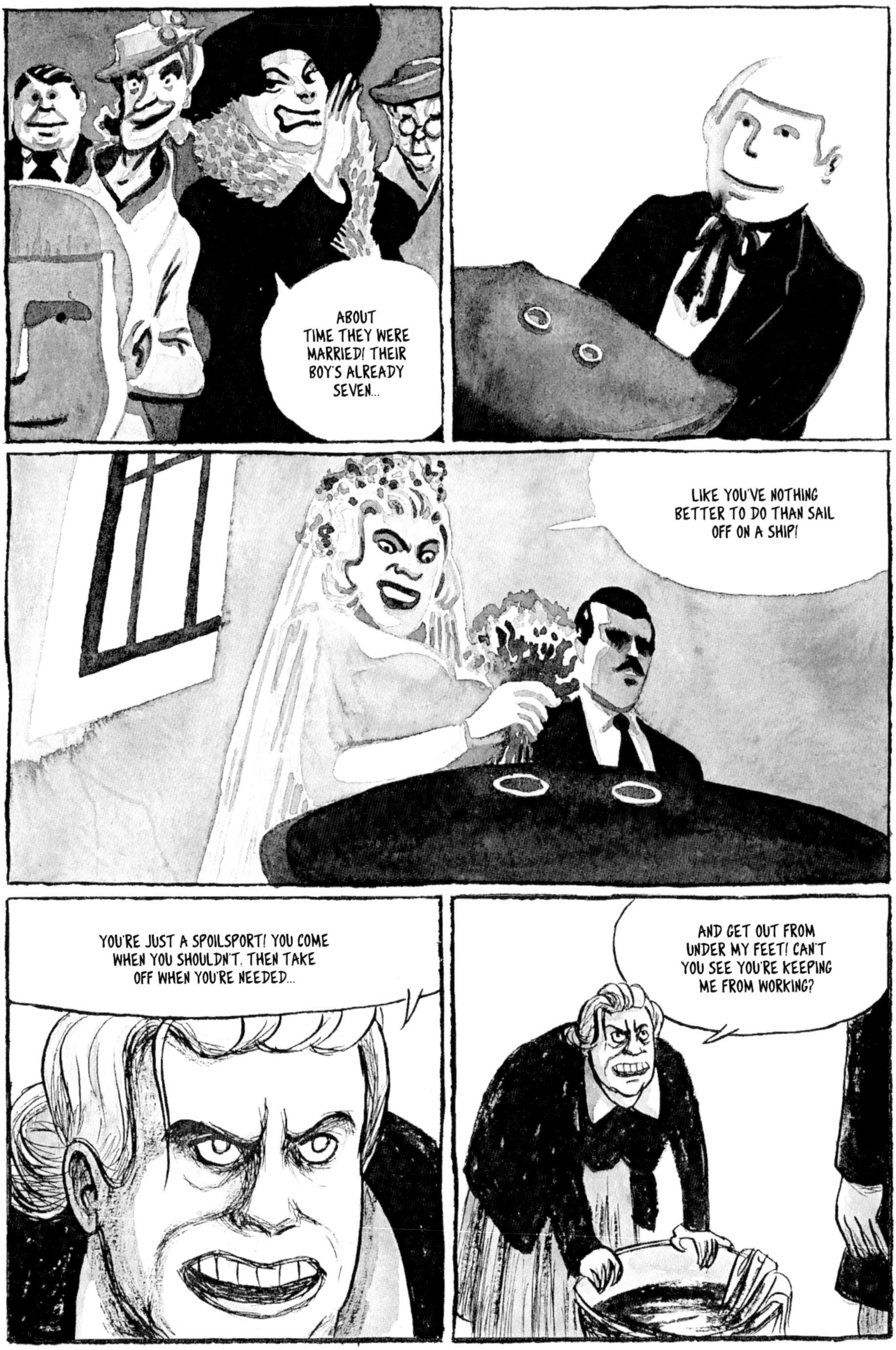
ABOUT TIME THEY WERE MARRIED! THEIR BOY'S ALREADY SEVEN...
LIKE YOU'VE NOTHING BETTER TO DO THAN SAIL OFF ON A SHIP!
YOU'RE JUST A SPOILSPORT! YOU COME WHEN YOU SHOULDN'T, THEN TAKE OFF WHEN YOU'RE NEEDED...
AND GET OUT FROM UNDER MY FEET! CAN'T YOU SEE YOU'RE KEEPING ME FROM WORKING?

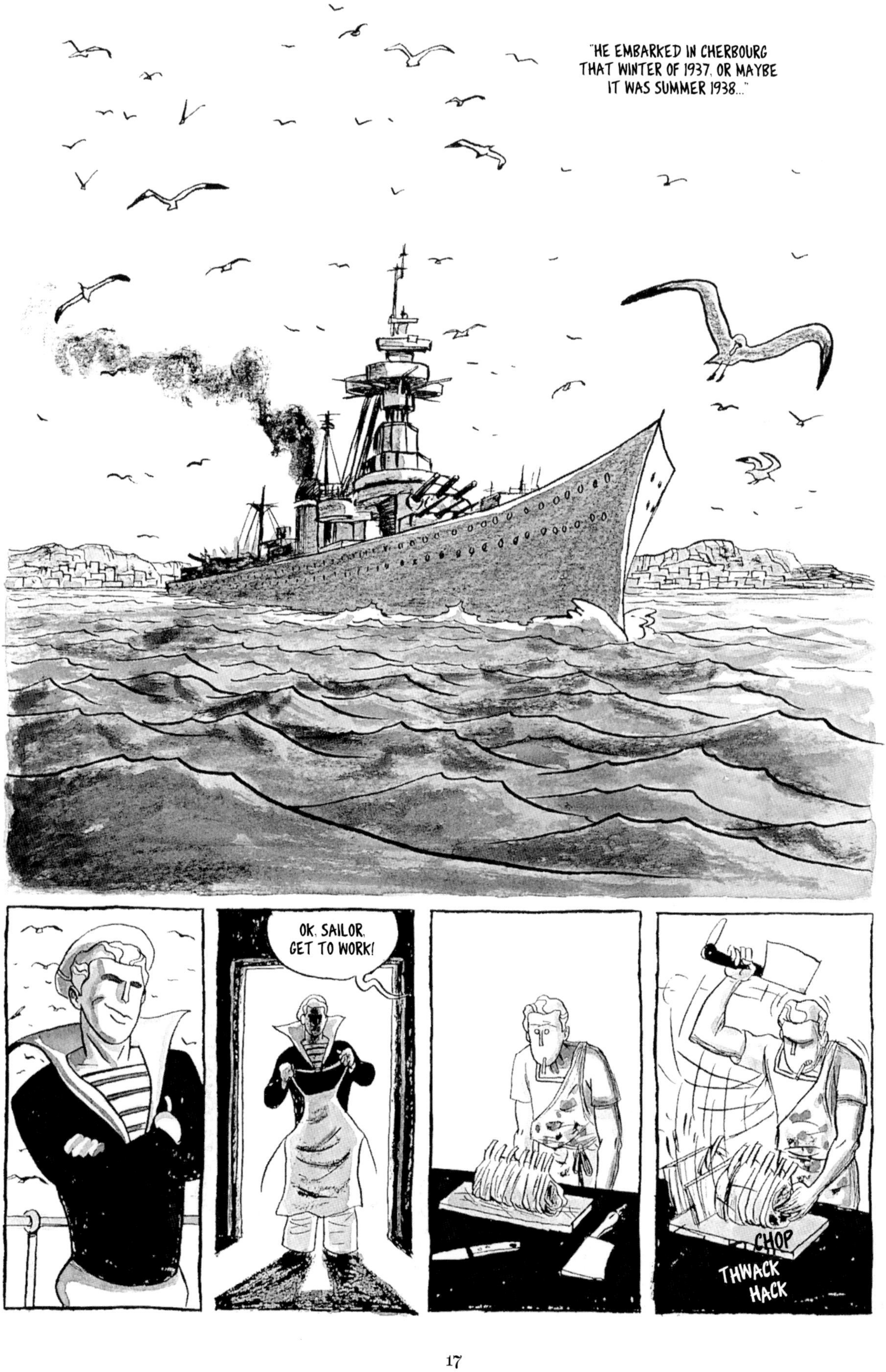
"HE EMBARKED IN CHERBOURG THAT WINTER OF 1937, OR MAYBE IT WAS SUMMER 1938..."
OK, SAILOR, GET TO WORK!
CHOP
THWACK
HACK

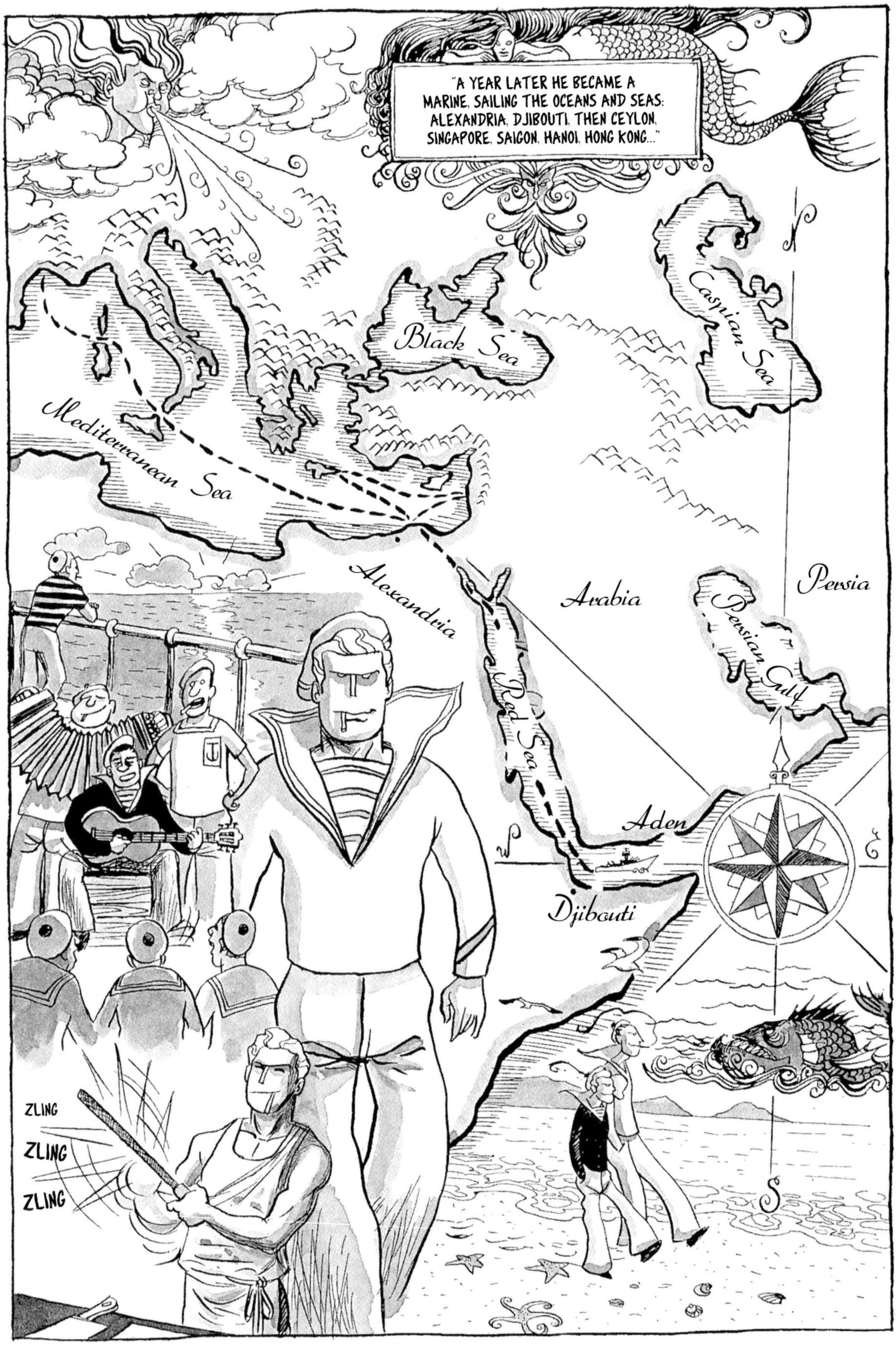

"A YEAR LATER HE BECAME A MARINE, SAILING THE OCEANS AND SEAS: ALEXANDRIA, DJIBOUTI, THEN CEYLON, SINGAPORE, SAIGON, HANOI, HONG KONG..."
Black Sea
Caspian Sea
Mediterranean Sea
Alexandria
Arabia
Persia
Persian Gulf
Red Sea
Aden
Djibouti
N
W
E
S
ZLING
ZLING
ZLING

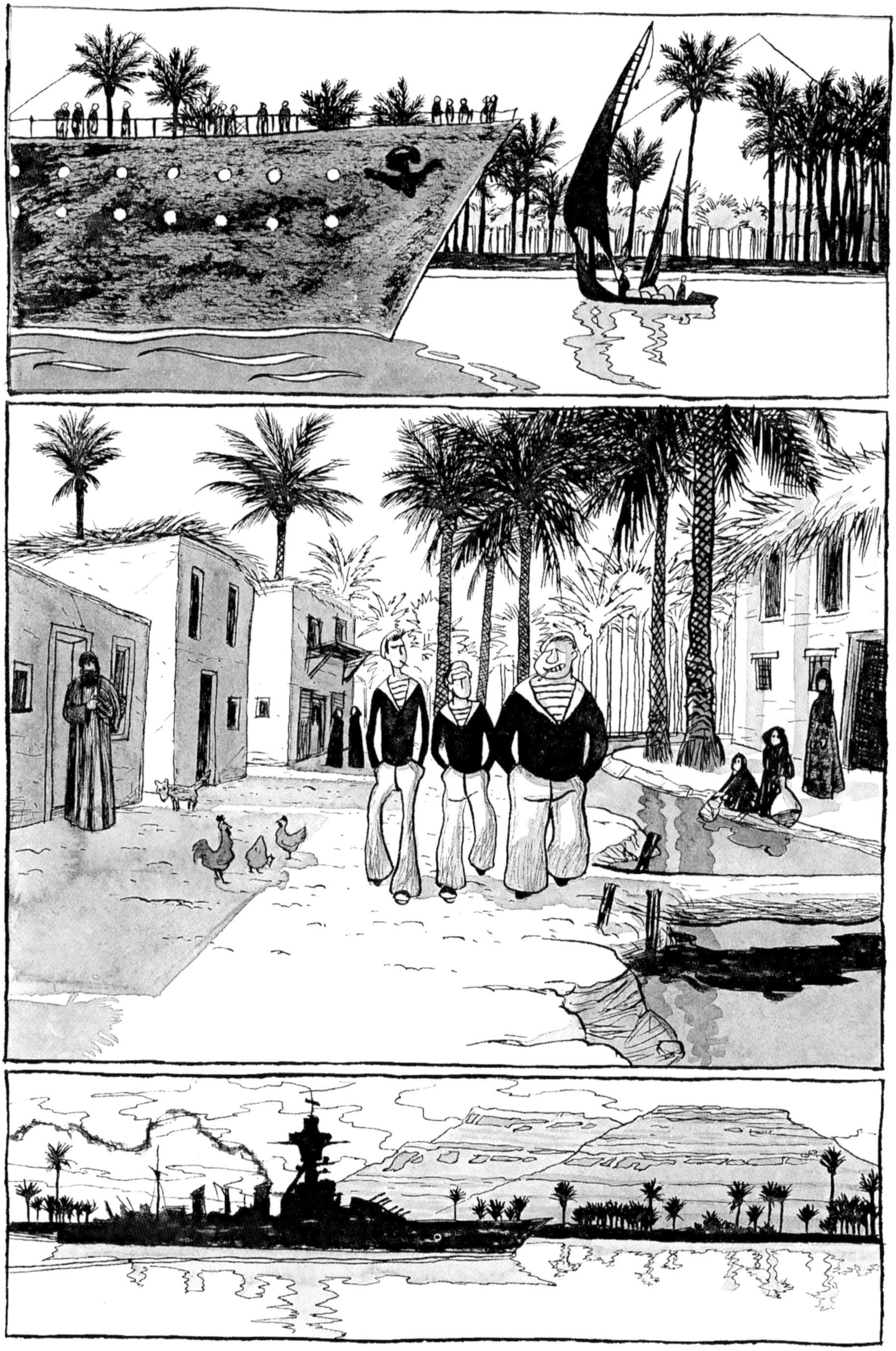

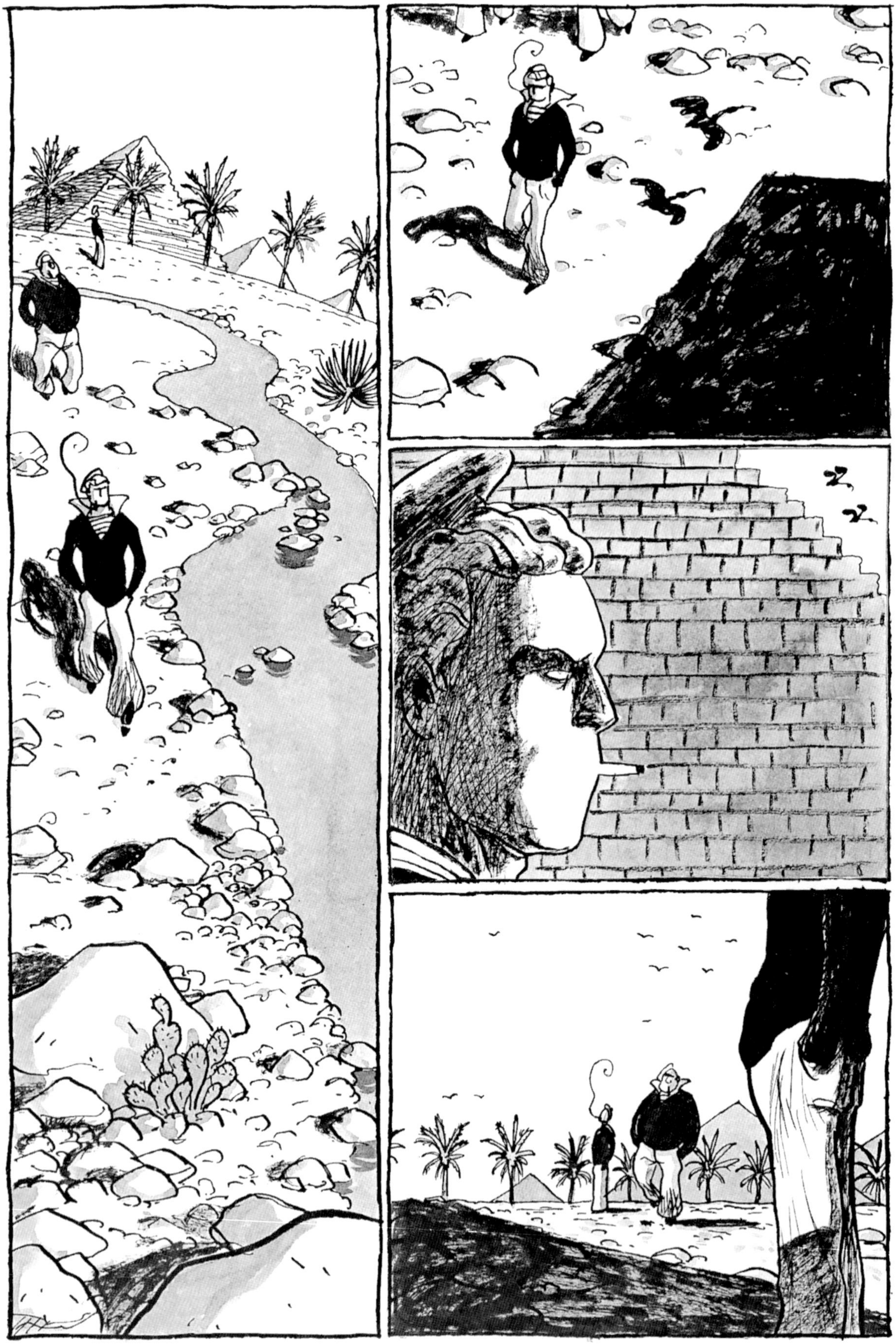

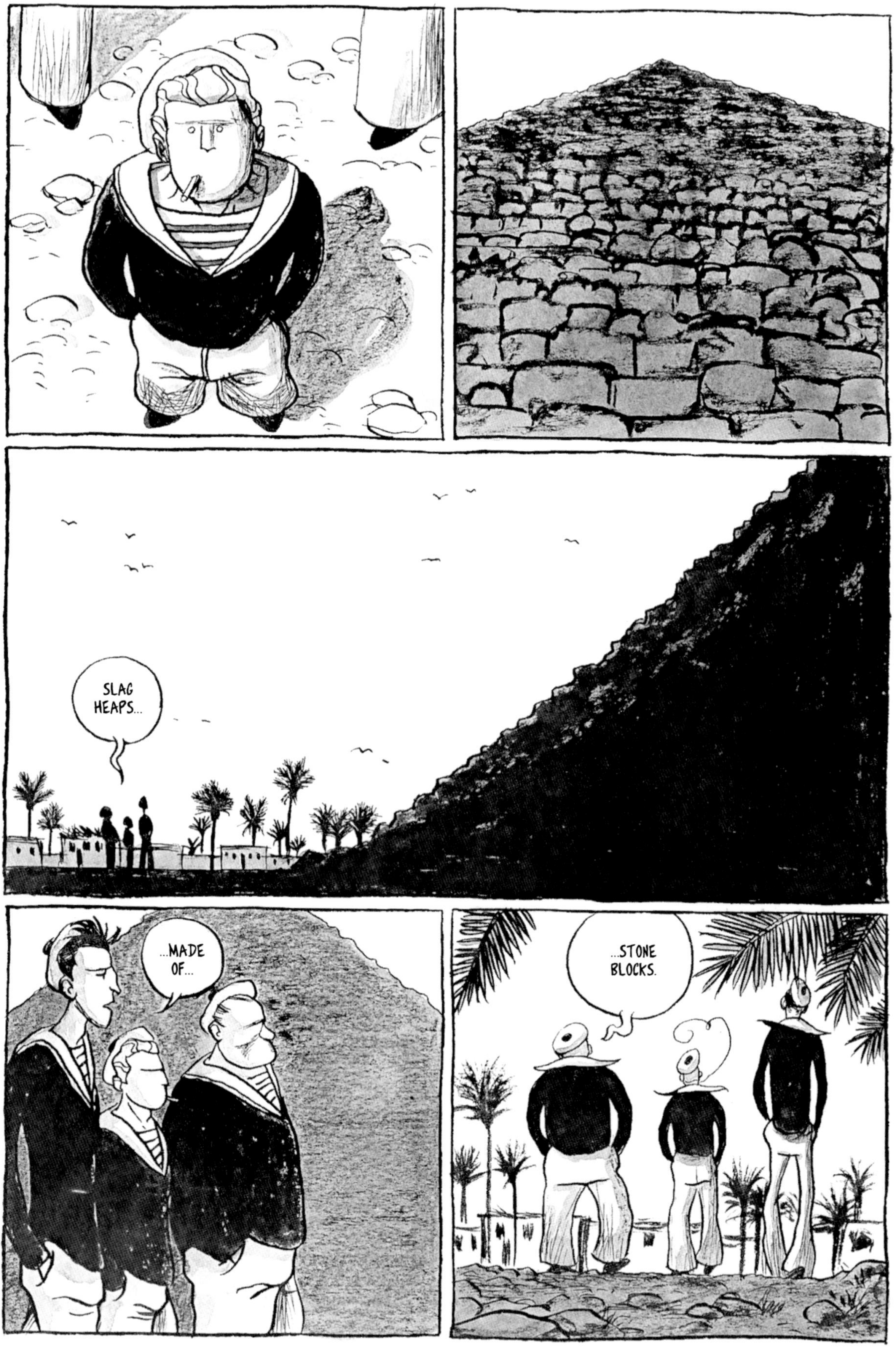
SLAG HEAPS...
...MADE OF...
...STONE BLOCKS.

ALL SET FOR THE PHOTO, GENTLEMEN?

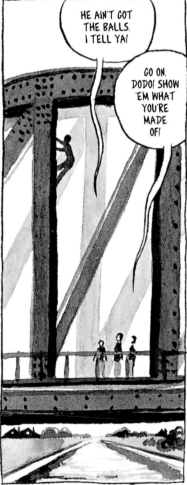

HE AIN'T GOT THE BALLS, I TELL YA!

GO ON, DODO! SHOW 'EM WHAT YOU'RE MADE OF!

AIN'T GOT THE BALLS, HUH, LADS?!

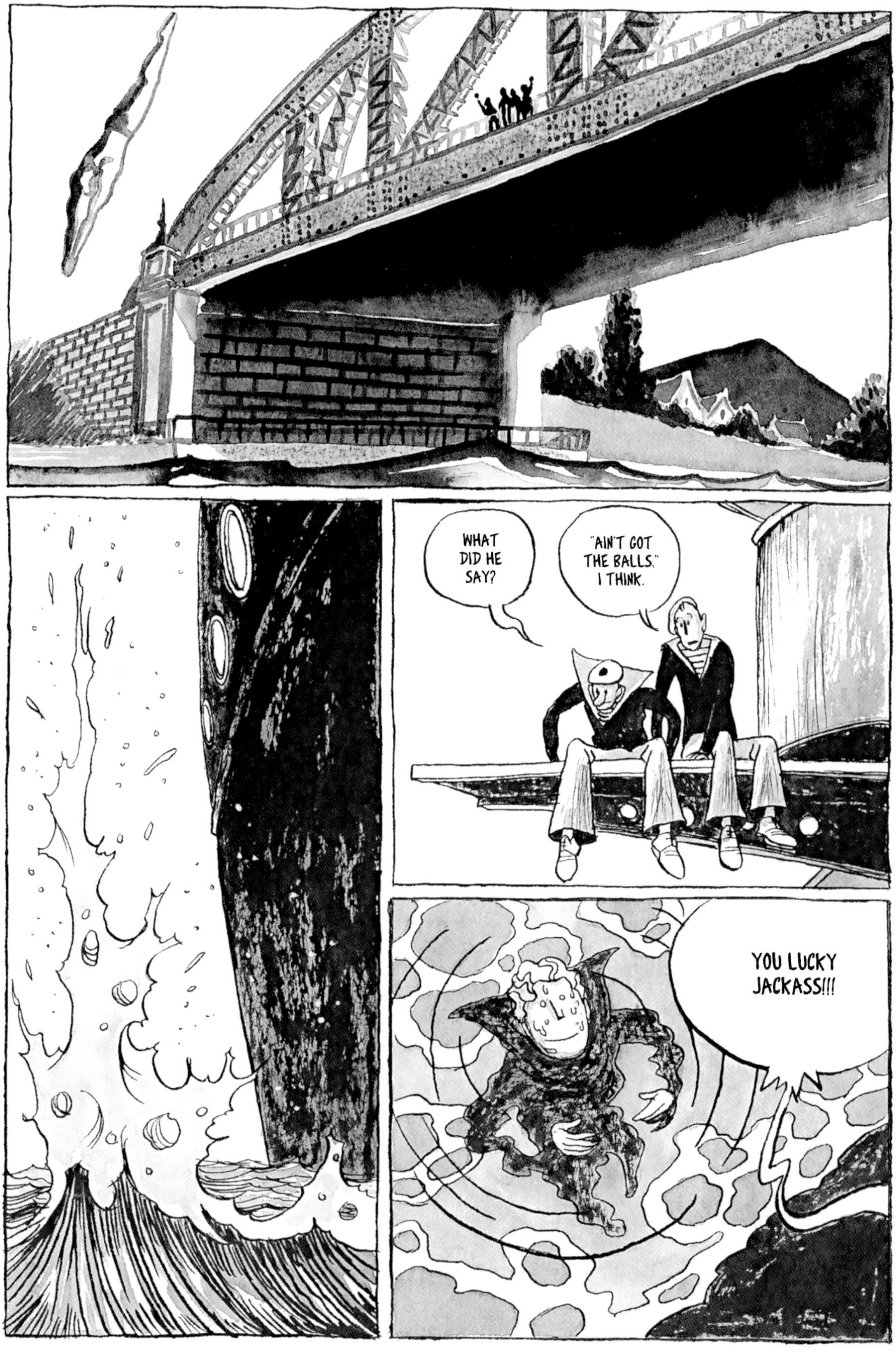
WHAT DID HE SAY?
"AIN'T GOT THE BALLS," I THINK.
YOU LUCKY JACKASS!!!

YOU COULD'VE BEEN KILLED! 20 DAYS IN THE BRIG FOR YOU!

YES, CAPTAIN, SIR!

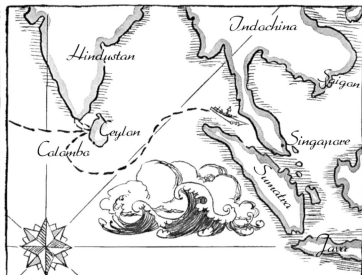

Hindustan

Indochina

Saigon

Ceylon

Colombo

Singapore

Sumatra

Java

DID THE MAIL COME?

YEAH, BUT NONE FOR YOU. SORRY, DODO.

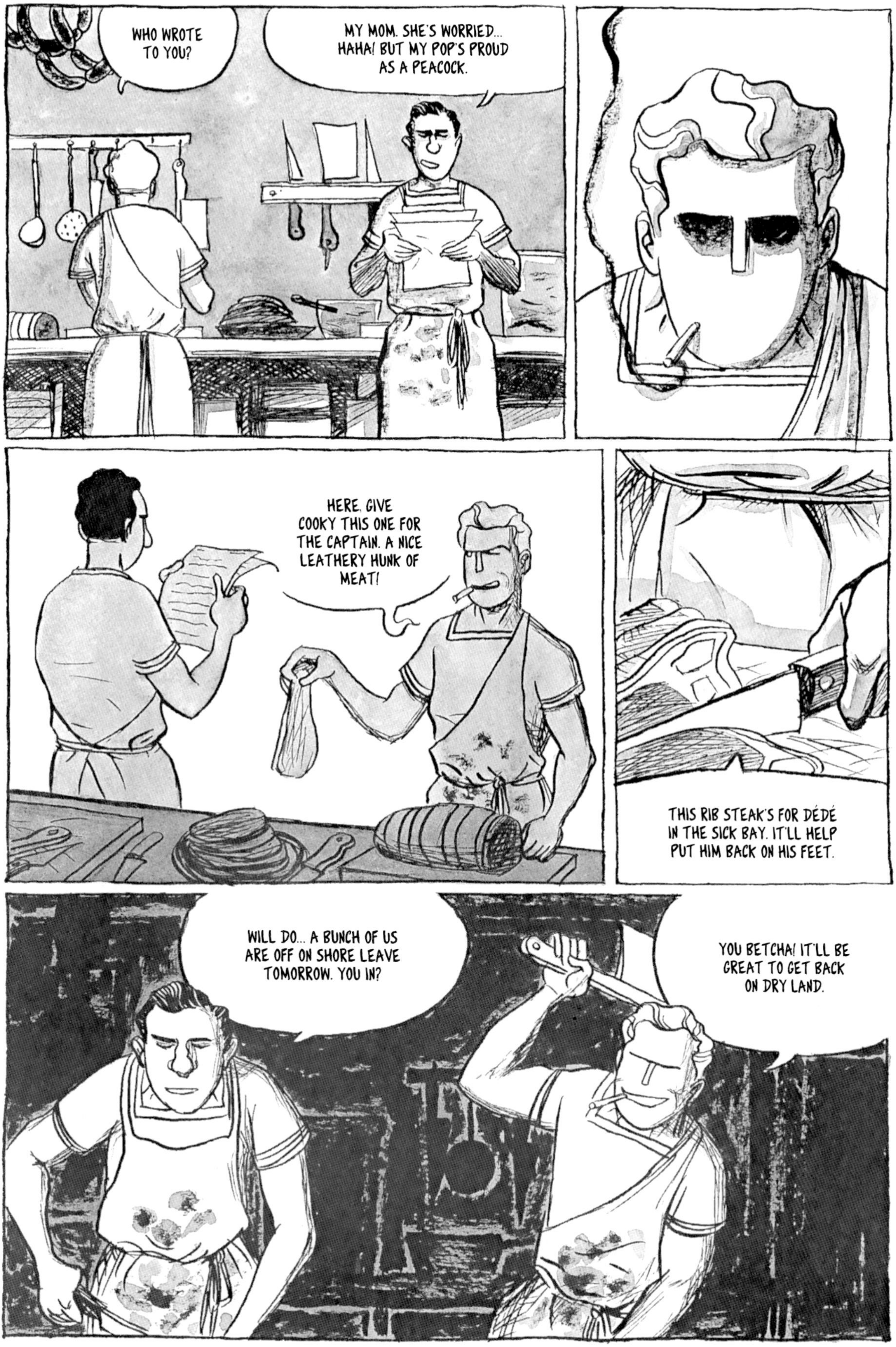
WHO WROTE TO YOU?
MY MOM. SHE'S WORRIED... HAHA! BUT MY POP'S PROUD AS A PEACOCK.
HERE. GIVE COOKY THIS ONE FOR THE CAPTAIN. A NICE LEATHERY HUNK OF MEAT!
THIS RIB STEAK'S FOR DÉDÉ IN THE SICK BAY. IT'LL HELP PUT HIM BACK ON HIS FEET.
WILL DO... A BUNCH OF US ARE OFF ON SHORE LEAVE TOMORROW. YOU IN?
YOU BETCHA! IT'LL BE GREAT TO GET BACK ON DRY LAND.

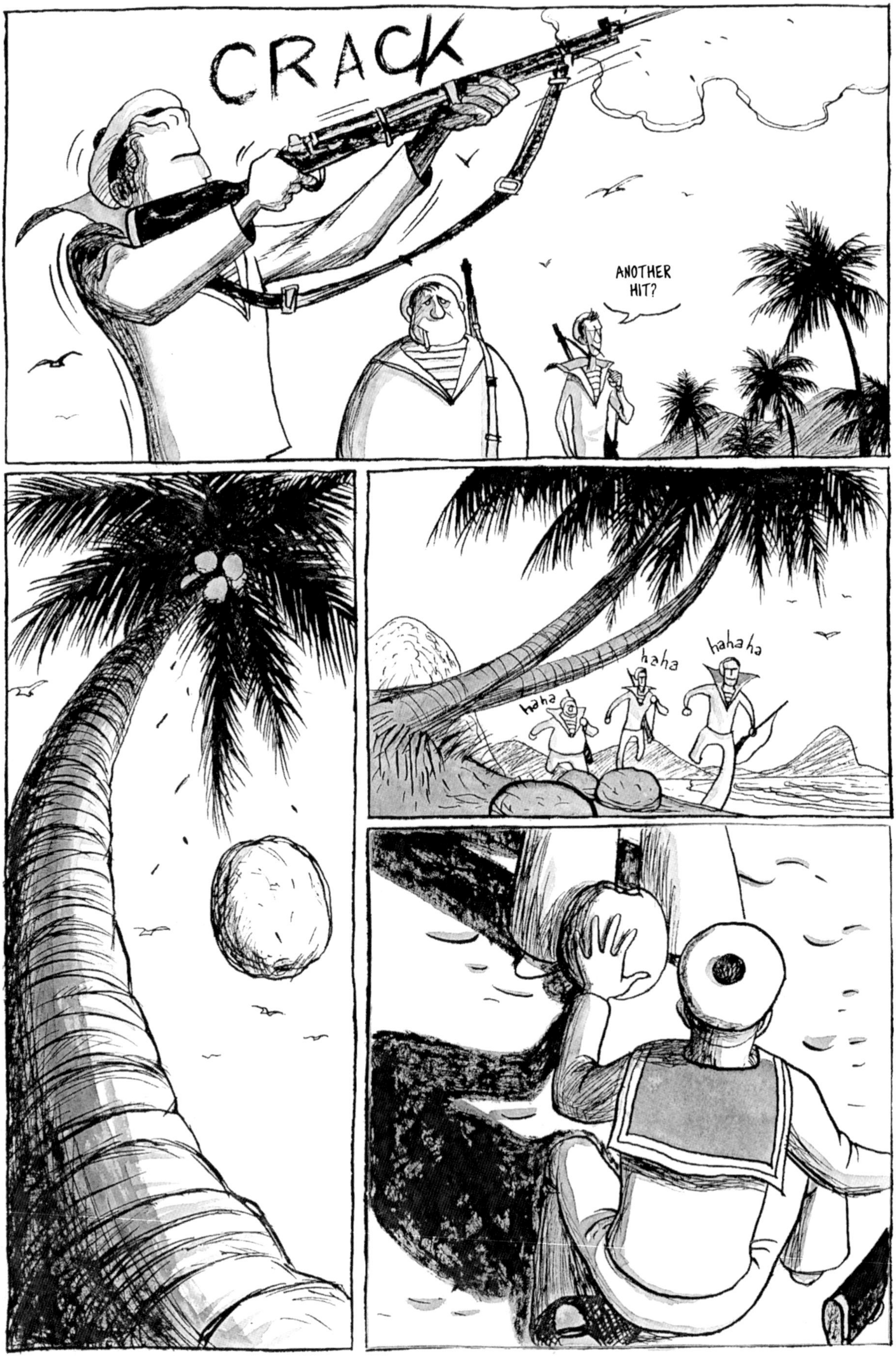
CRACK
ANOTHER HIT?
haha
haha
hahaha

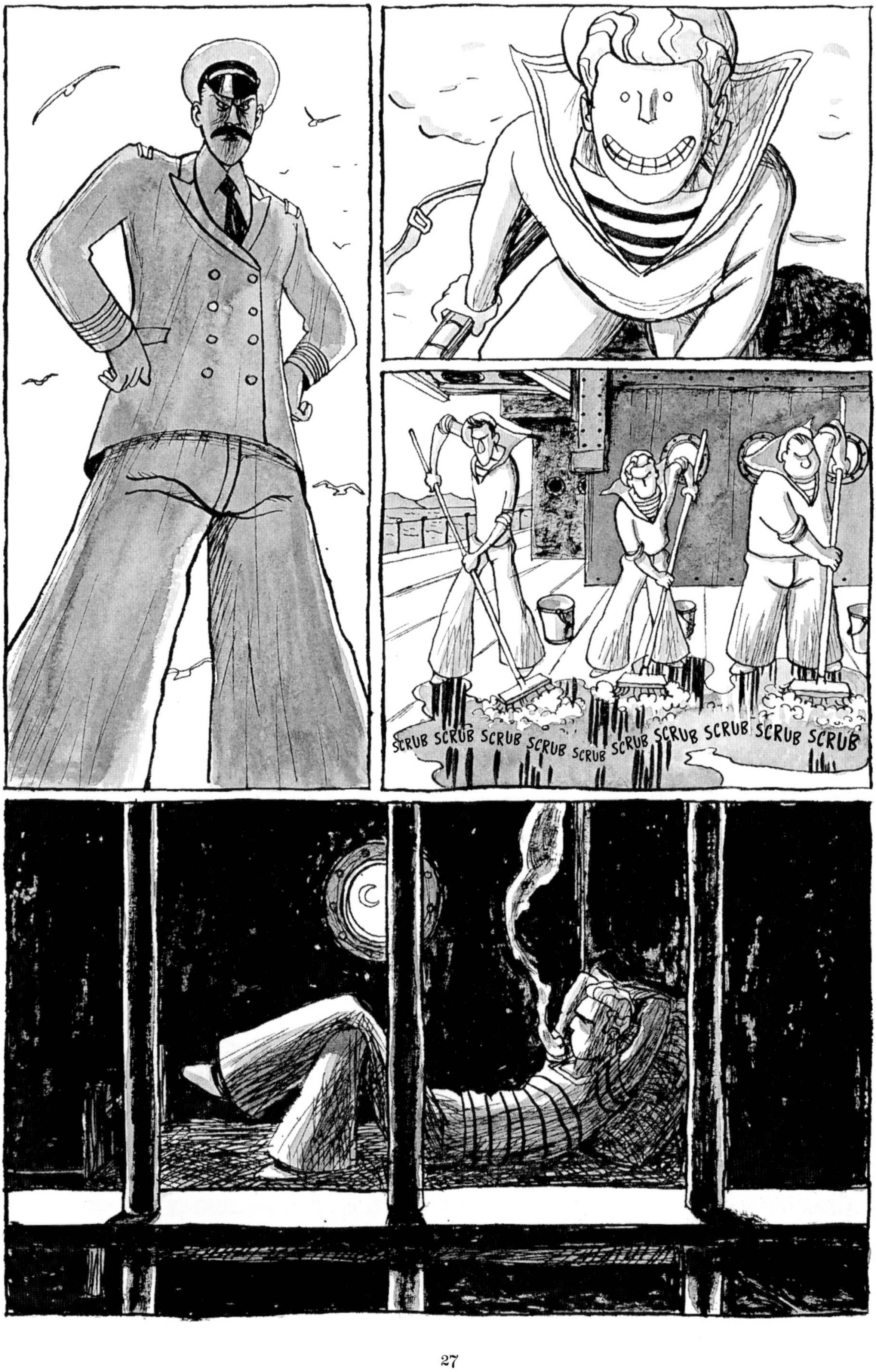
SCRUB SCRUB SCRUB SCRUB SCRUB SCRUB SCRUB SCRUB SCRUB SCRUB

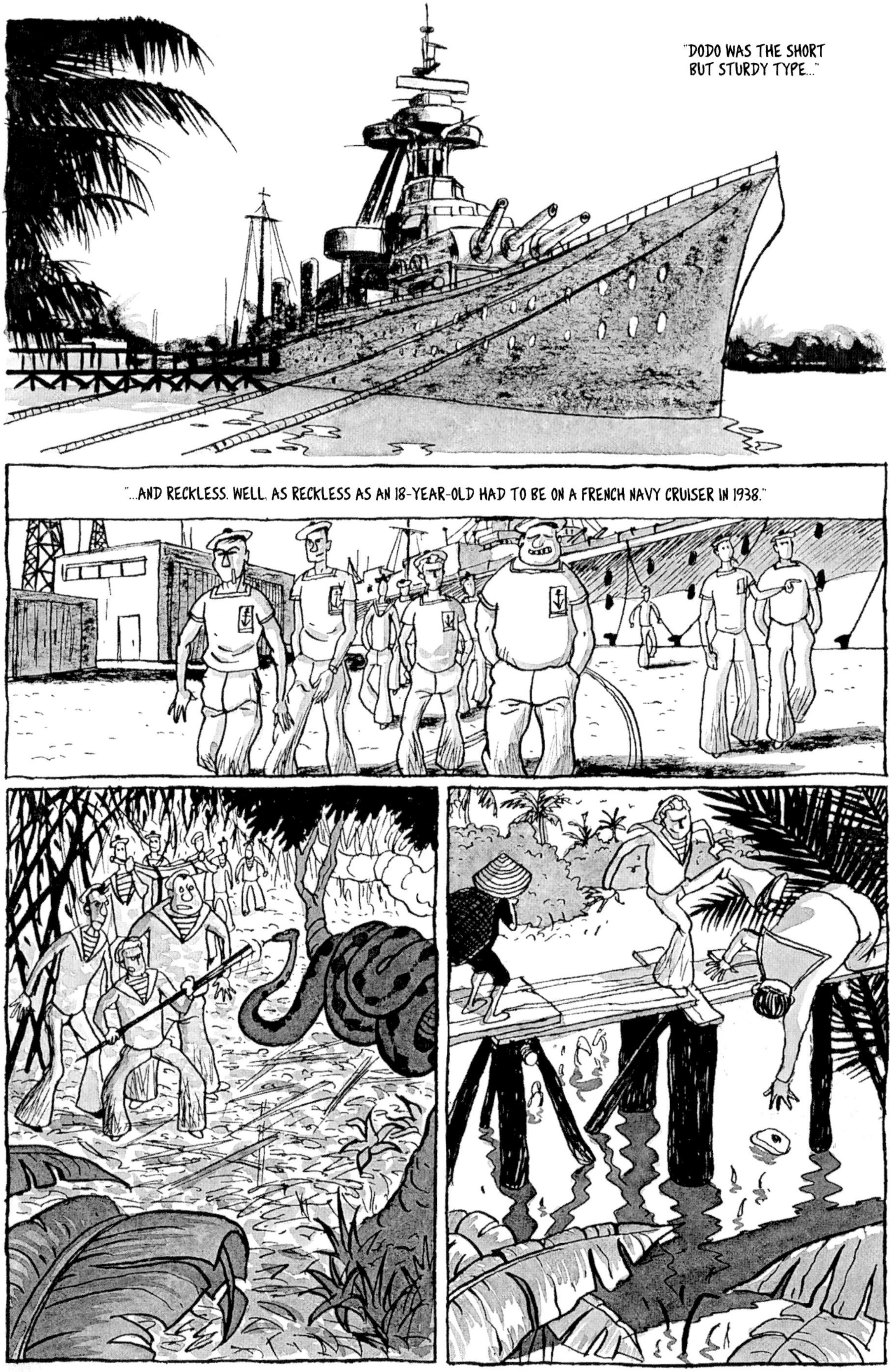
"DODO WAS THE SHORT BUT STURDY TYPE..."
"...AND RECKLESS. WELL, AS RECKLESS AS AN 18-YEAR-OLD HAD TO BE ON A FRENCH NAVY CRUISER IN 1938."

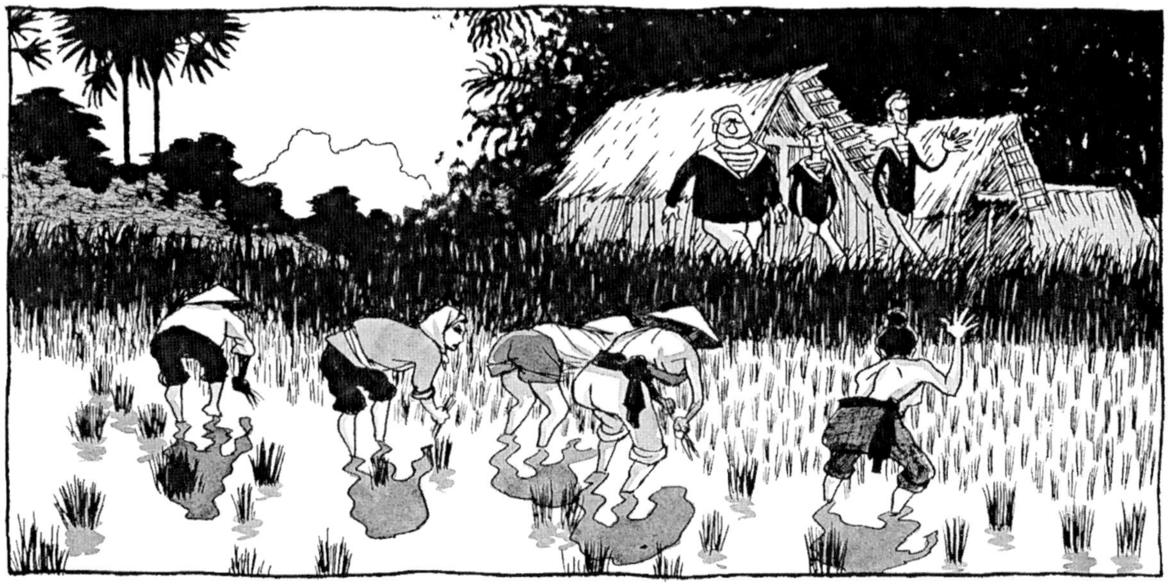

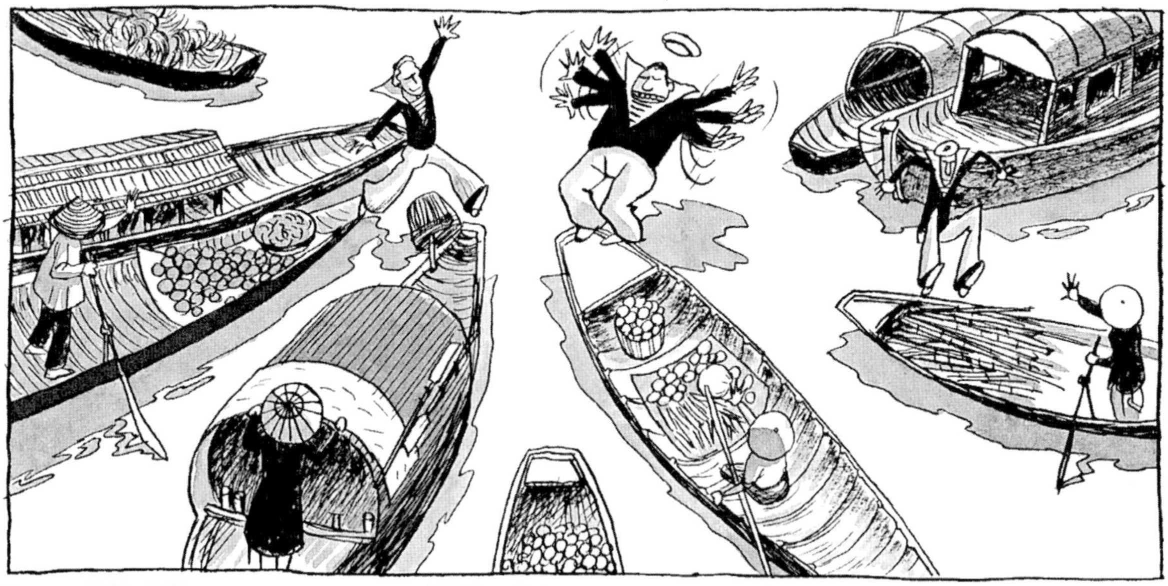

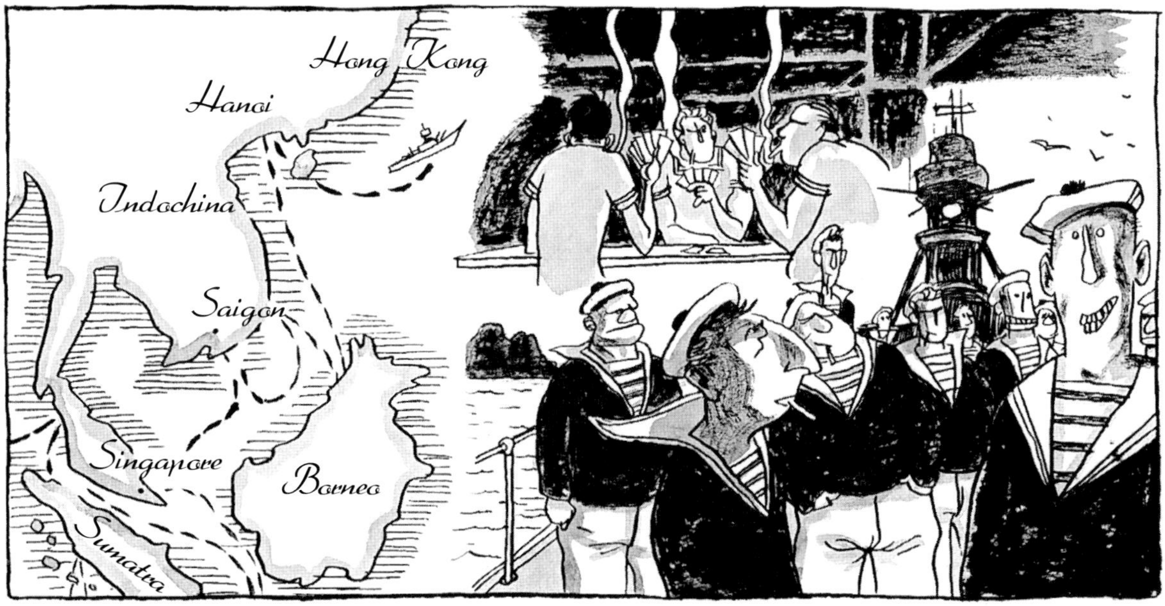
Hong Kong
Hanoi
Indochina
Saigon
Singapore
Borneo
Sumatra

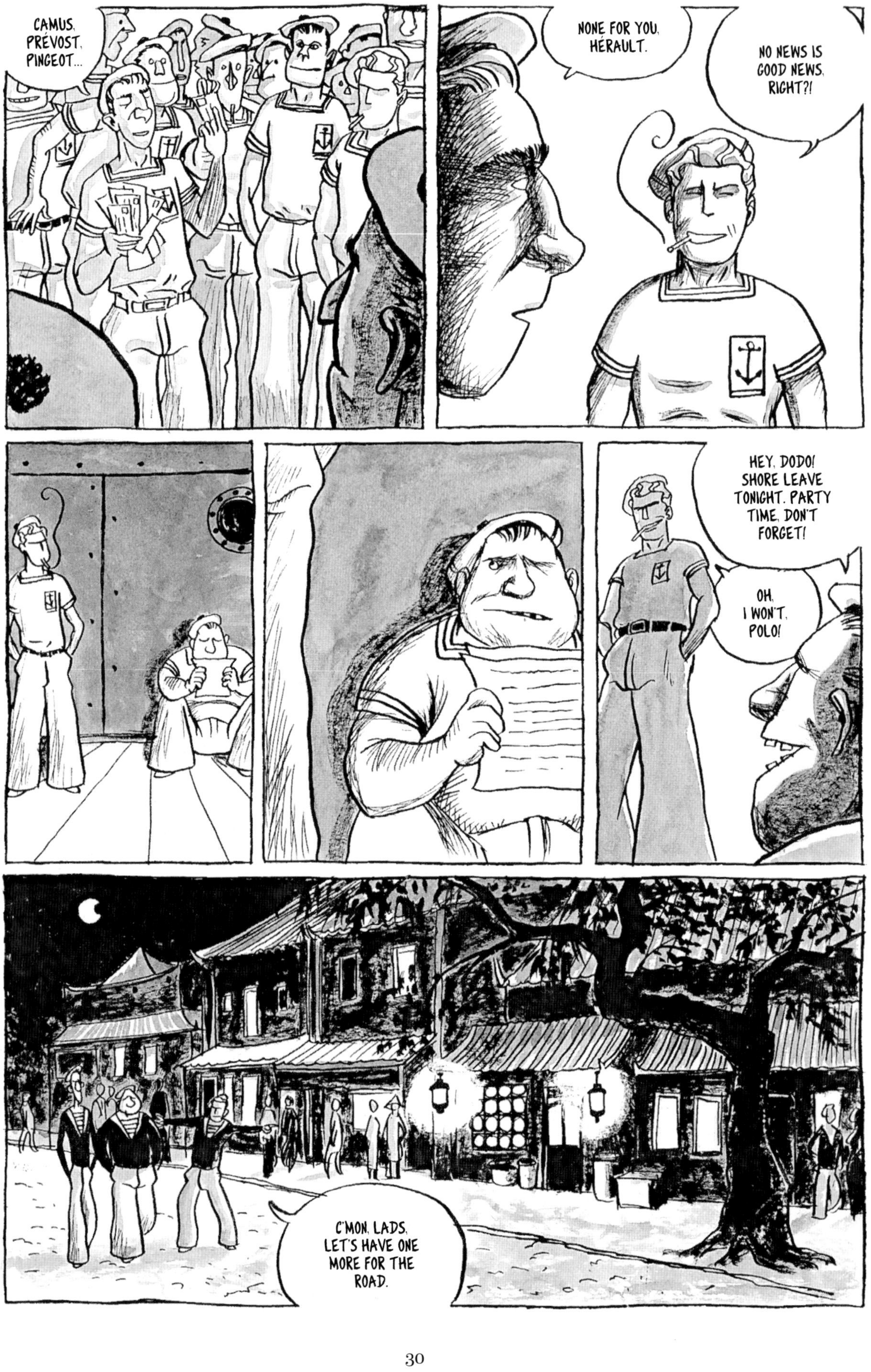
CAMUS, PRÉVOST, PINGEOT...
NONE FOR YOU, HÉRAULT.
NO NEWS IS GOOD NEWS, RIGHT?!
HEY, DODO! SHORE LEAVE TONIGHT. PARTY TIME, DON'T FORGET!
OH, I WON'T, POLO!
C'MON, LADS, LET'S HAVE ONE MORE FOR THE ROAD.

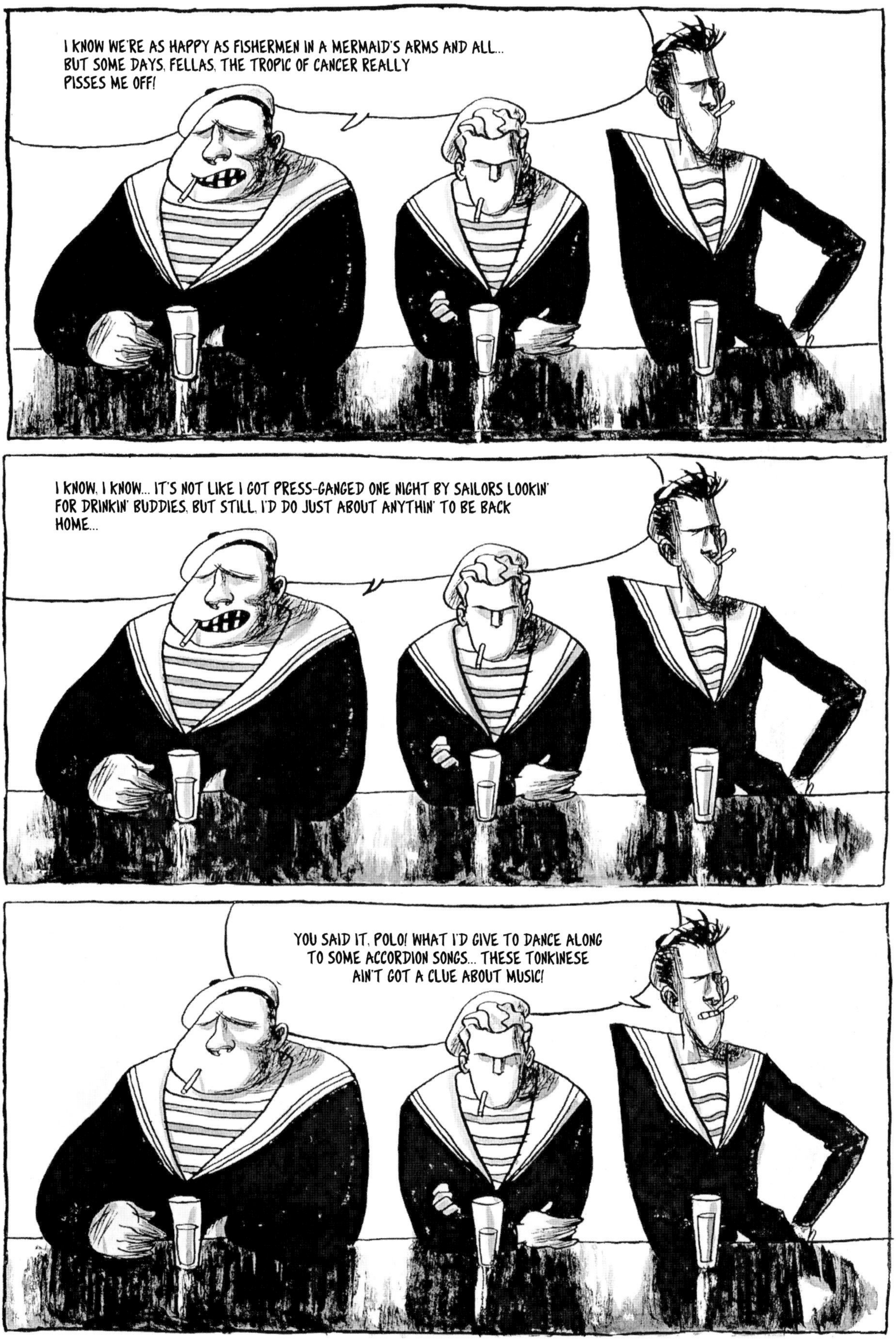
I KNOW WE'RE AS HAPPY AS FISHERMEN IN A MERMAID'S ARMS AND ALL... BUT SOME DAYS, FELLAS, THE TROPIC OF CANCER REALLY PISSES ME OFF!
I KNOW, I KNOW... IT'S NOT LIKE I GOT PRESS-GANGED ONE NIGHT BY SAILORS LOOKIN' FOR DRINKIN' BUDDIES, BUT STILL, I'D DO JUST ABOUT ANYTHIN' TO BE BACK HOME...
YOU SAID IT, POLO! WHAT I'D GIVE TO DANCE ALONG TO SOME ACCORDION SONGS... THESE TONKINESE AIN'T GOT A CLUE ABOUT MUSIC!

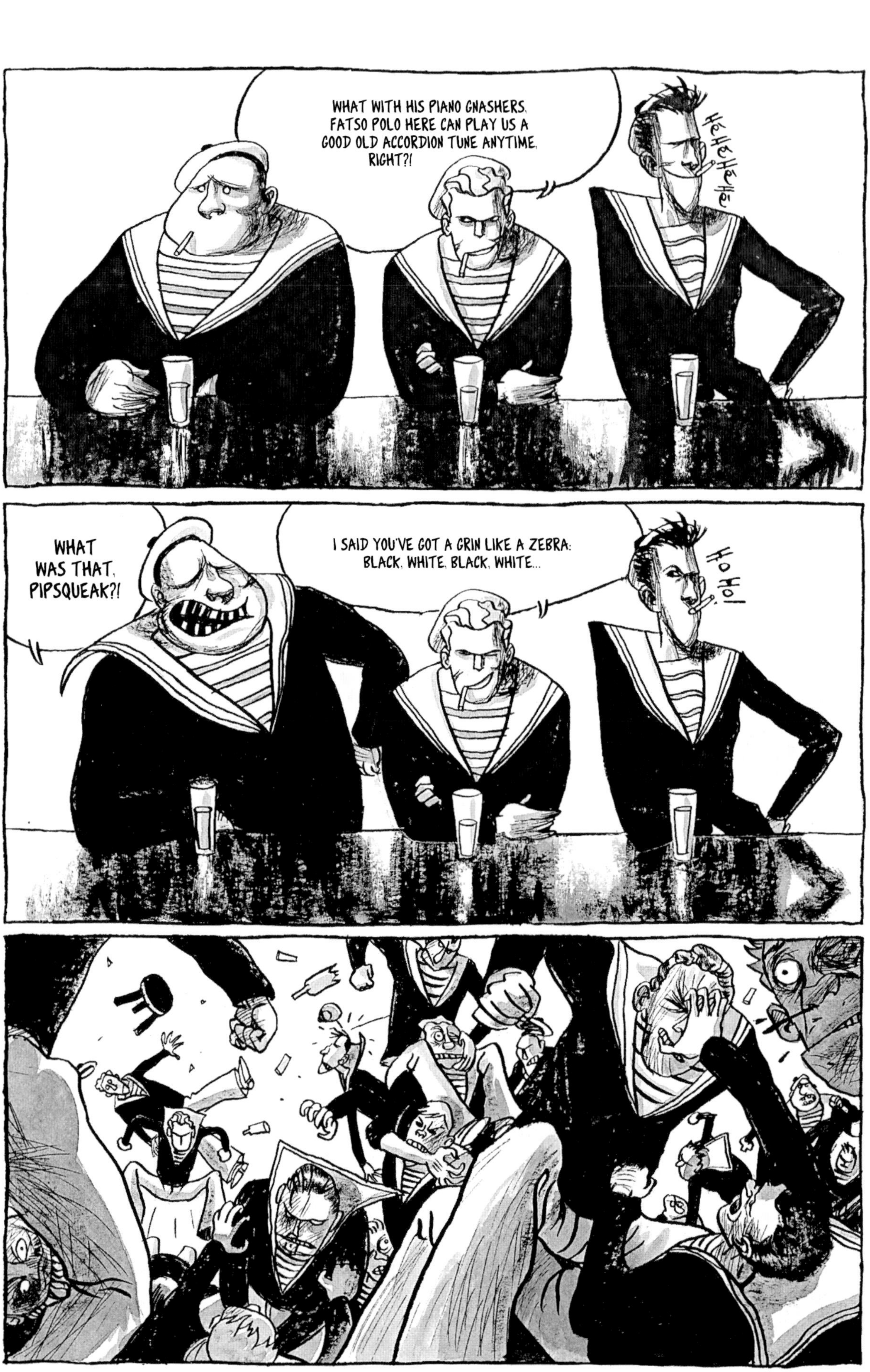
WHAT WITH HIS PIANO GNASHERS, FATSO POLO HERE CAN PLAY US A GOOD OLD ACCORDION TUNE ANYTIME, RIGHT?!
HéHéHéHéHé
WHAT WAS THAT, PIPSQUEAK?!
I SAID YOU'VE GOT A GRIN LIKE A ZEBRA: BLACK, WHITE, BLACK, WHITE...
Ho Ho!

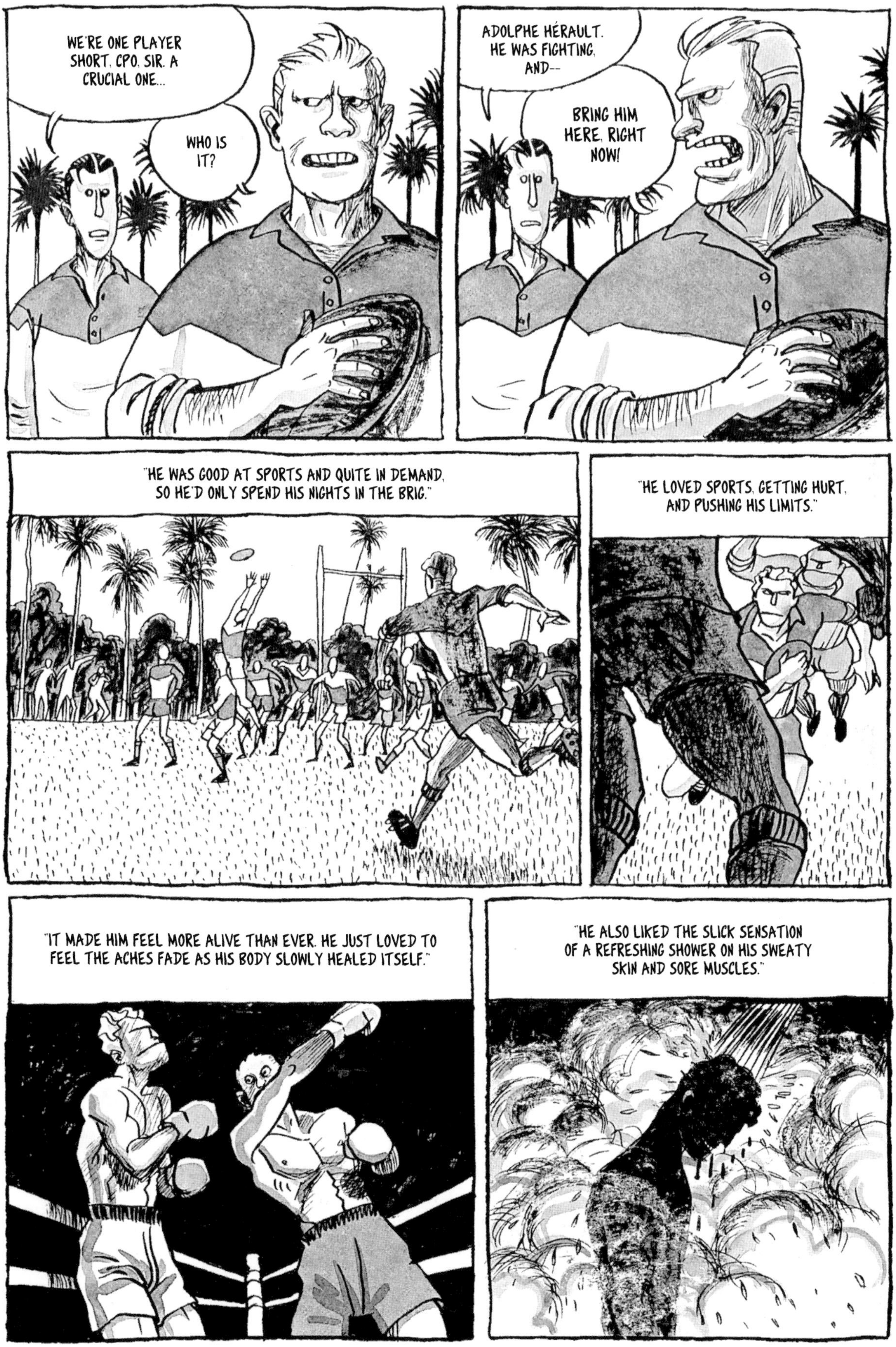
WE'RE ONE PLAYER SHORT, CPO, SIR. A CRUCIAL ONE...
WHO IS IT?
ADOLPHE HÉRAULT. HE WAS FIGHTING, AND--
BRING HIM HERE, RIGHT NOW!
"HE WAS GOOD AT SPORTS AND QUITE IN DEMAND, SO HE'D ONLY SPEND HIS NIGHTS IN THE BRIG."
"HE LOVED SPORTS, GETTING HURT, AND PUSHING HIS LIMITS."
"IT MADE HIM FEEL MORE ALIVE THAN EVER. HE JUST LOVED TO FEEL THE ACHES FADE AS HIS BODY SLOWLY HEALED ITSELF."
"HE ALSO LIKED THE SLICK SENSATION OF A REFRESHING SHOWER ON HIS SWEATY SKIN AND SORE MUSCLES."

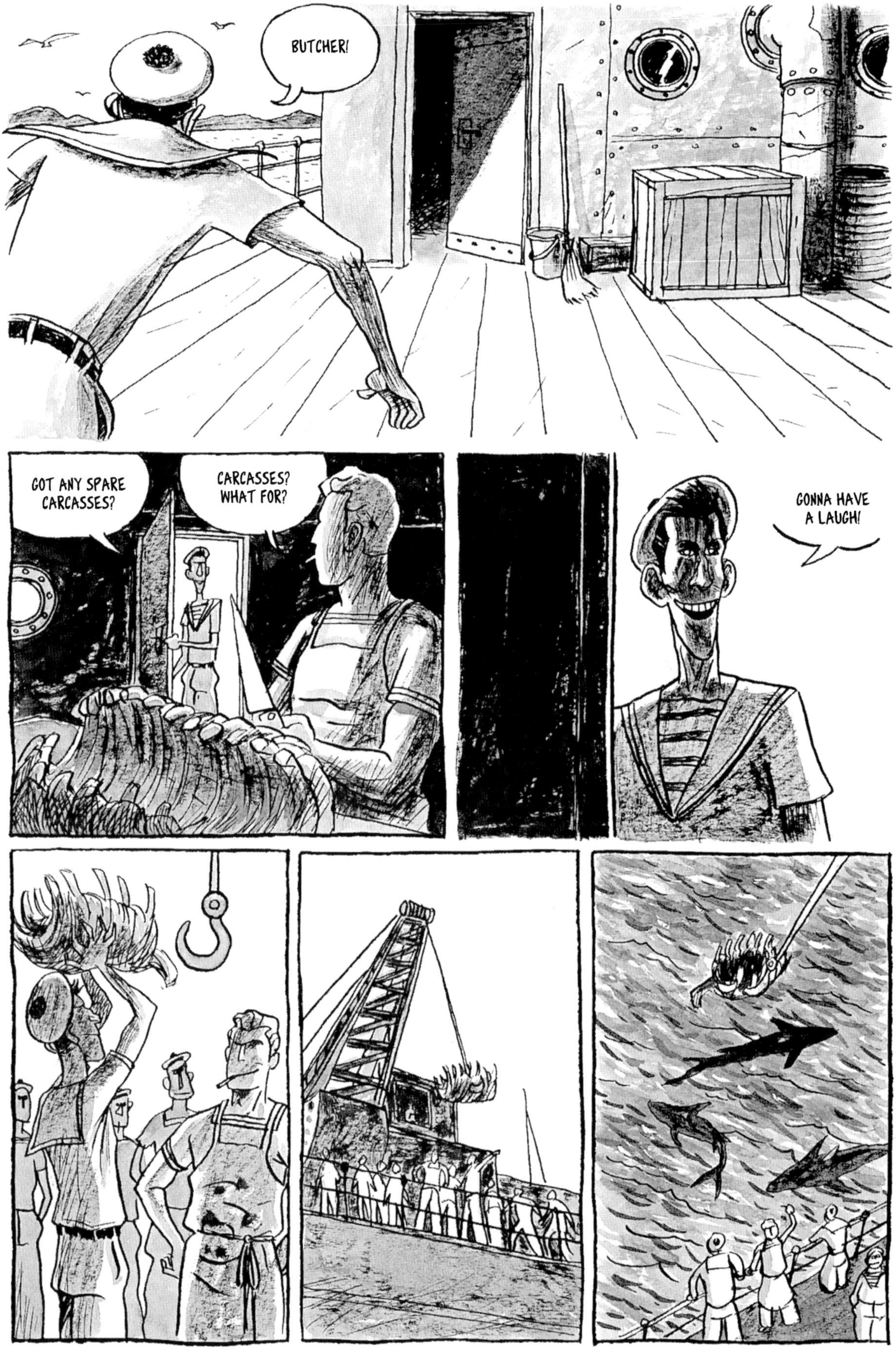
BUTCHER!
GOT ANY SPARE CARCASSES?
CARCASSES? WHAT FOR?
GONNA HAVE A LAUGH!

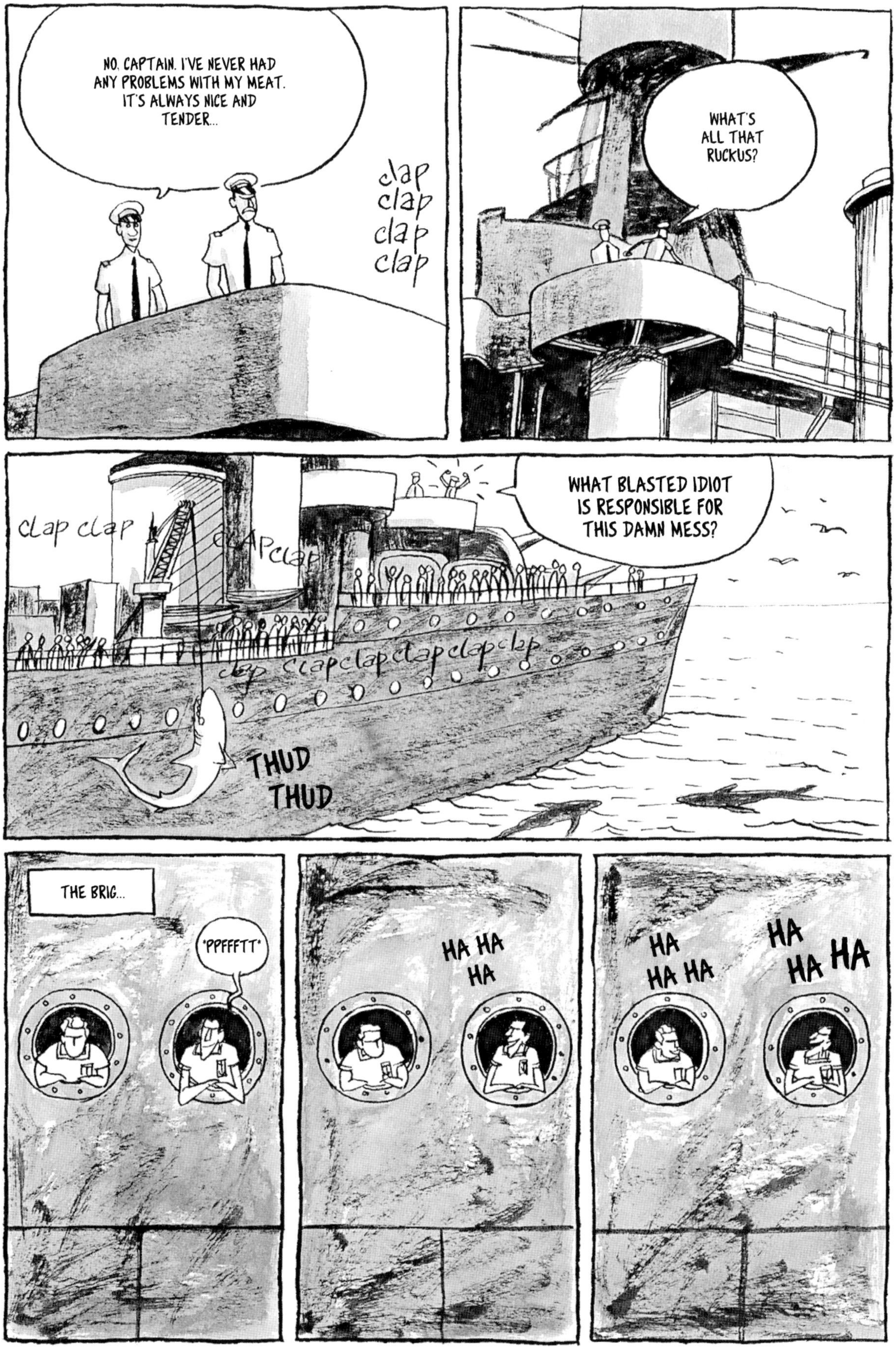
NO. CAPTAIN. I'VE NEVER HAD ANY PROBLEMS WITH MY MEAT. IT'S ALWAYS NICE AND TENDER...
clap clap clap clap
WHAT'S ALL THAT RUCKUS?
WHAT BLASTED IDIOT IS RESPONSIBLE FOR THIS DAMN MESS?
clap clap
clap clap
clap clap clap clap clap clap
THUD THUD
THE BRIG...
PPFFFTT
HA HA HA
HA HA HA
HA HA HA

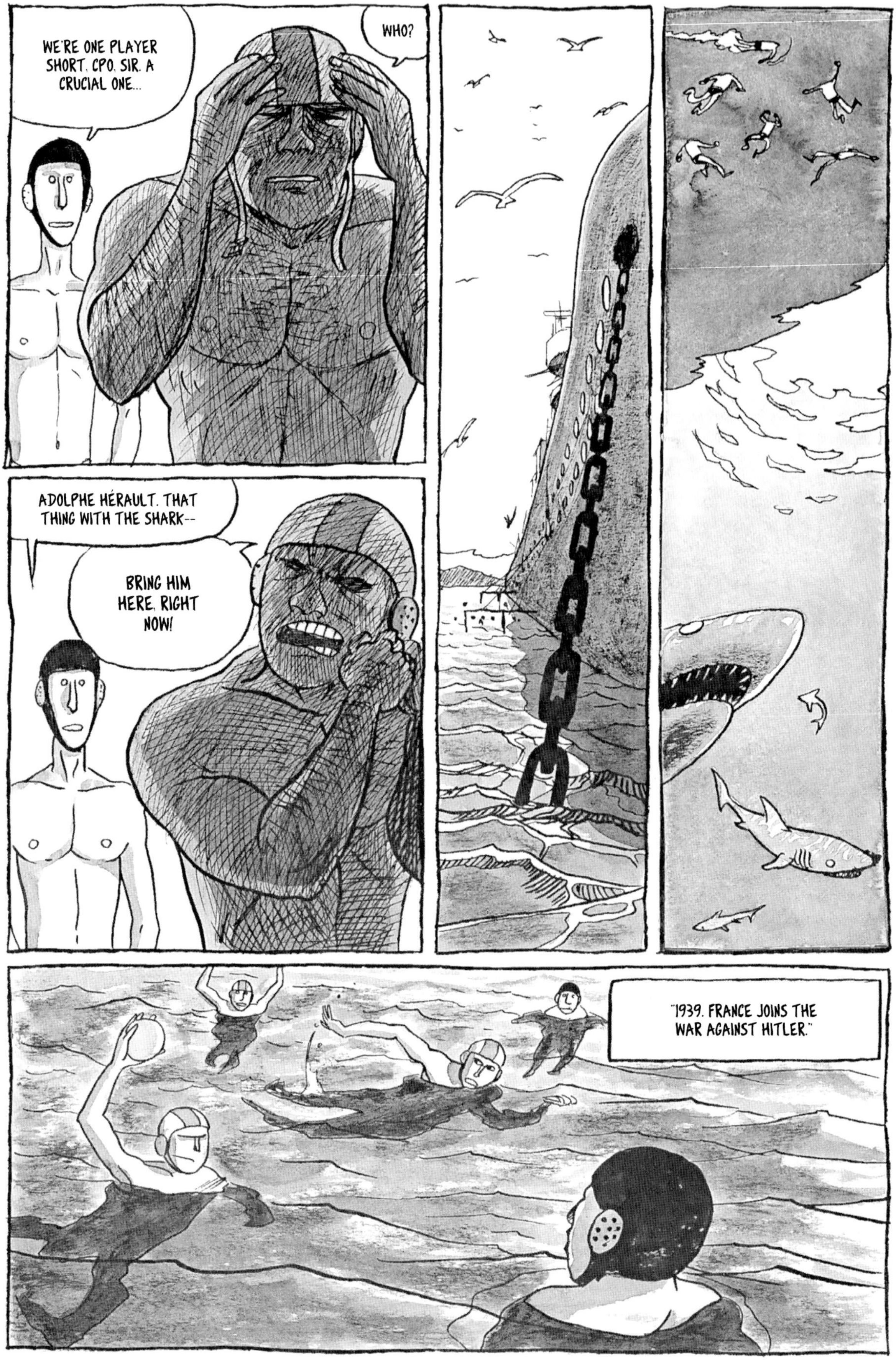

WE'RE ONE PLAYER SHORT, CPO, SIR. A CRUCIAL ONE...
WHO?
ADOLPHE HÉRAULT. THAT THING WITH THE SHARK--
BRING HIM HERE, RIGHT NOW!
"1939. FRANCE JOINS THE WAR AGAINST HITLER."

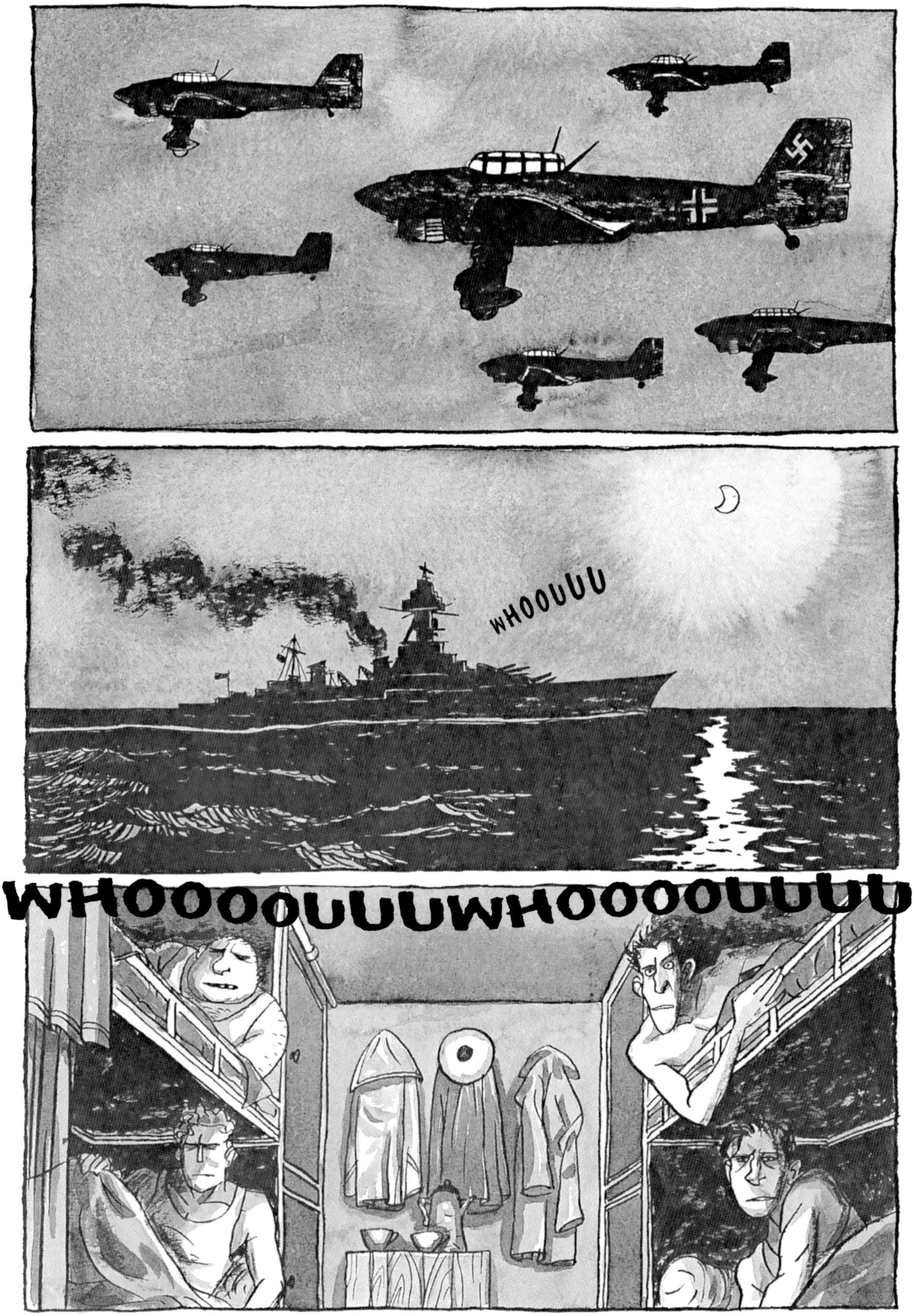
WHOOUUU
WHOOOOUUUWHOOOOUUUU

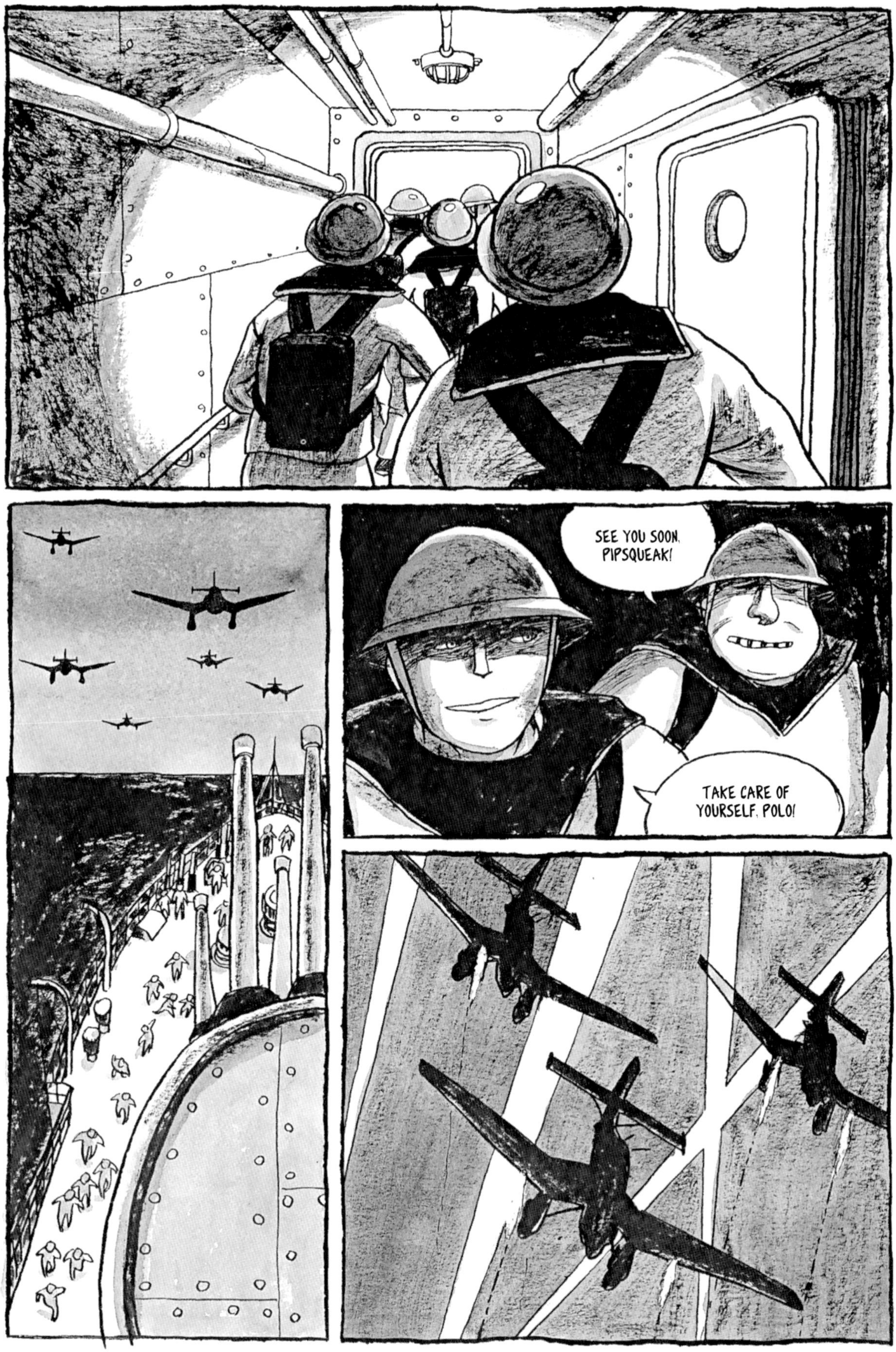

SEE YOU SOON, PIPSQUEAK!
TAKE CARE OF YOURSELF, POLO!

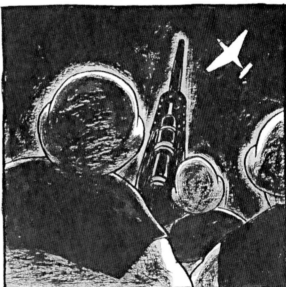

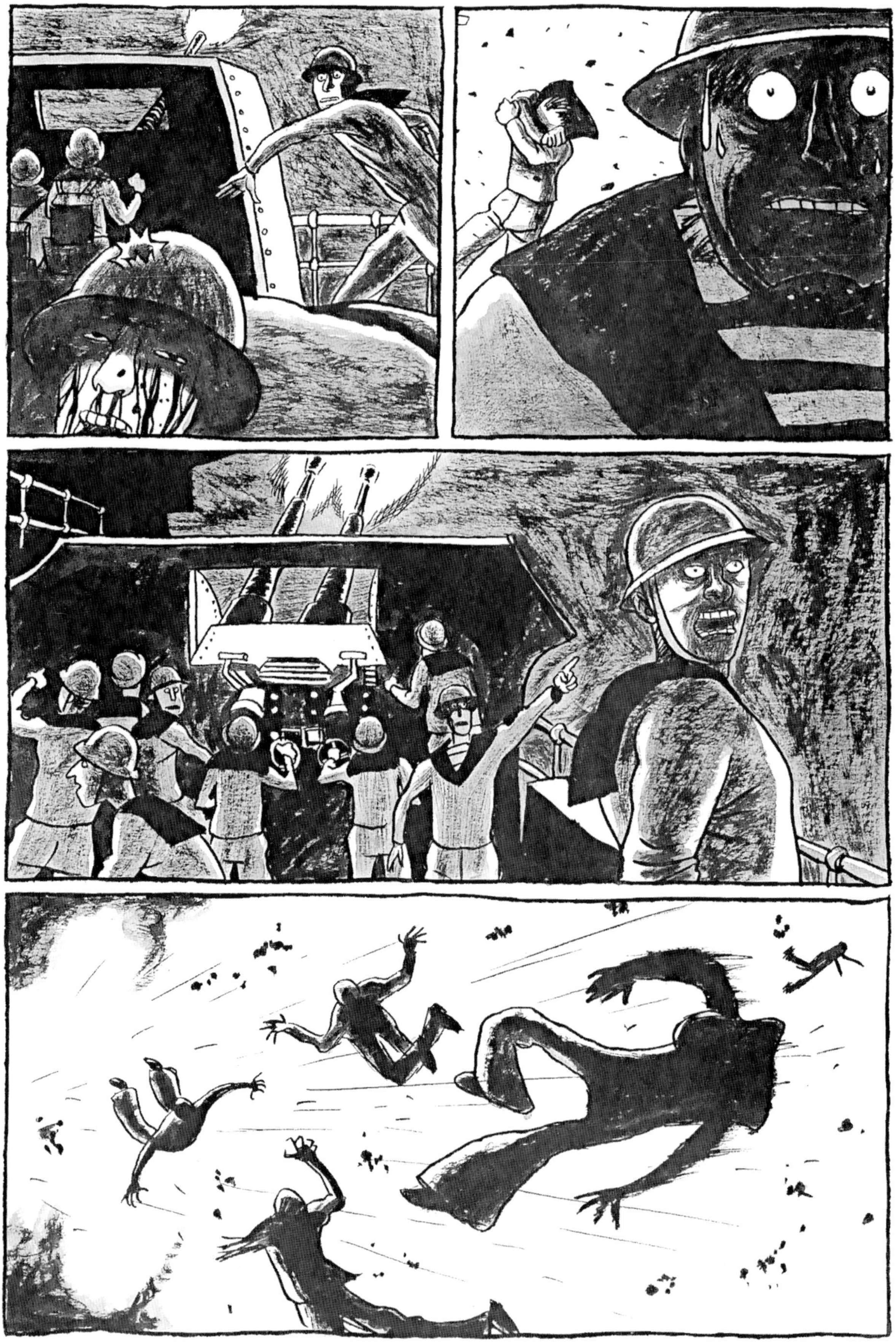

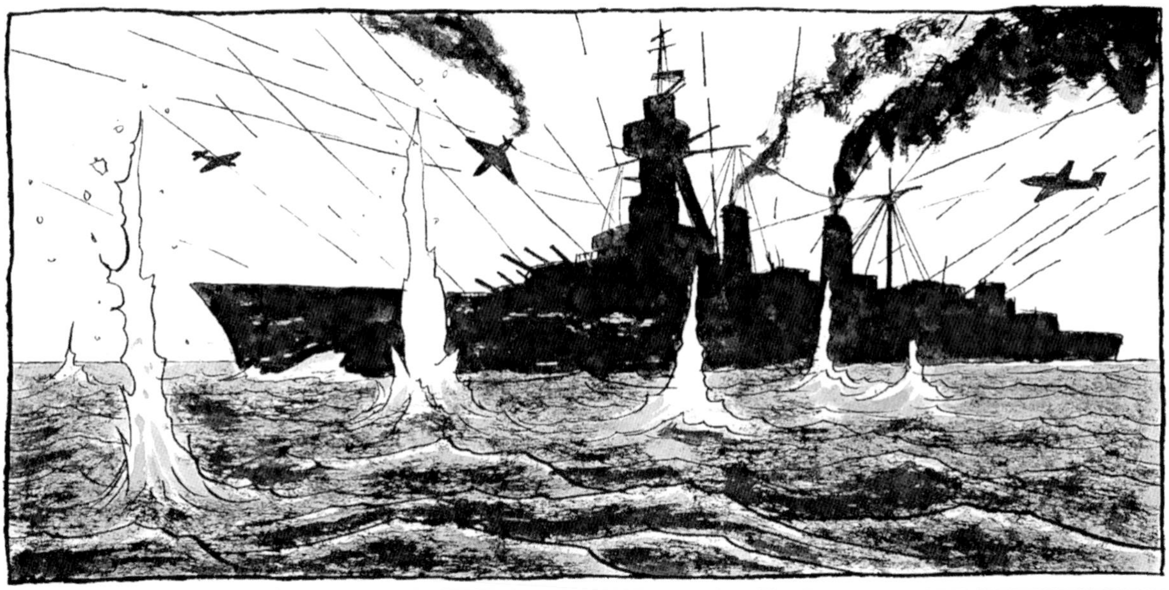

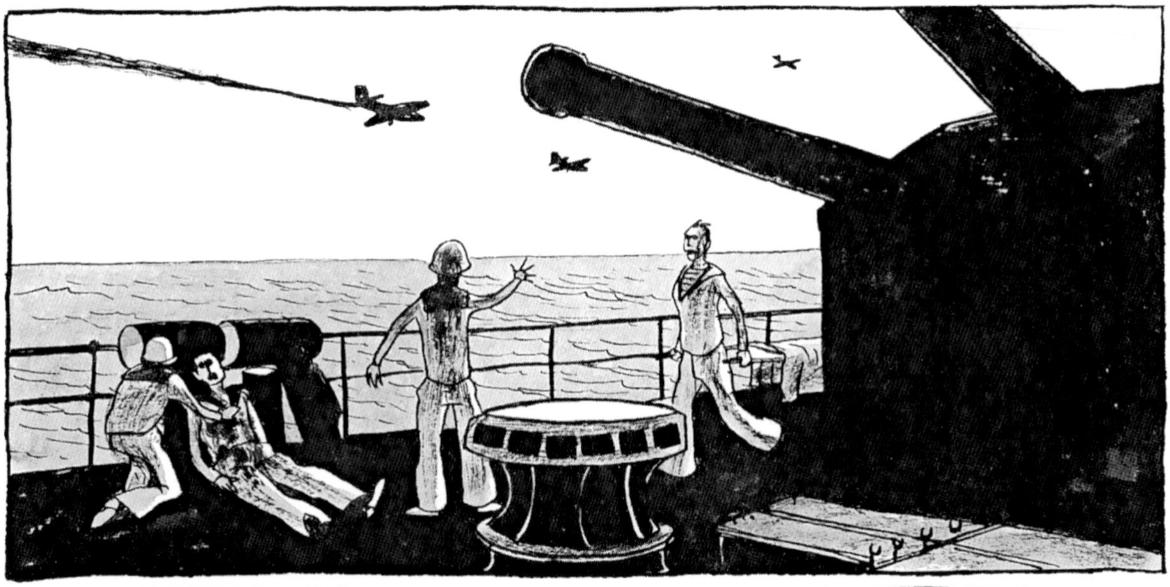

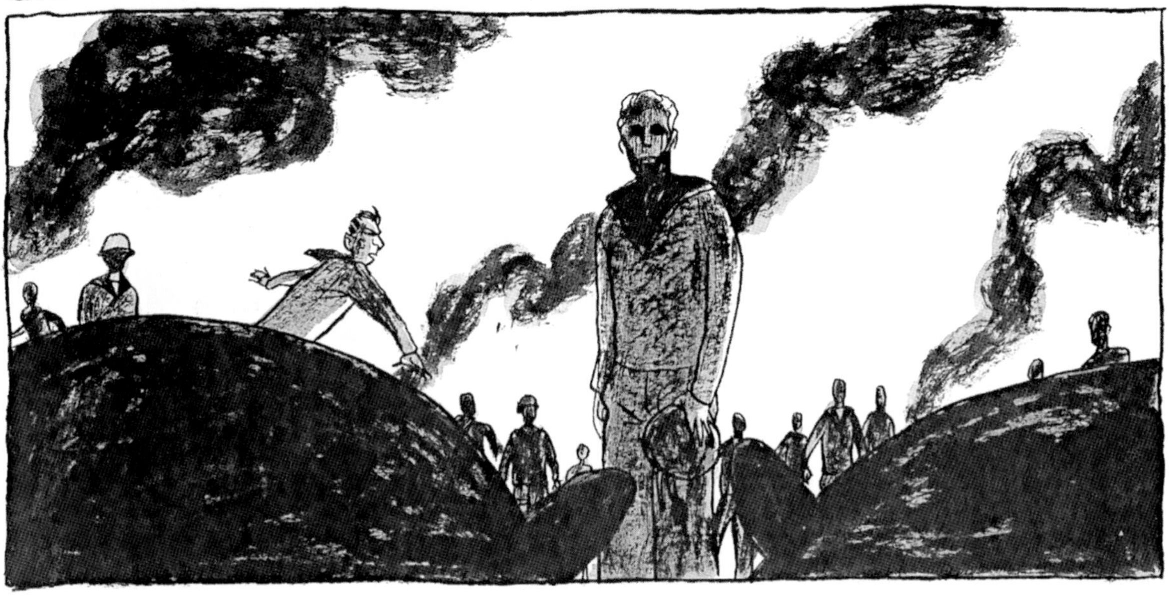

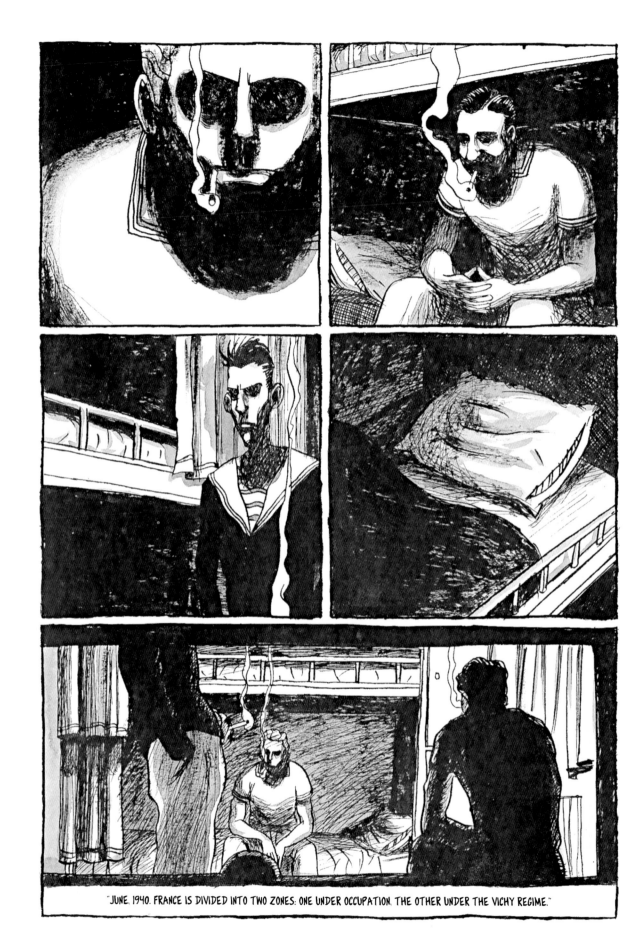

"JUNE, 1940. FRANCE IS DIVIDED INTO TWO ZONES: ONE UNDER OCCUPATION, THE OTHER UNDER THE VICHY REGIME."

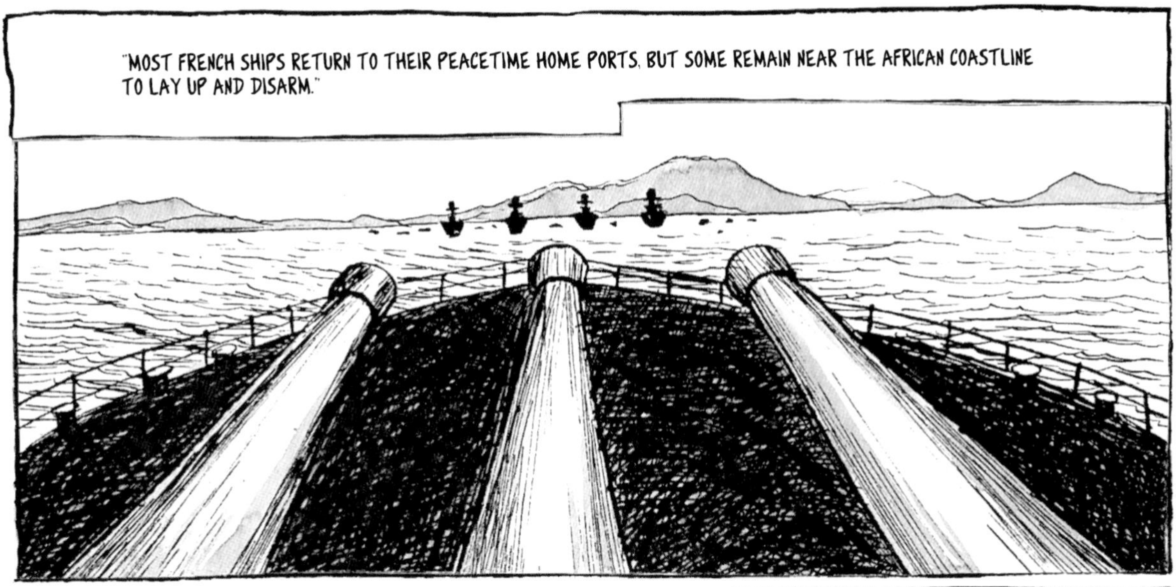
"MOST FRENCH SHIPS RETURN TO THEIR PEACETIME HOME PORTS, BUT SOME REMAIN NEAR THE AFRICAN COASTLINE TO LAY UP AND DISARM."

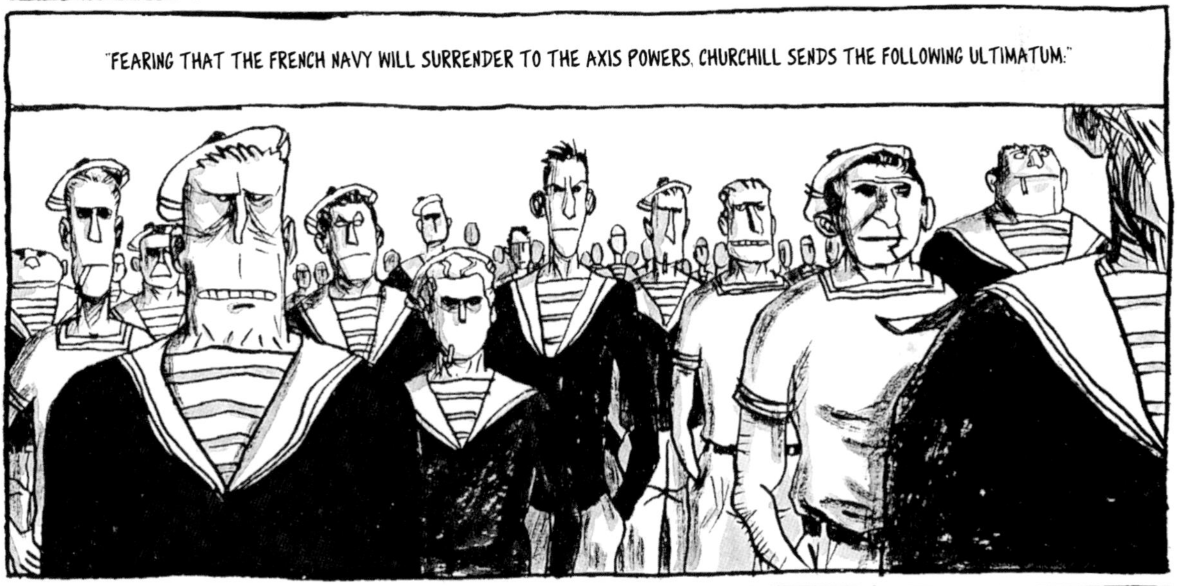
"FEARING THAT THE FRENCH NAVY WILL SURRENDER TO THE AXIS POWERS, CHURCHILL SENDS THE FOLLOWING ULTIMATUM:"

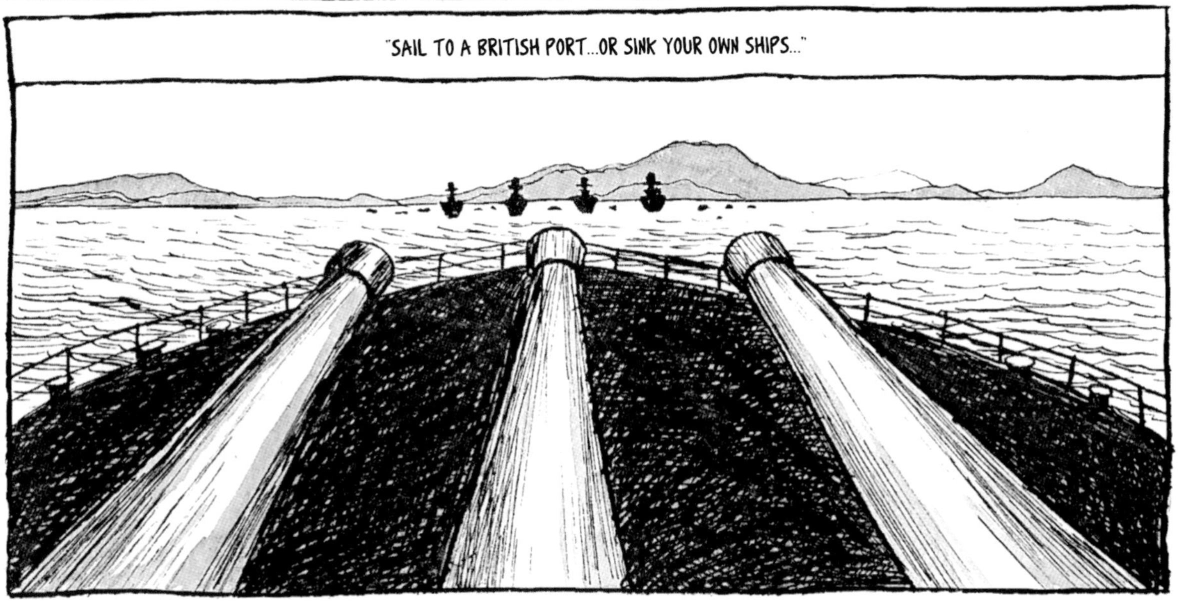
"SAIL TO A BRITISH PORT...OR SINK YOUR OWN SHIPS..."

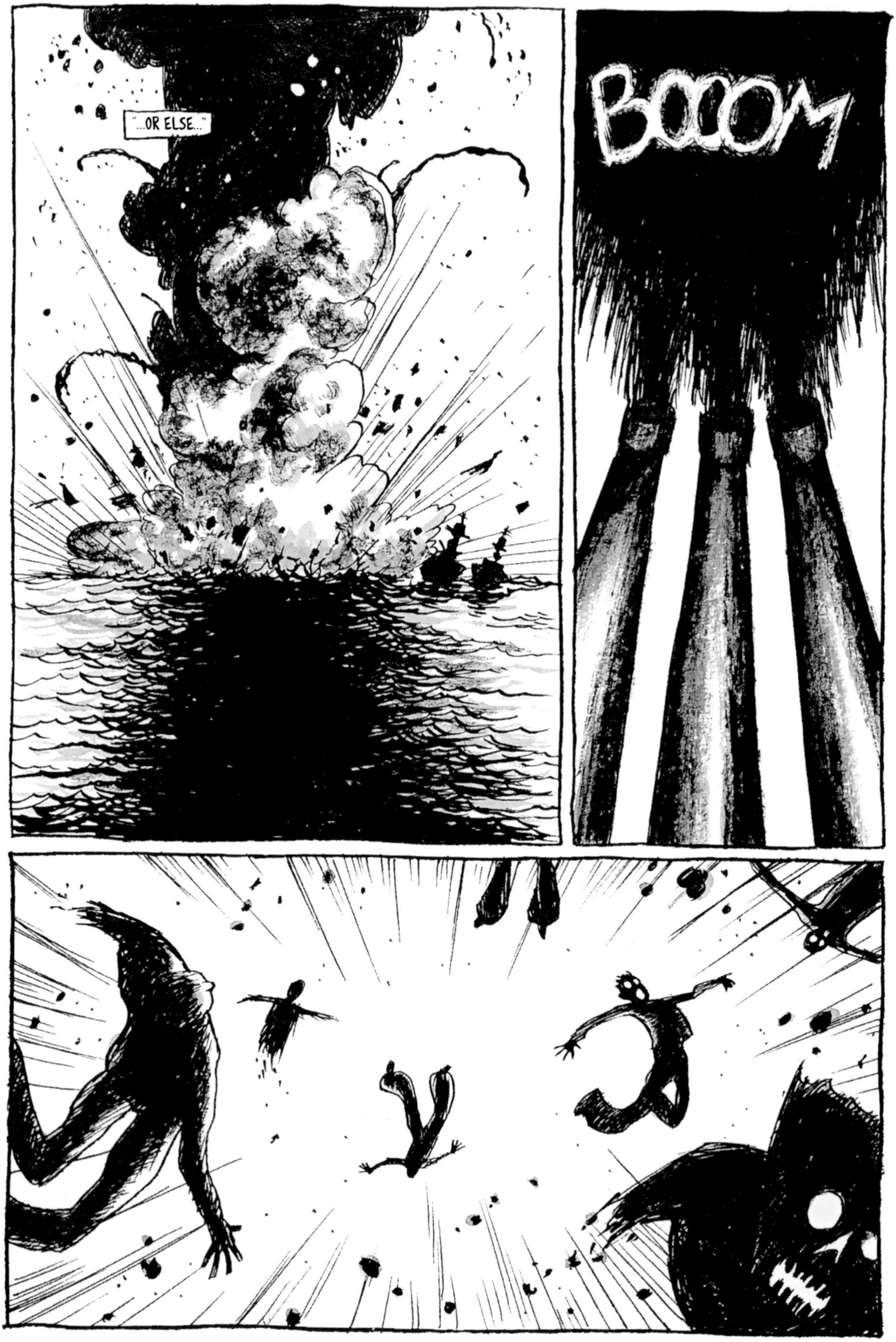
"...OR ELSE..."
BOOOM

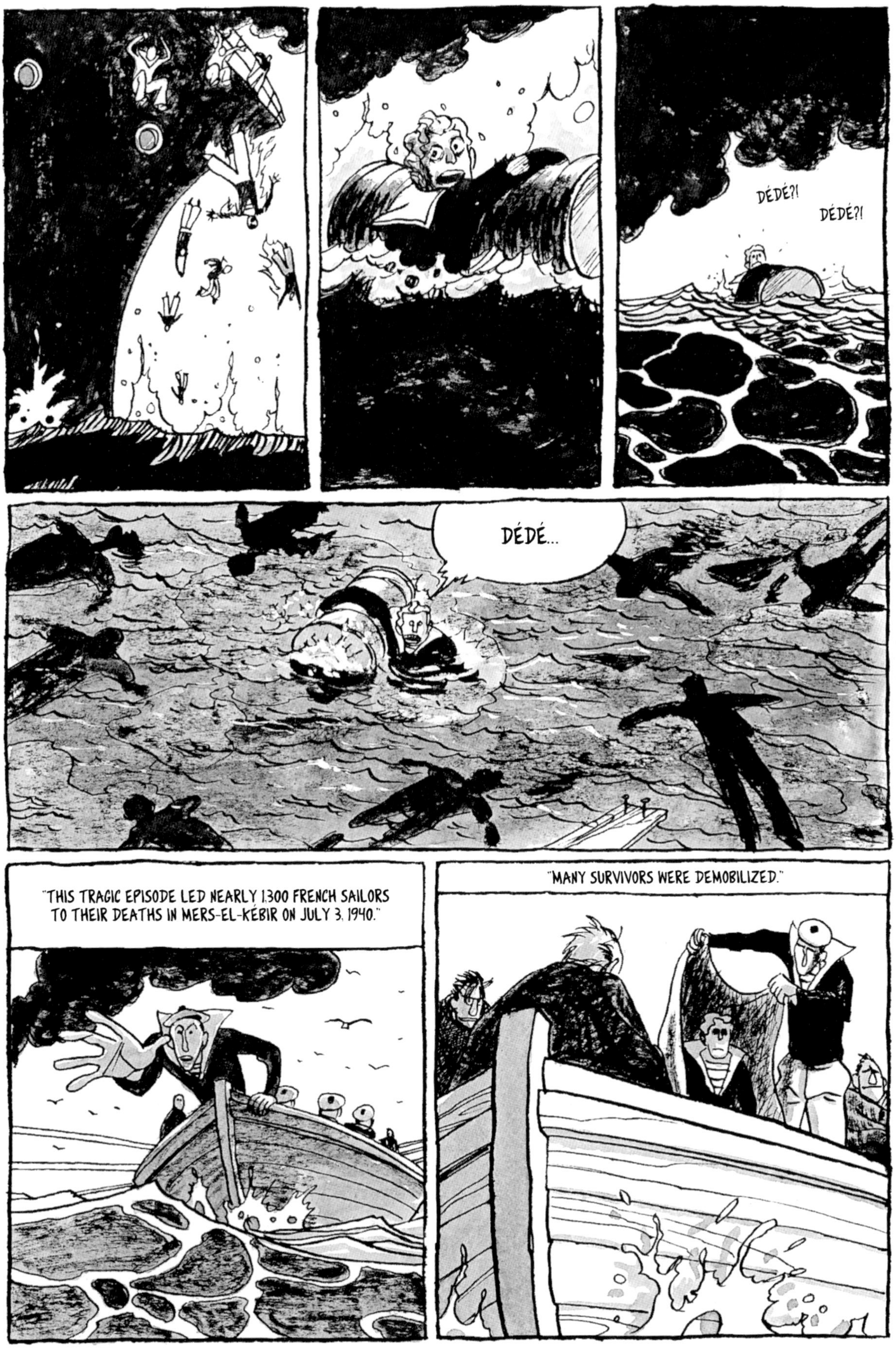
DÉDÉ?!
DÉDÉ?!
DÉDÉ...
"THIS TRAGIC EPISODE LED NEARLY 1,300 FRENCH SAILORS TO THEIR DEATHS IN MERS-EL-KÉBIR ON JULY 3, 1940."
"MANY SURVIVORS WERE DEMOBILIZED."

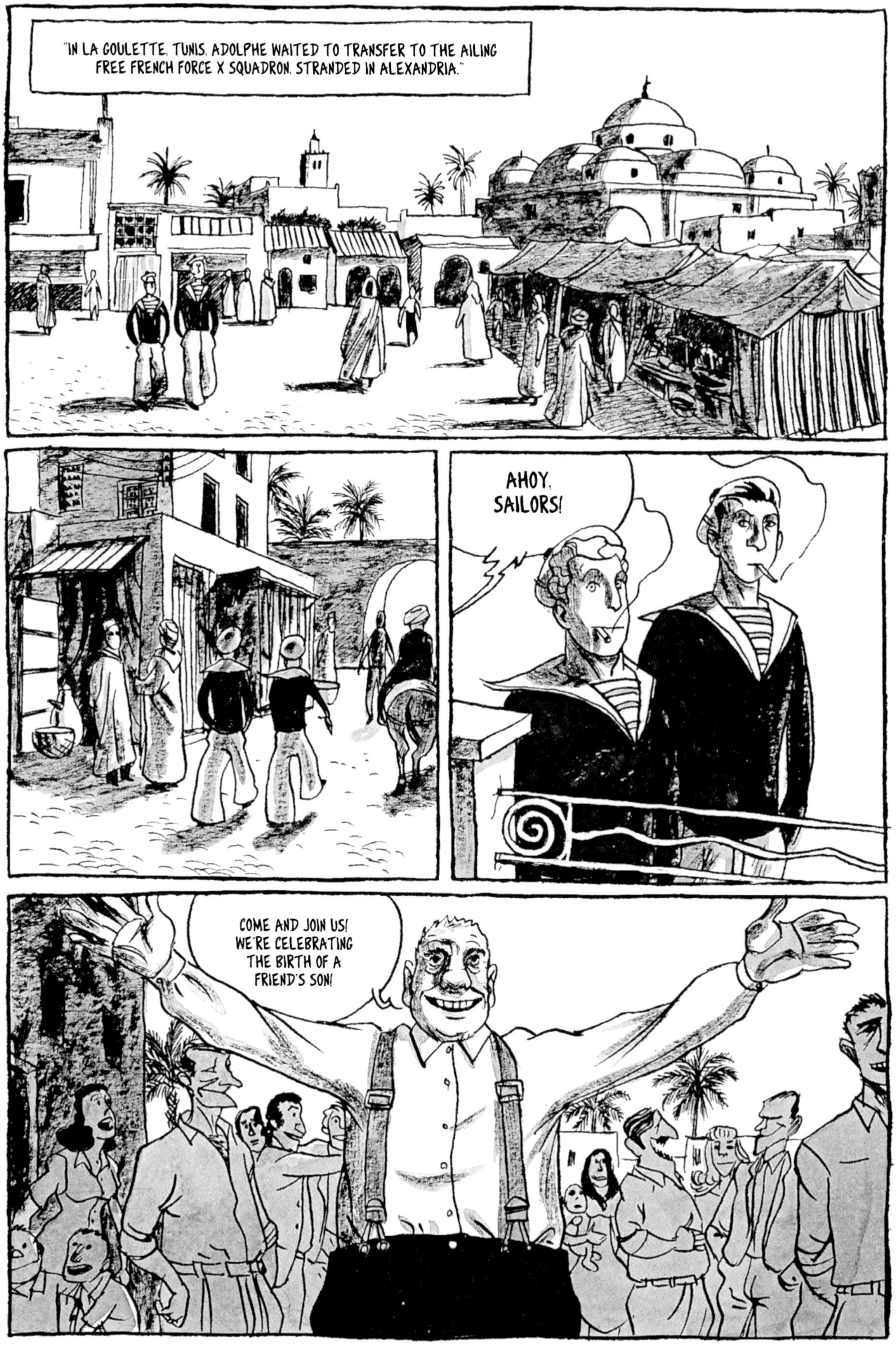
"IN LA GOULETTE, TUNIS, ADOLPHE WAITED TO TRANSFER TO THE AILING FREE FRENCH FORCE X SQUADRON, STRANDED IN ALEXANDRIA."
AHOY, SAILORS!
COME AND JOIN US! WE'RE CELEBRATING THE BIRTH OF A FRIEND'S SON!

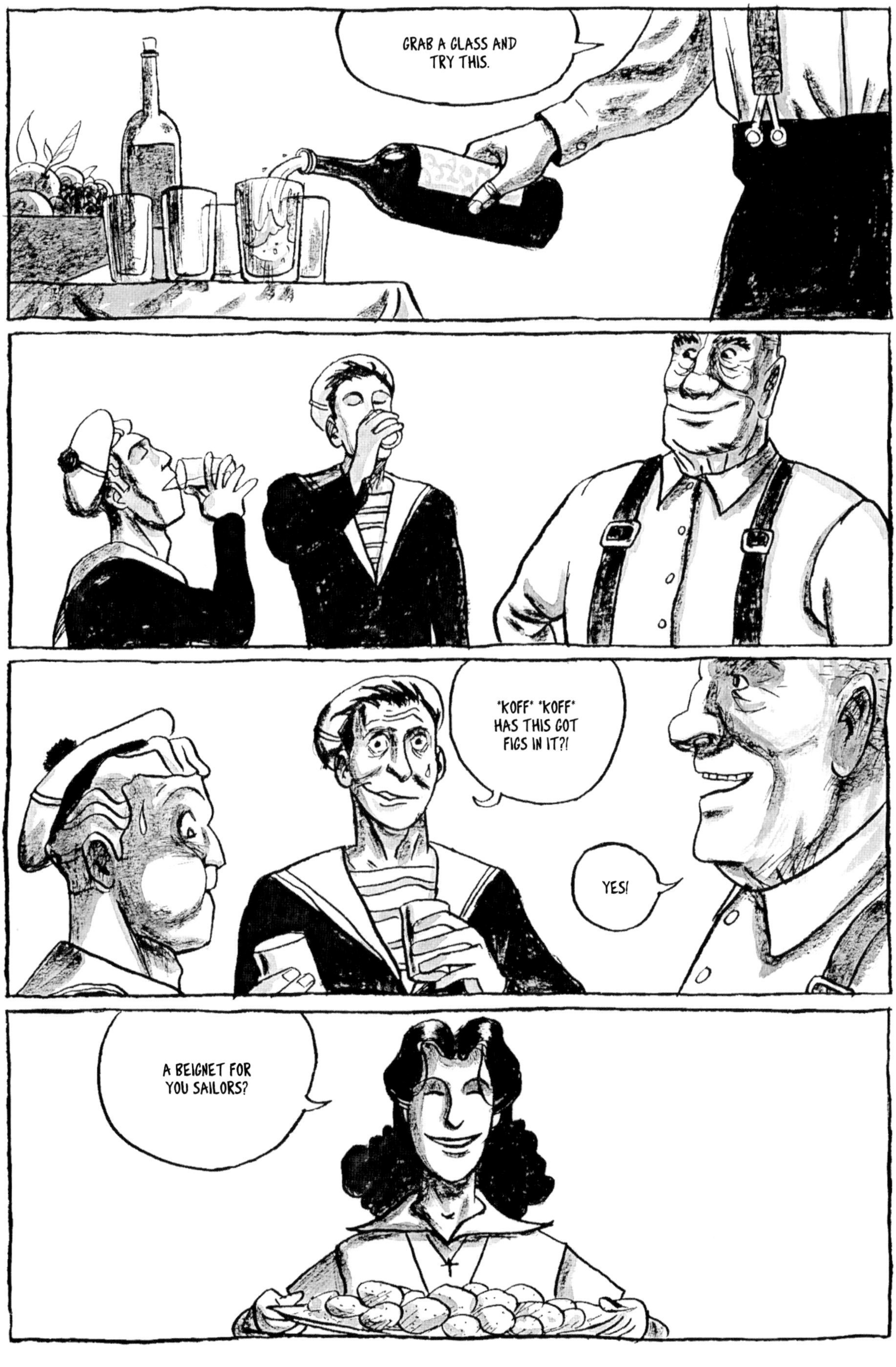
GRAB A GLASS AND TRY THIS.
KOFF *KOFF* HAS THIS GOT FIGS IN IT?!
YES!
A BEIGNET FOR YOU SAILORS?

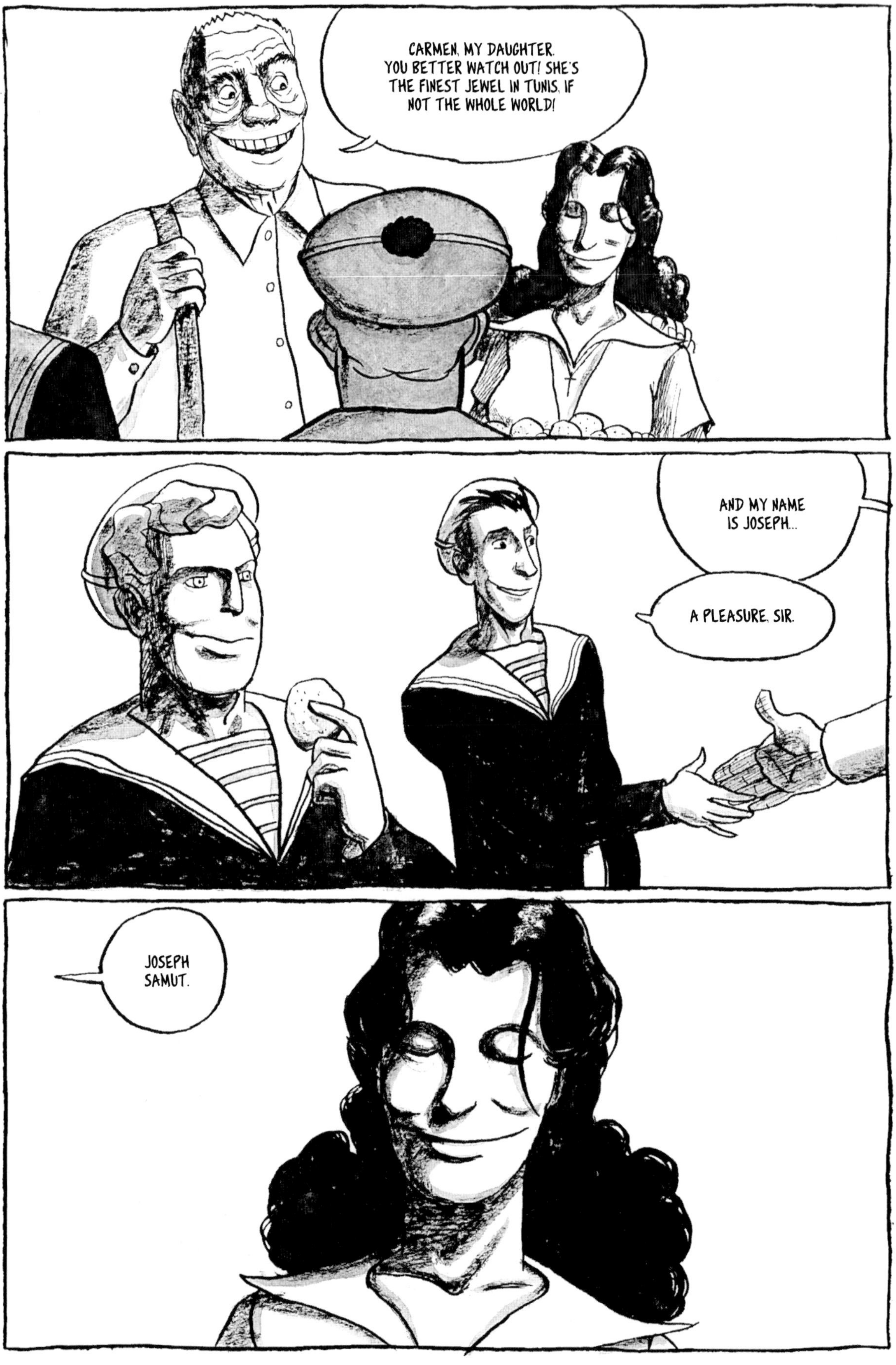
CARMEN, MY DAUGHTER. YOU BETTER WATCH OUT! SHE'S THE FINEST JEWEL IN TUNIS, IF NOT THE WHOLE WORLD!
AND MY NAME IS JOSEPH...
A PLEASURE, SIR.
JOSEPH SAMUT.

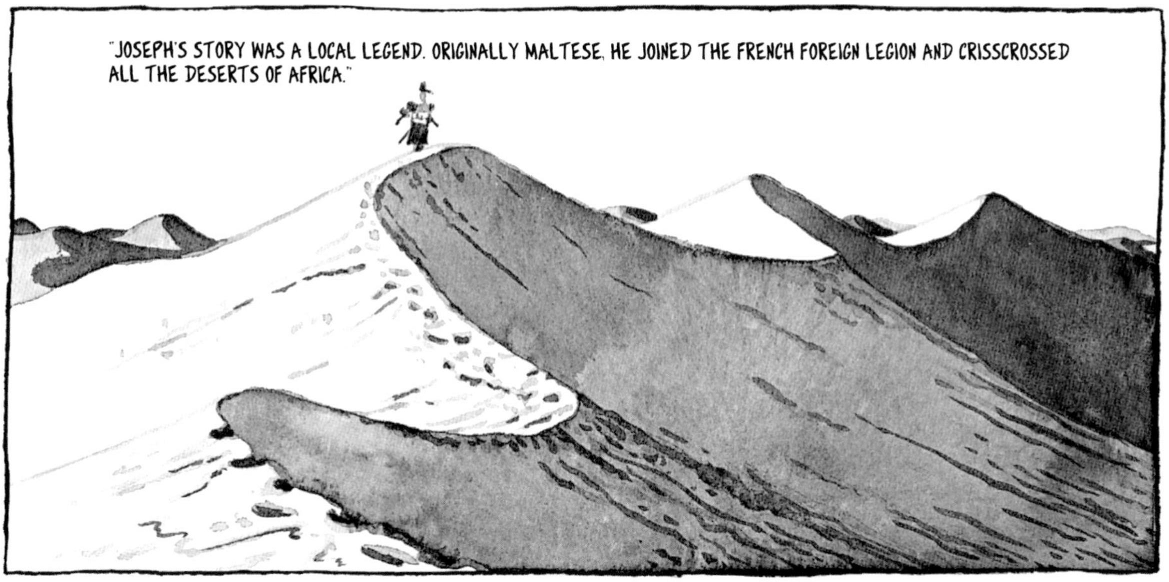
"JOSEPH'S STORY WAS A LOCAL LEGEND. ORIGINALLY MALTESE, HE JOINED THE FRENCH FOREIGN LEGION AND CRISSCROSSED ALL THE DESERTS OF AFRICA."

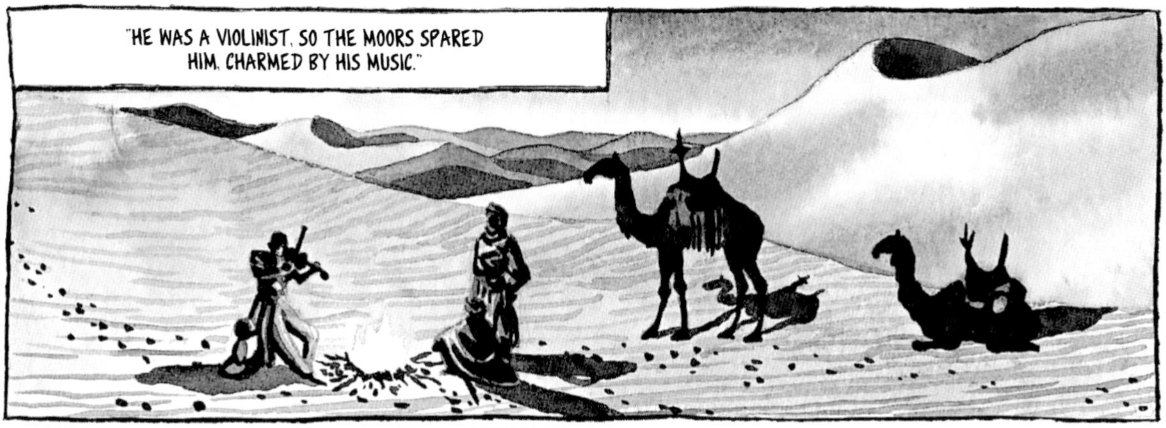
"HE WAS A VIOLINIST, SO THE MOORS SPARED HIM, CHARMED BY HIS MUSIC."

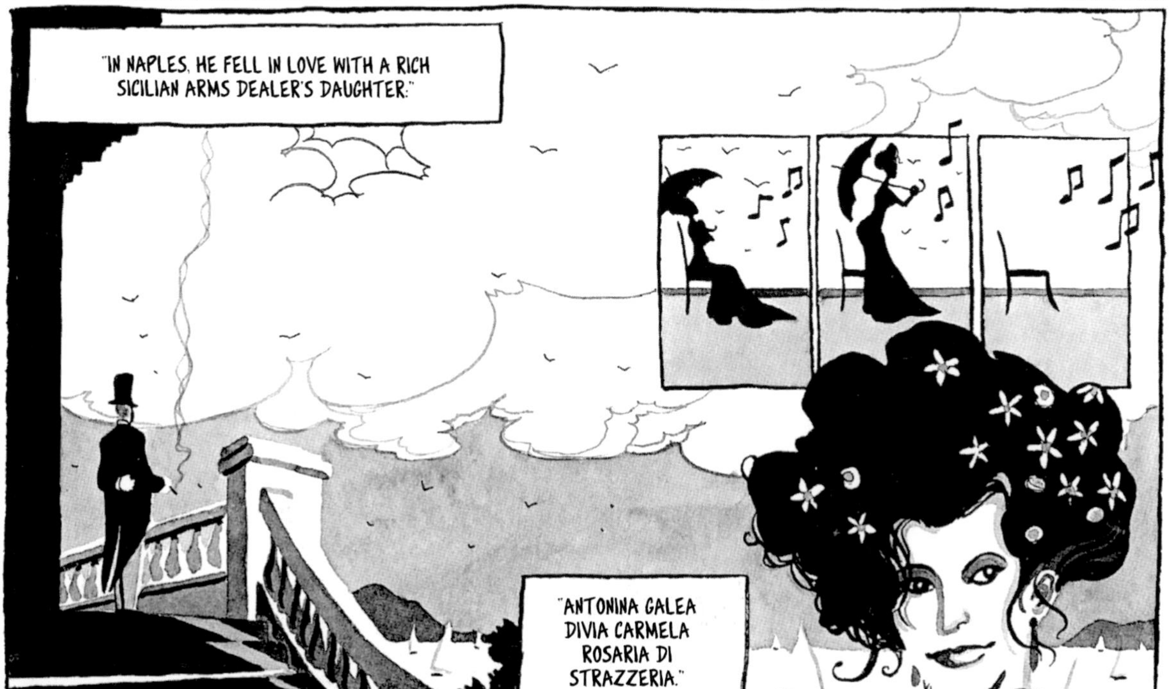
"IN NAPLES, HE FELL IN LOVE WITH A RICH SICILIAN ARMS DEALER'S DAUGHTER:
"ANTONINA GALEA DIVIA CARMELA ROSARIA DI STRAZZERIA."

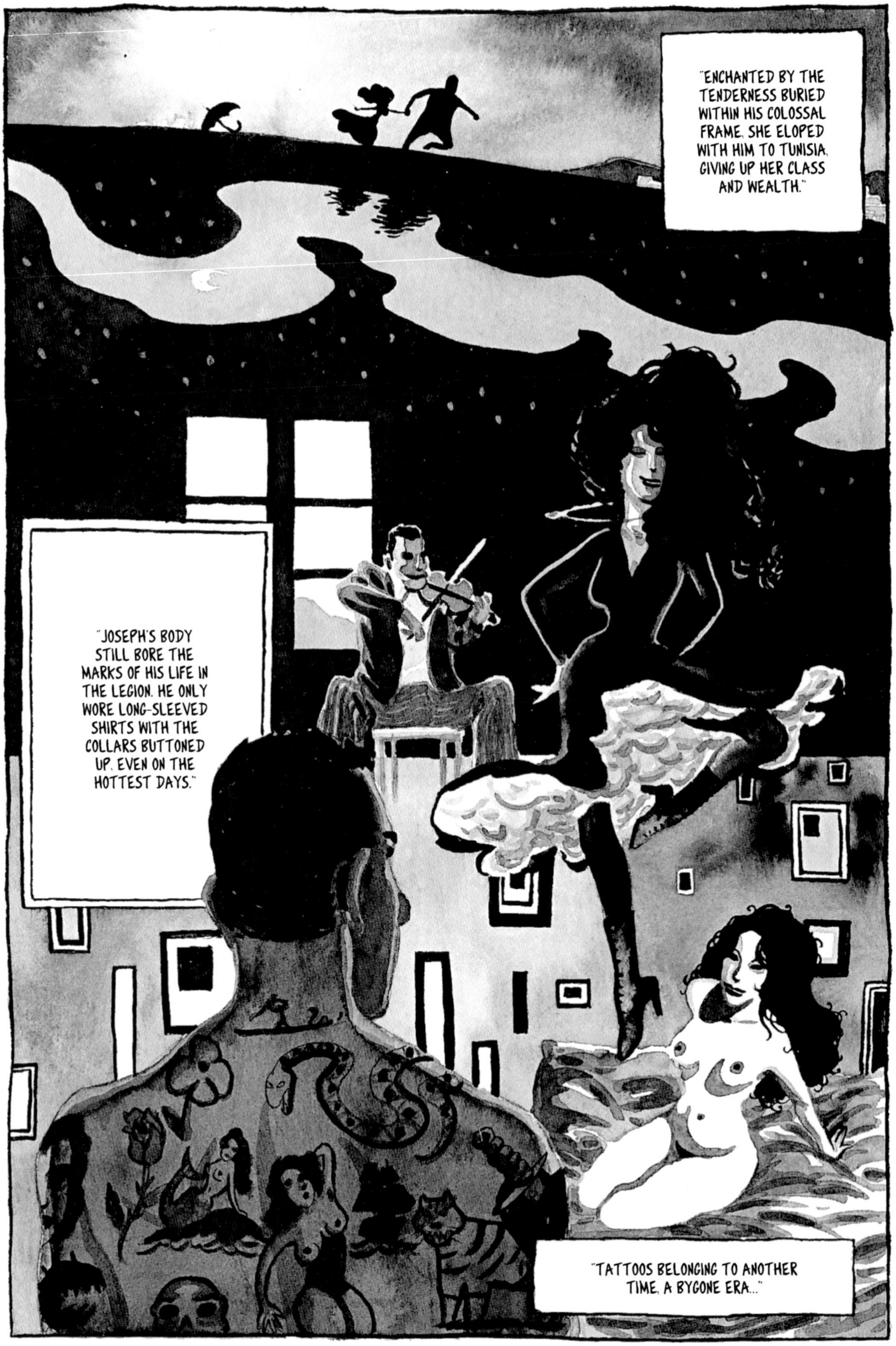
"ENCHANTED BY THE TENDERNESS BURIED WITHIN HIS COLOSSAL FRAME, SHE ELOPED WITH HIM TO TUNISIA, GIVING UP HER CLASS AND WEALTH."
"JOSEPH'S BODY STILL BORE THE MARKS OF HIS LIFE IN THE LEGION. HE ONLY WORE LONG-SLEEVED SHIRTS WITH THE COLLARS BUTTONED UP, EVEN ON THE HOTTEST DAYS."
"TATTOOS BELONGING TO ANOTHER TIME, A BYGONE ERA..."

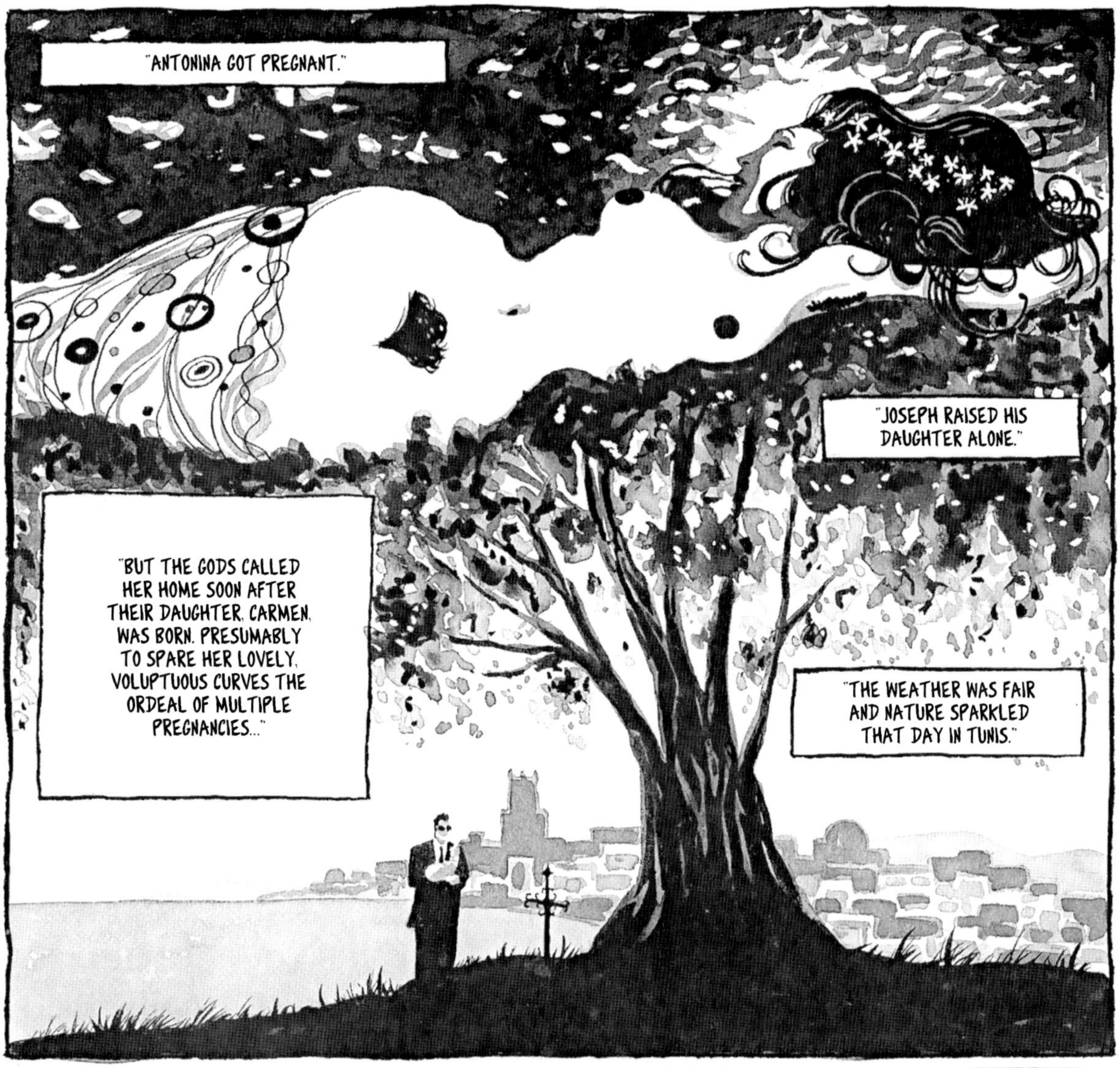
"ANTONINA GOT PREGNANT."
"BUT THE GODS CALLED HER HOME SOON AFTER THEIR DAUGHTER, CARMEN, WAS BORN. PRESUMABLY TO SPARE HER LOVELY, VOLUPTUOUS CURVES THE ORDEAL OF MULTIPLE PREGNANCIES..."
"JOSEPH RAISED HIS DAUGHTER ALONE."
"THE WEATHER WAS FAIR AND NATURE SPARKLED THAT DAY IN TUNIS."

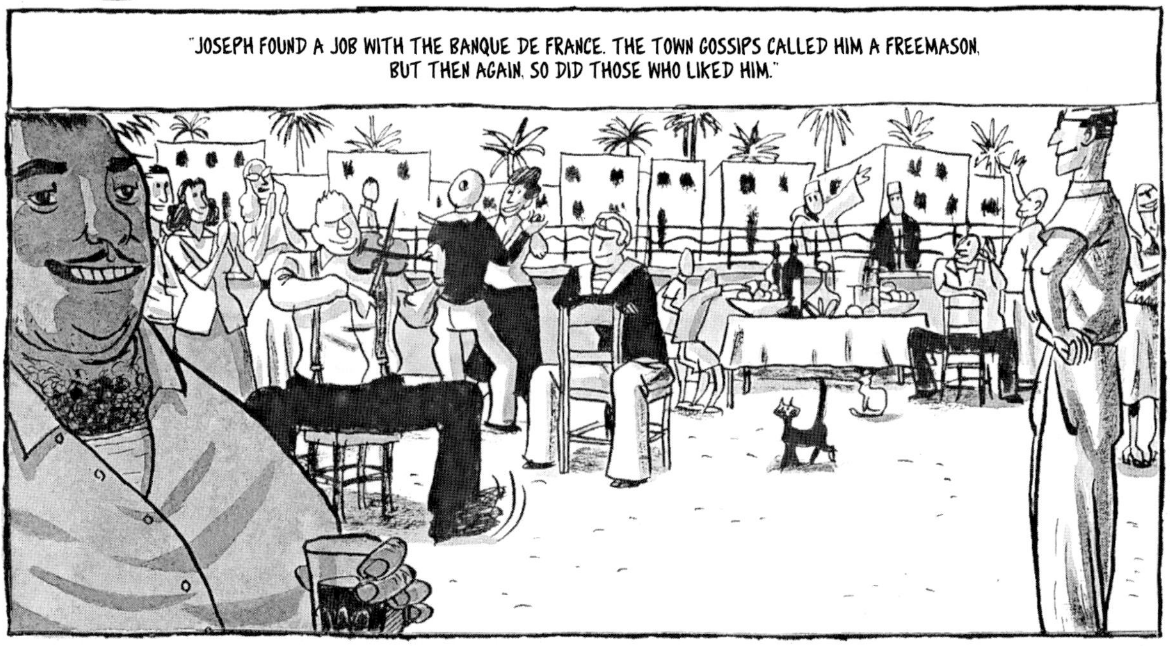
"JOSEPH FOUND A JOB WITH THE BANQUE DE FRANCE. THE TOWN GOSSIPS CALLED HIM A FREEMASON, BUT THEN AGAIN, SO DID THOSE WHO LIKED HIM."

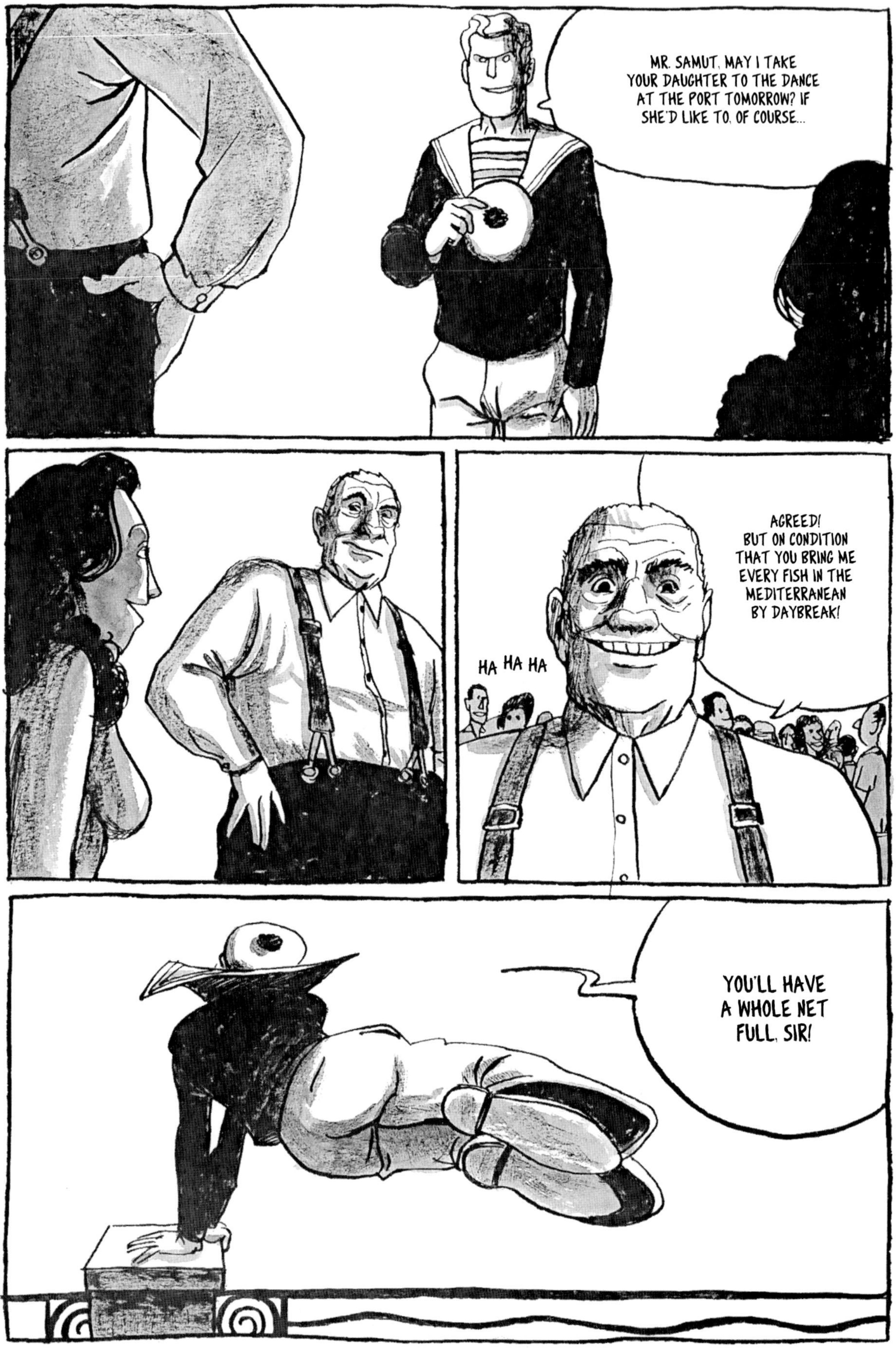
MR. SAMUT, MAY I TAKE YOUR DAUGHTER TO THE DANCE AT THE PORT TOMORROW? IF SHE'D LIKE TO, OF COURSE...
AGREED! BUT ON CONDITION THAT YOU BRING ME EVERY FISH IN THE MEDITERRANEAN BY DAYBREAK!
HA HA HA
YOU'LL HAVE A WHOLE NET FULL, SIR!

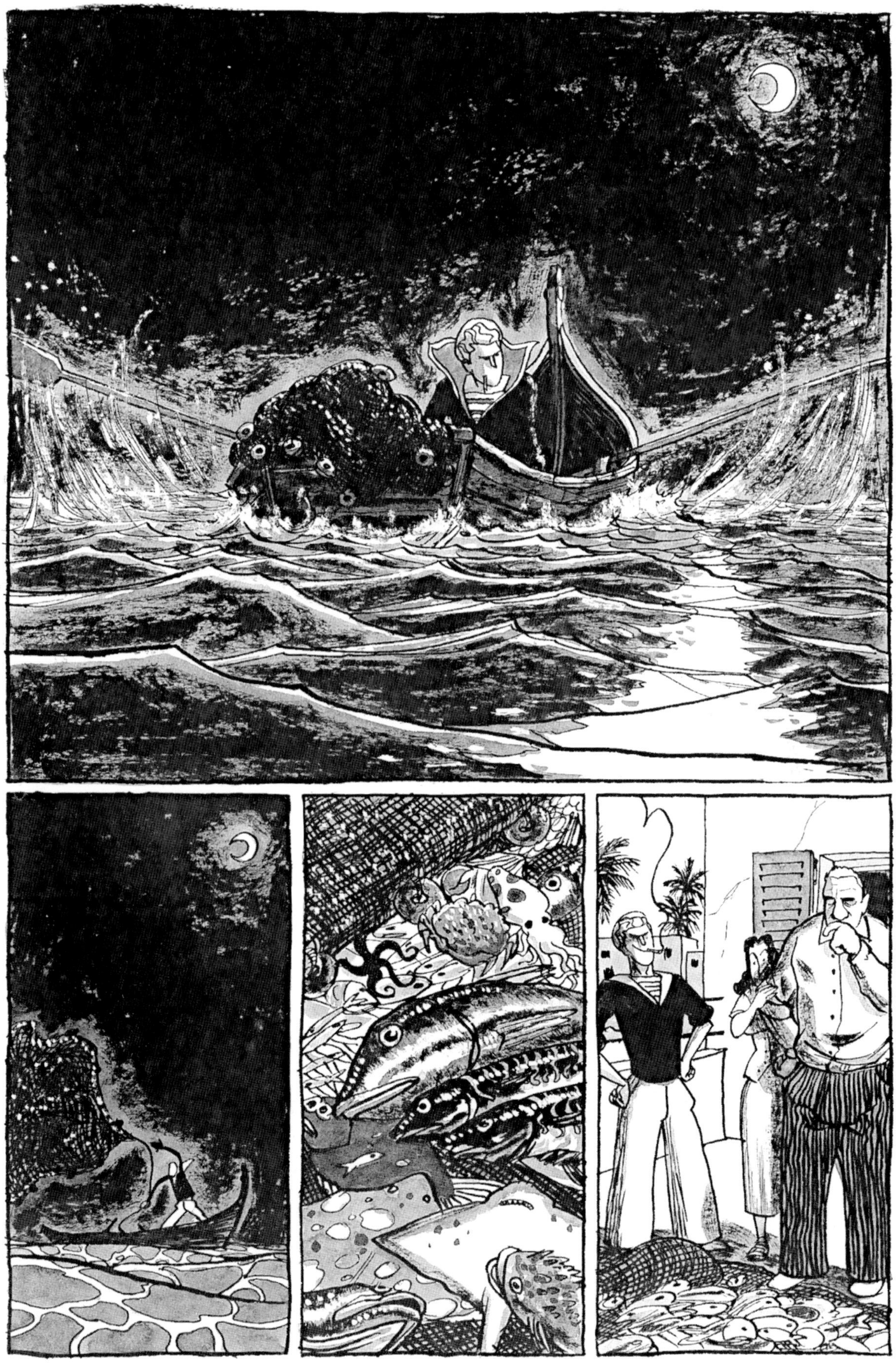

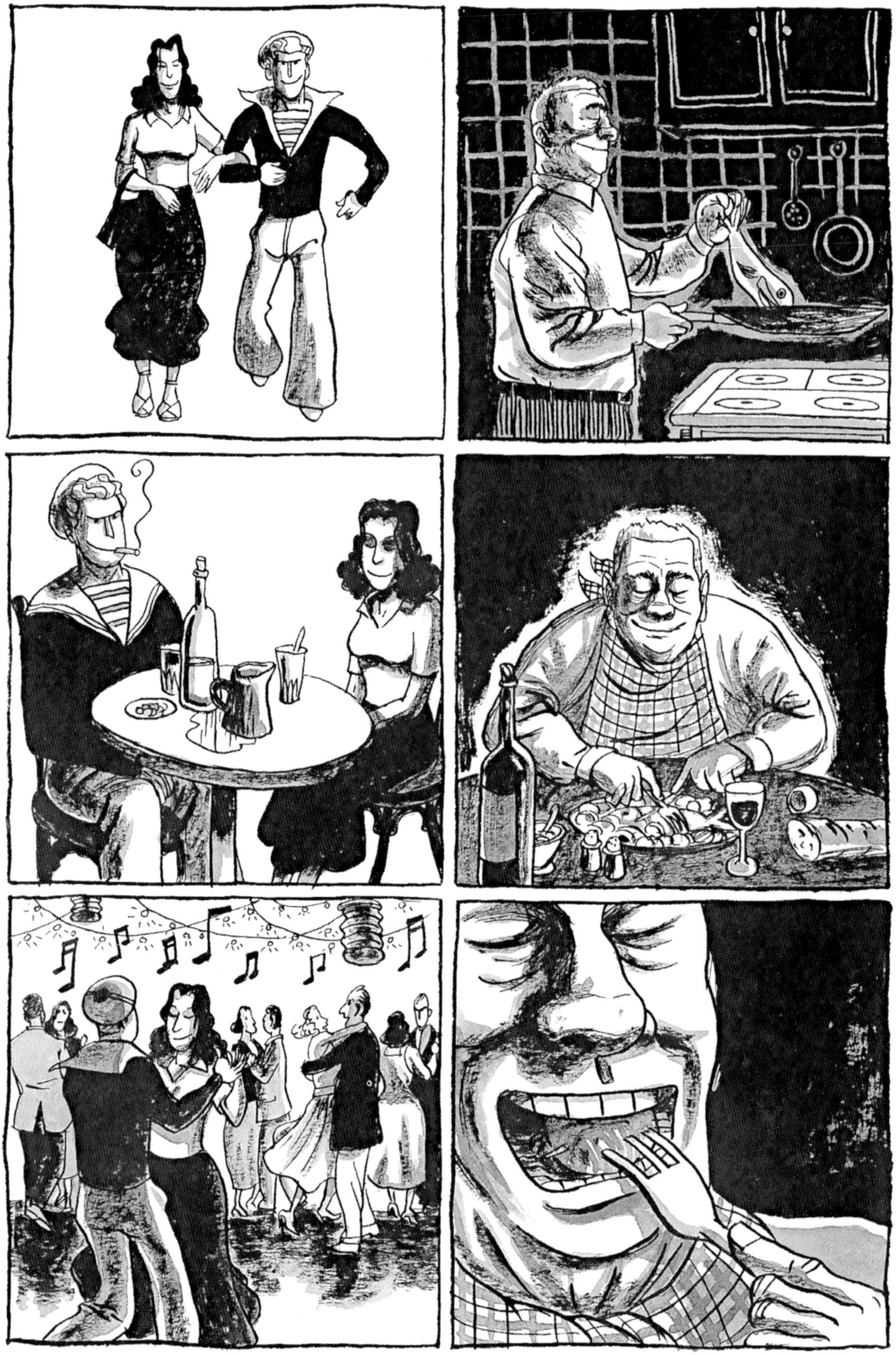

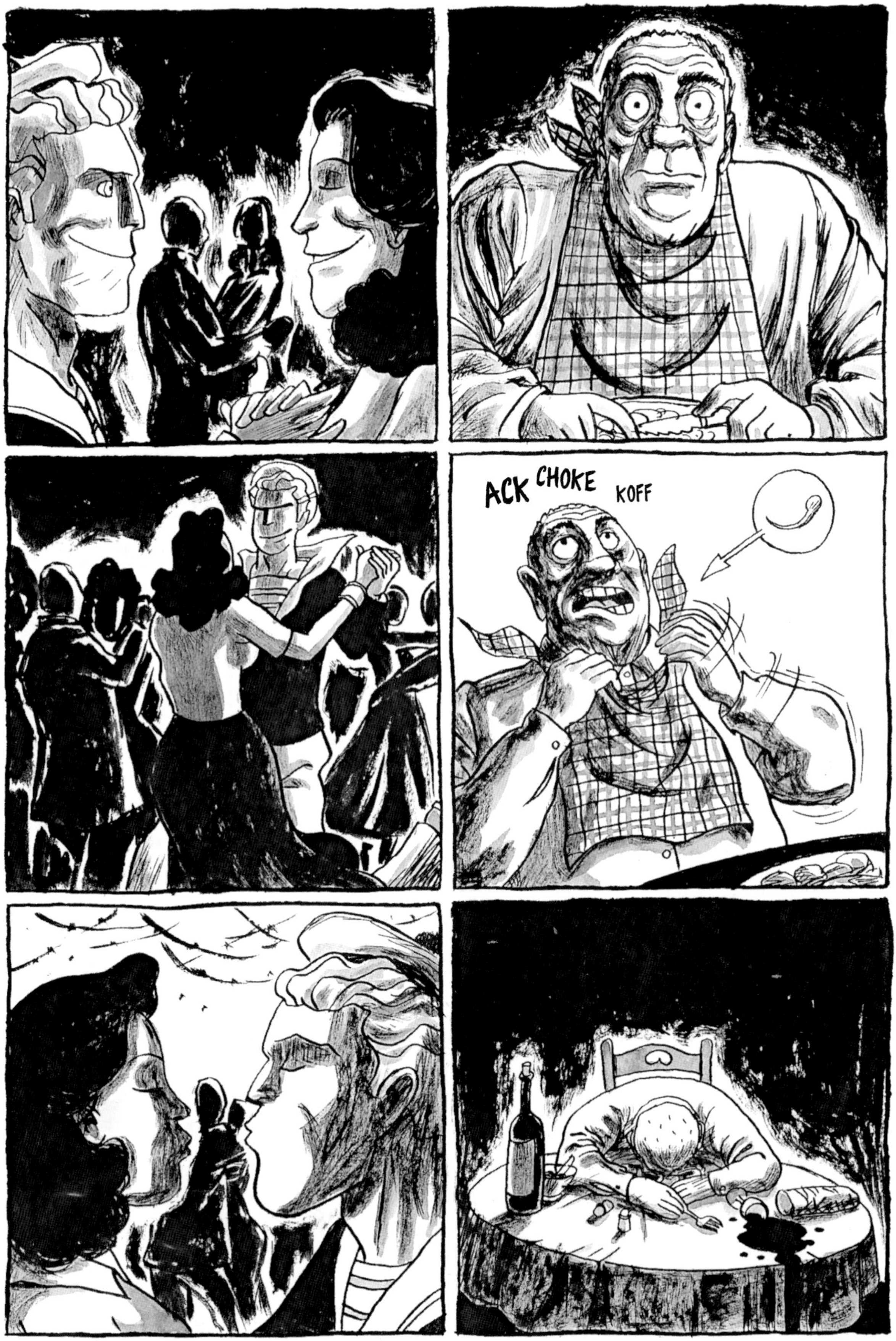
ACK CHOKE KOFF

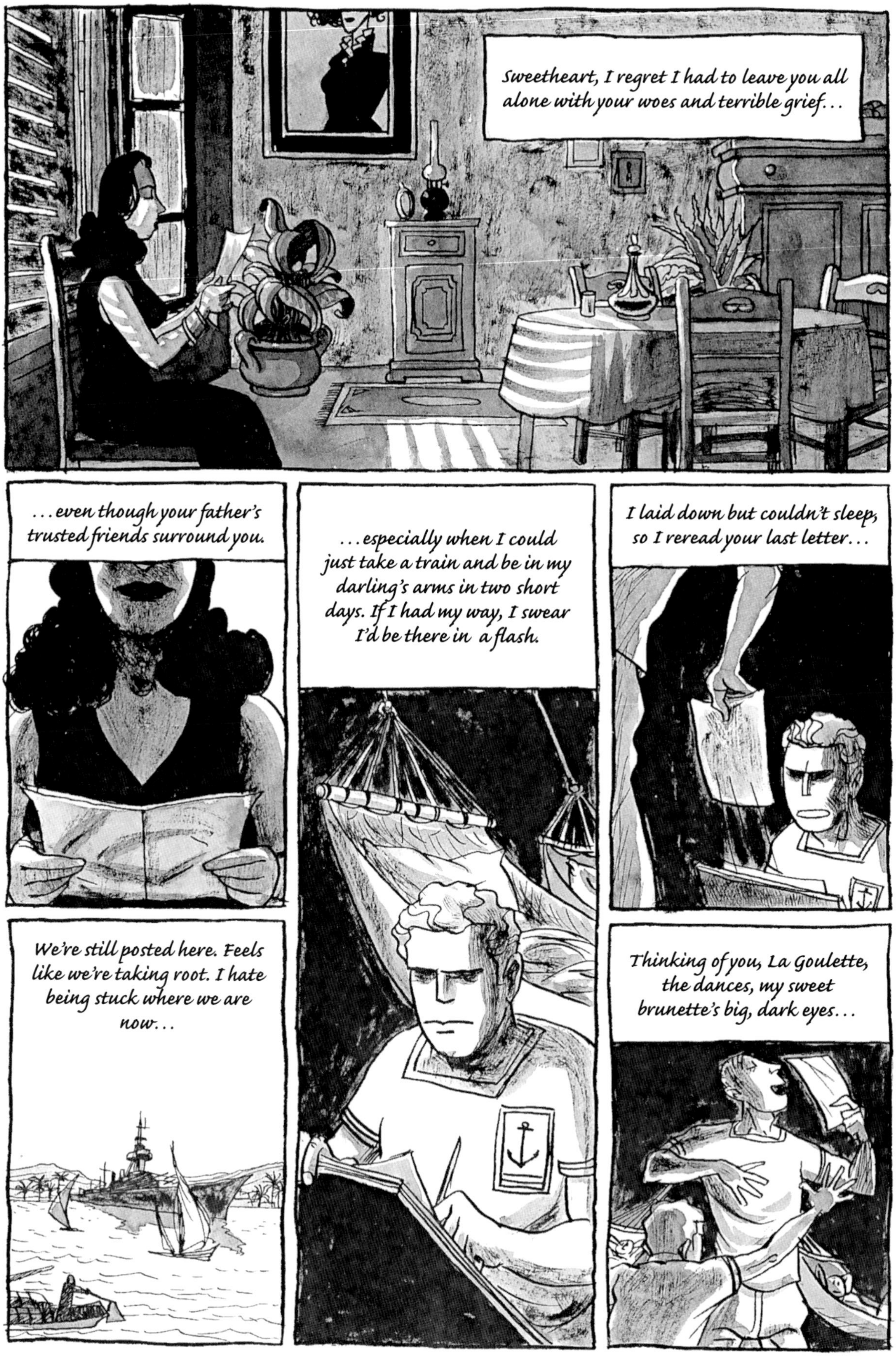
Sweetheart, I regret I had to leave you all alone with your woes and terrible grief...
...even though your father's trusted friends surround you.
...especially when I could just take a train and be in my darling's arms in two short days. If I had my way, I swear I'd be there in a flash.
I laid down but couldn't sleep, so I reread your last letter...
We're still posted here. Feels like we're taking root. I hate being stuck where we are now...
Thinking of you, La Goulette, the dances, my sweet brunette's big, dark eyes...

I hopped into my hammock with a pen and paper, but some of the guys noticed me...

They laughed and cracked jokes, but they all hope I'll get my shore leave soon.

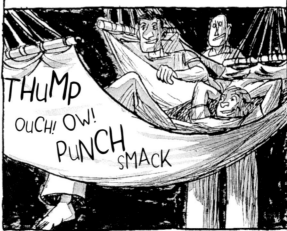

THUMP
OUCH! OW!
PUNCH SMACK

I hope it'll be soon too. Goodnight, my little desert rose. Tender, torrid kisses from your ever-loving...

...Dodo.

"ADOLPHE WAS DEMOBBED ON NOVEMBER 18, 1945."

"THEY MARRIED IN APRIL, 1946."

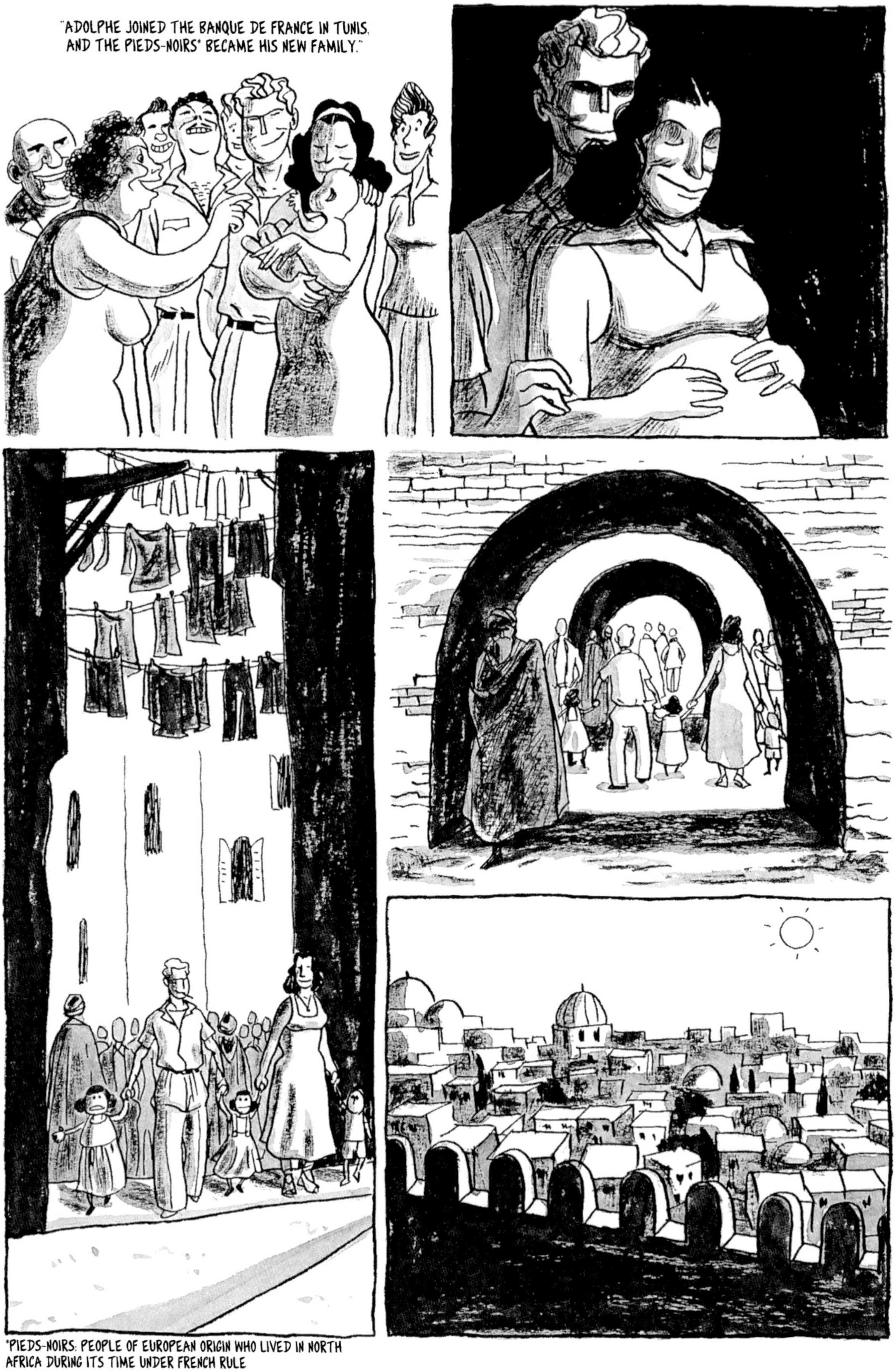
"ADOLPHE JOINED THE BANQUE DE FRANCE IN TUNIS, AND THE PIEDS-NOIRS* BECAME HIS NEW FAMILY."

*PIEDS-NOIRS: PEOPLE OF EUROPEAN ORIGIN WHO LIVED IN NORTH AFRICA DURING ITS TIME UNDER FRENCH RULE

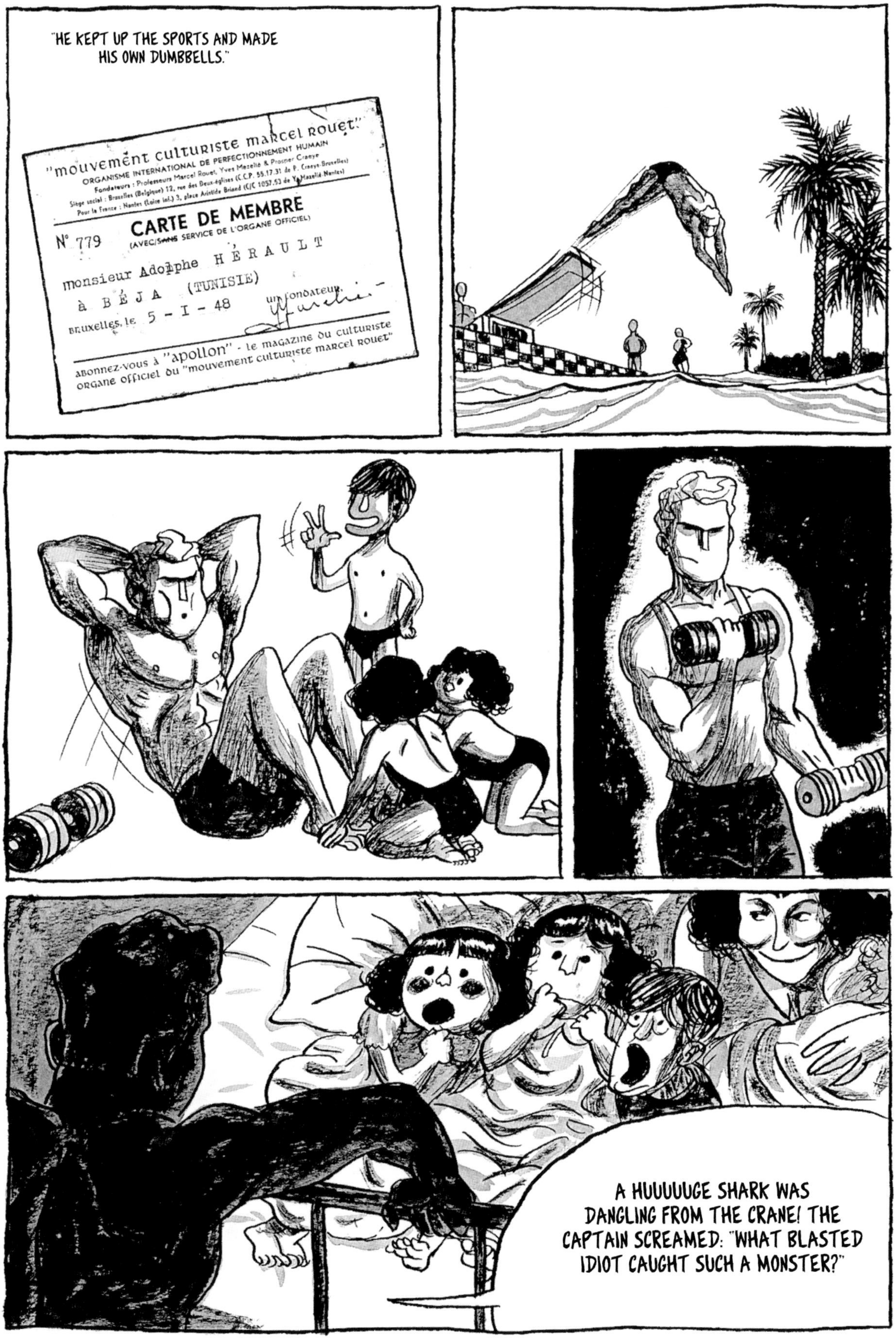
"HE KEPT UP THE SPORTS AND MADE HIS OWN DUMBBELLS."
"mouvement culturiste marcel rouet"
ORGANISME INTERNATIONAL DE PERFECTIONNEMENT HUMAIN
CARTE DE MEMBRE
(AVEC/SANS SERVICE DE L'ORGANE OFFICIEL)
N° 779
monsieur Adolphe HÉRAULT
à BÉJA (TUNISIE)
Bruxelles, le 5 - I - 48
un fondateur,
abonnez-vous à "apollon" - le magazine du culturiste
organe officiel du "mouvement culturiste marcel rouet"
A HUUUUUGE SHARK WAS DANGLING FROM THE CRANE! THE CAPTAIN SCREAMED: "WHAT BLASTED IDIOT CAUGHT SUCH A MONSTER?"

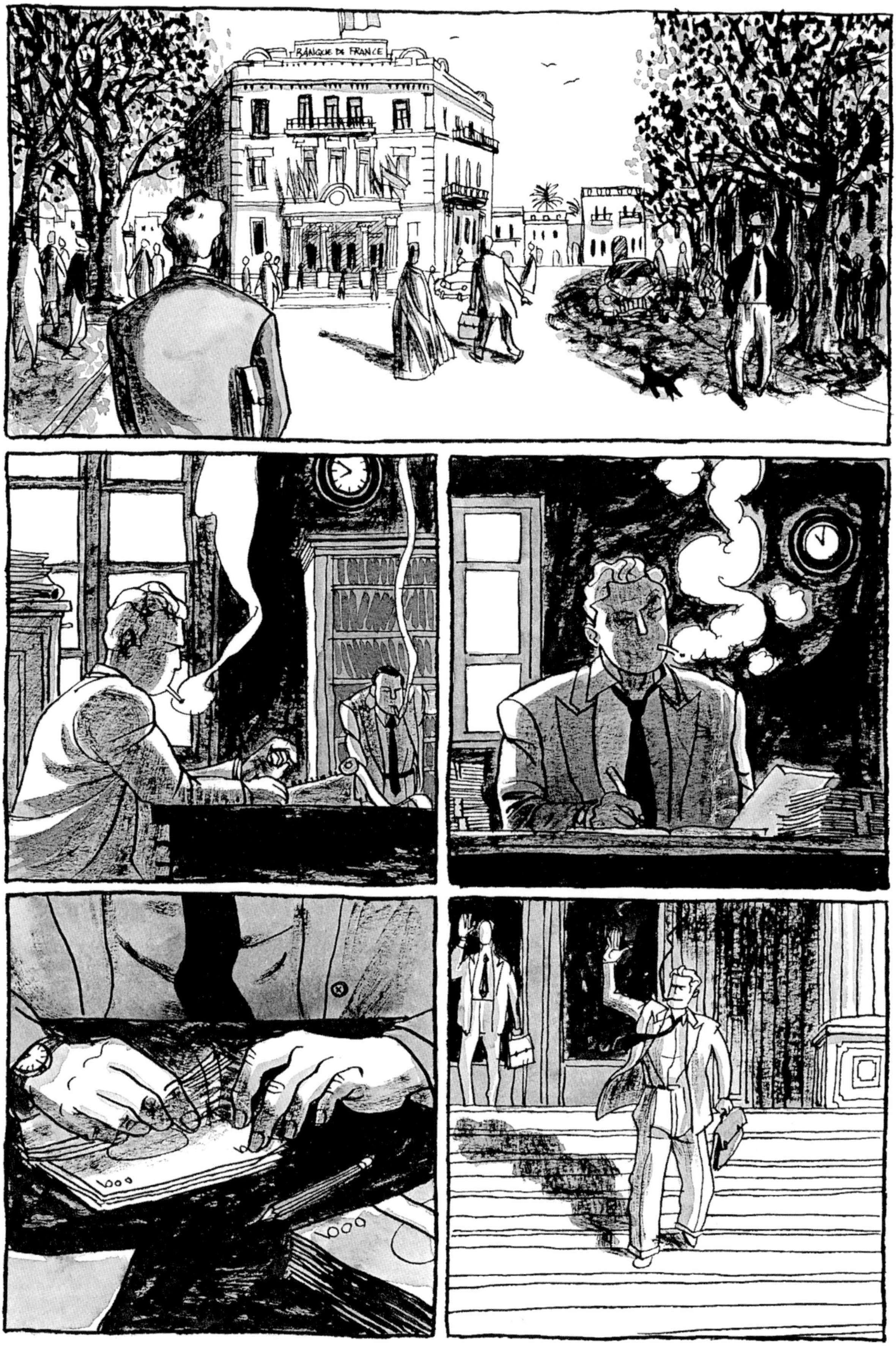
BANQUE DE FRANCE
1000
1000

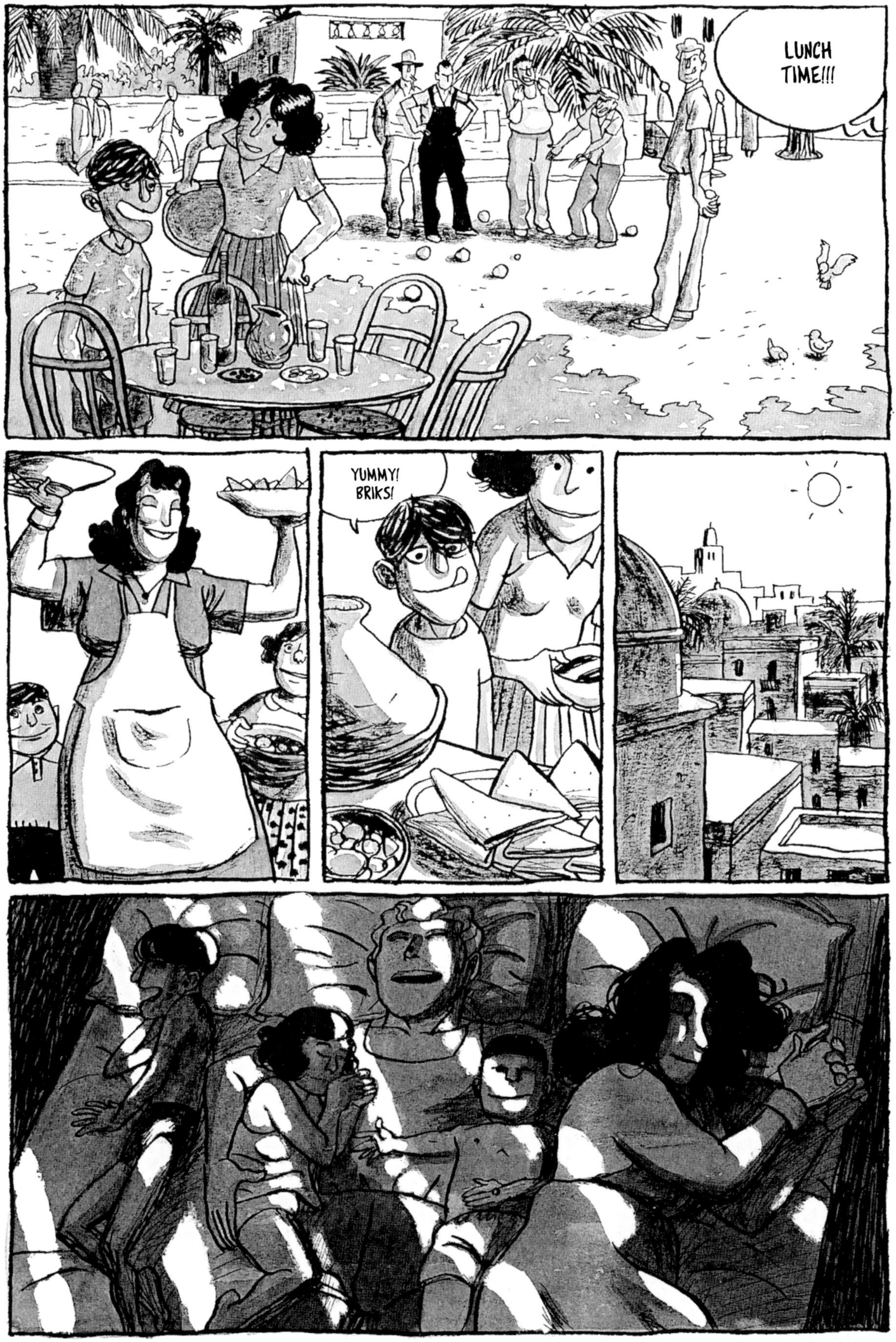
LUNCH TIME!!!
YUMMY! BRIKS!

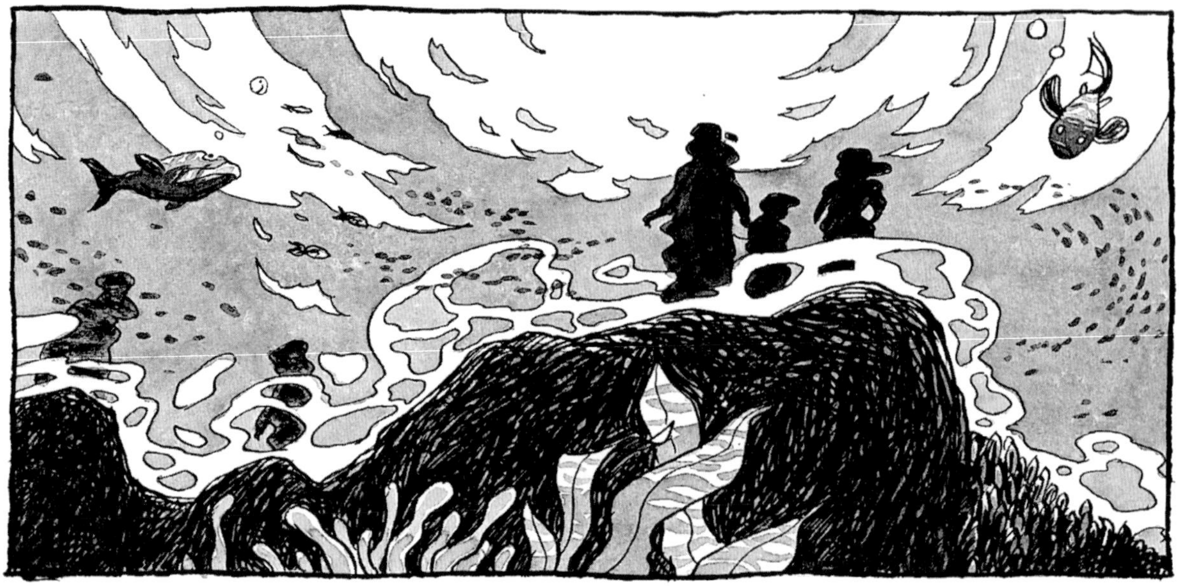

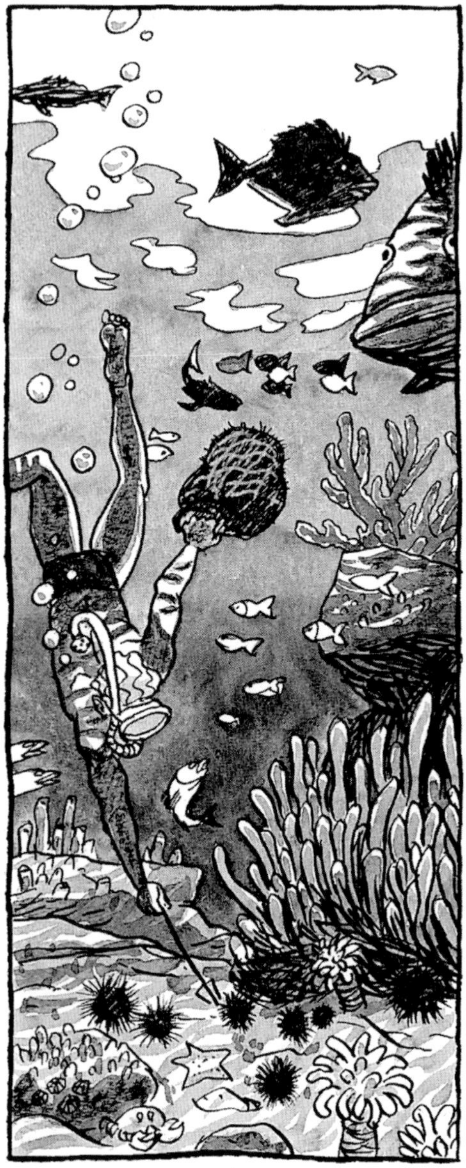

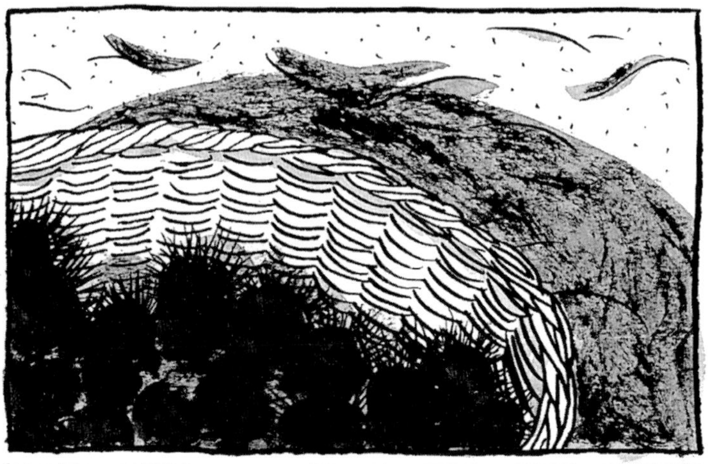

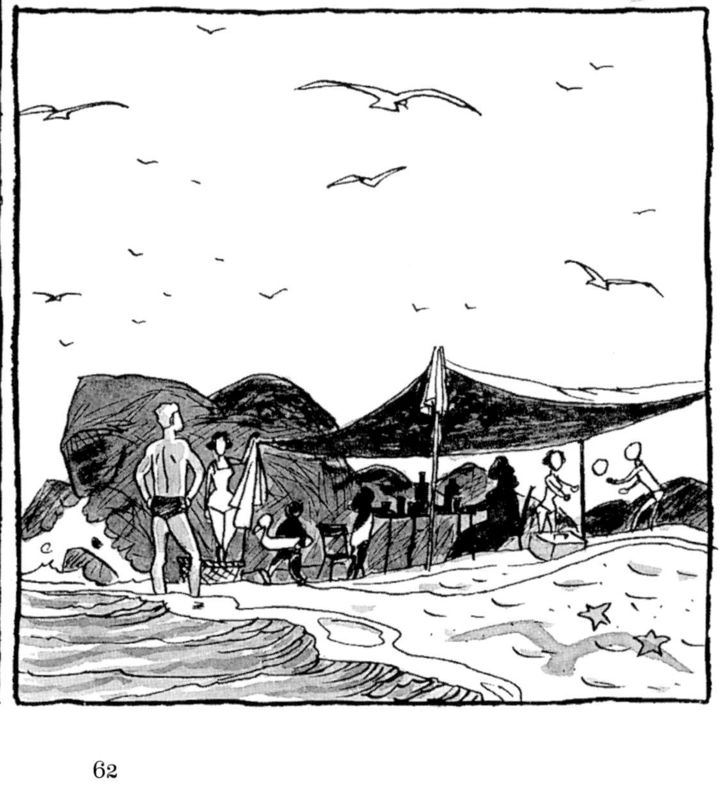

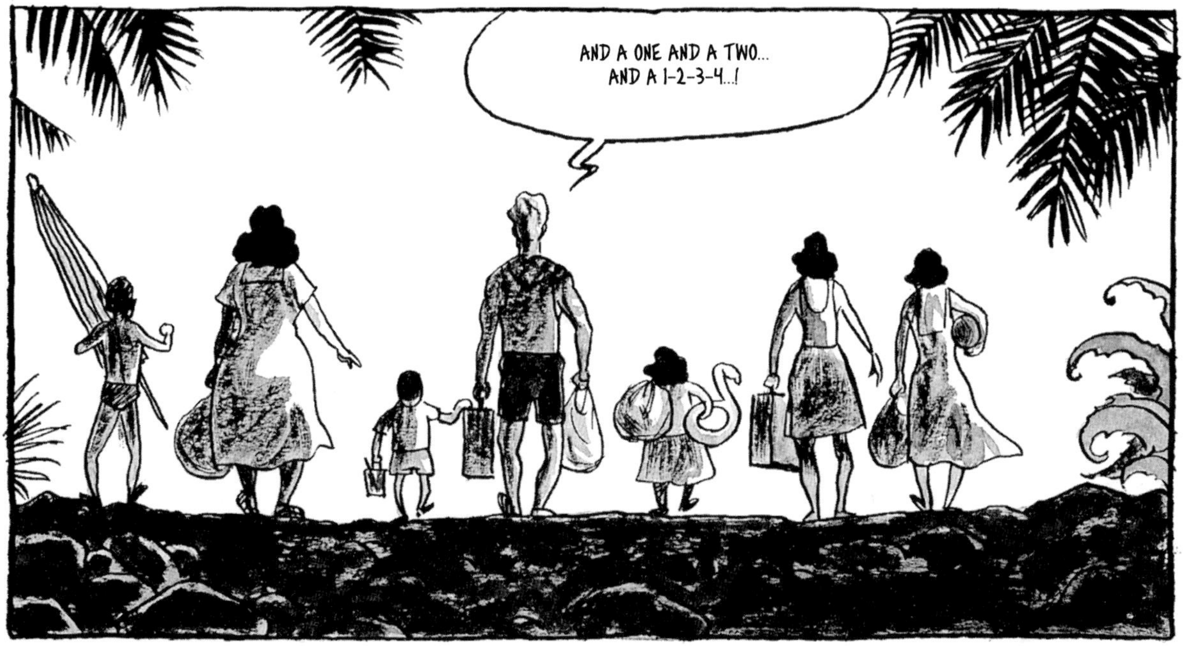
AND A ONE AND A TWO...
AND A 1-2-3-4...!

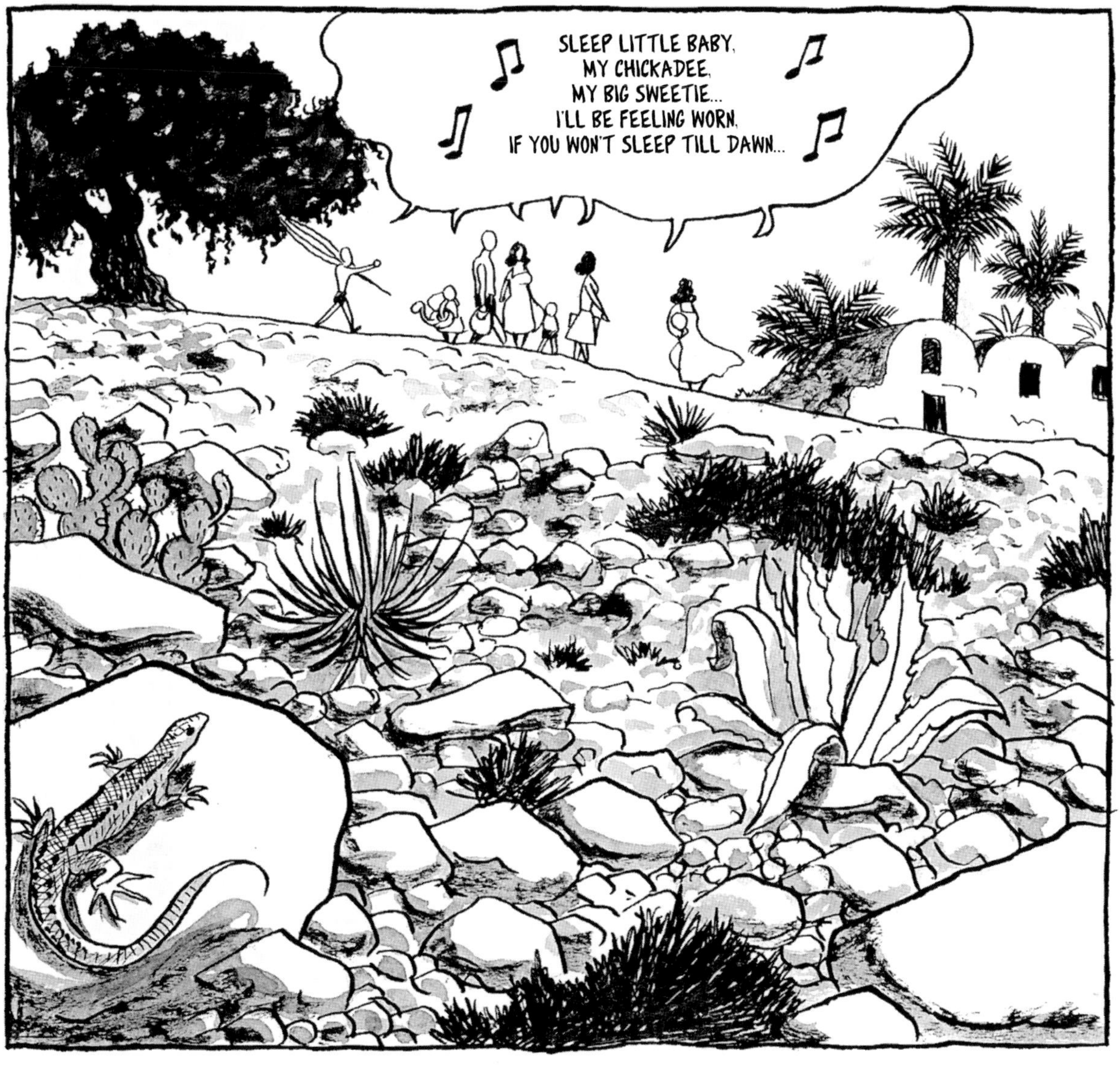
SLEEP LITTLE BABY,
MY CHICKADEE,
MY BIG SWEETIE...
I'LL BE FEELING WORN,
IF YOU WON'T SLEEP TILL DAWN...

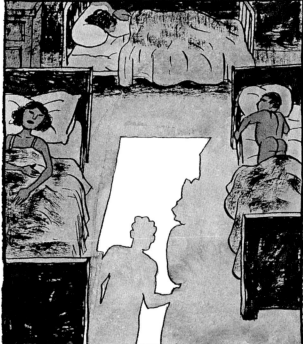

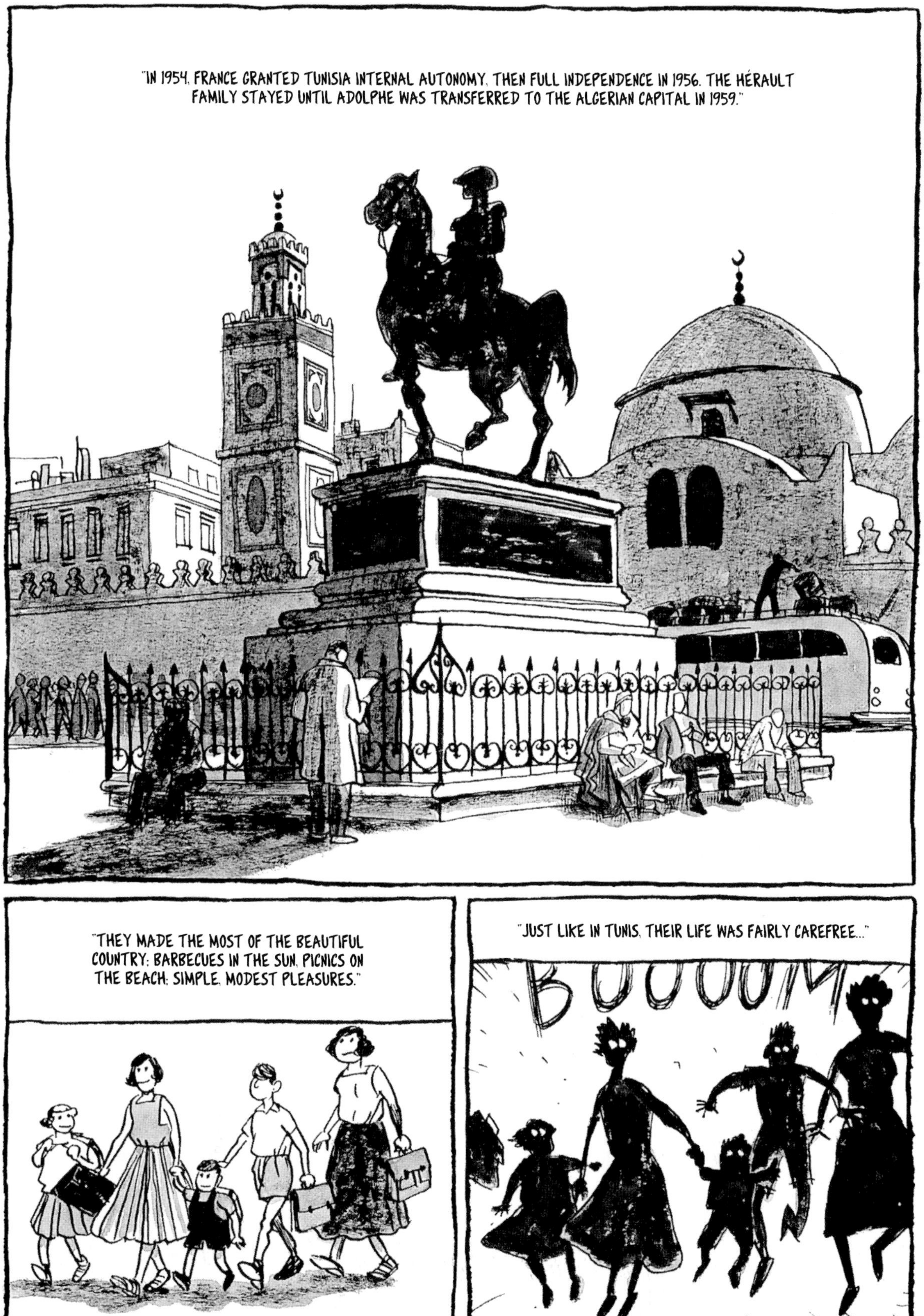
"IN 1954, FRANCE GRANTED TUNISIA INTERNAL AUTONOMY, THEN FULL INDEPENDENCE IN 1956. THE HÉRAULT FAMILY STAYED UNTIL ADOLPHE WAS TRANSFERRED TO THE ALGERIAN CAPITAL IN 1959."
"THEY MADE THE MOST OF THE BEAUTIFUL COUNTRY: BARBECUES IN THE SUN, PICNICS ON THE BEACH; SIMPLE, MODEST PLEASURES."
"JUST LIKE IN TUNIS, THEIR LIFE WAS FAIRLY CAREFREE..."
BOOOOM

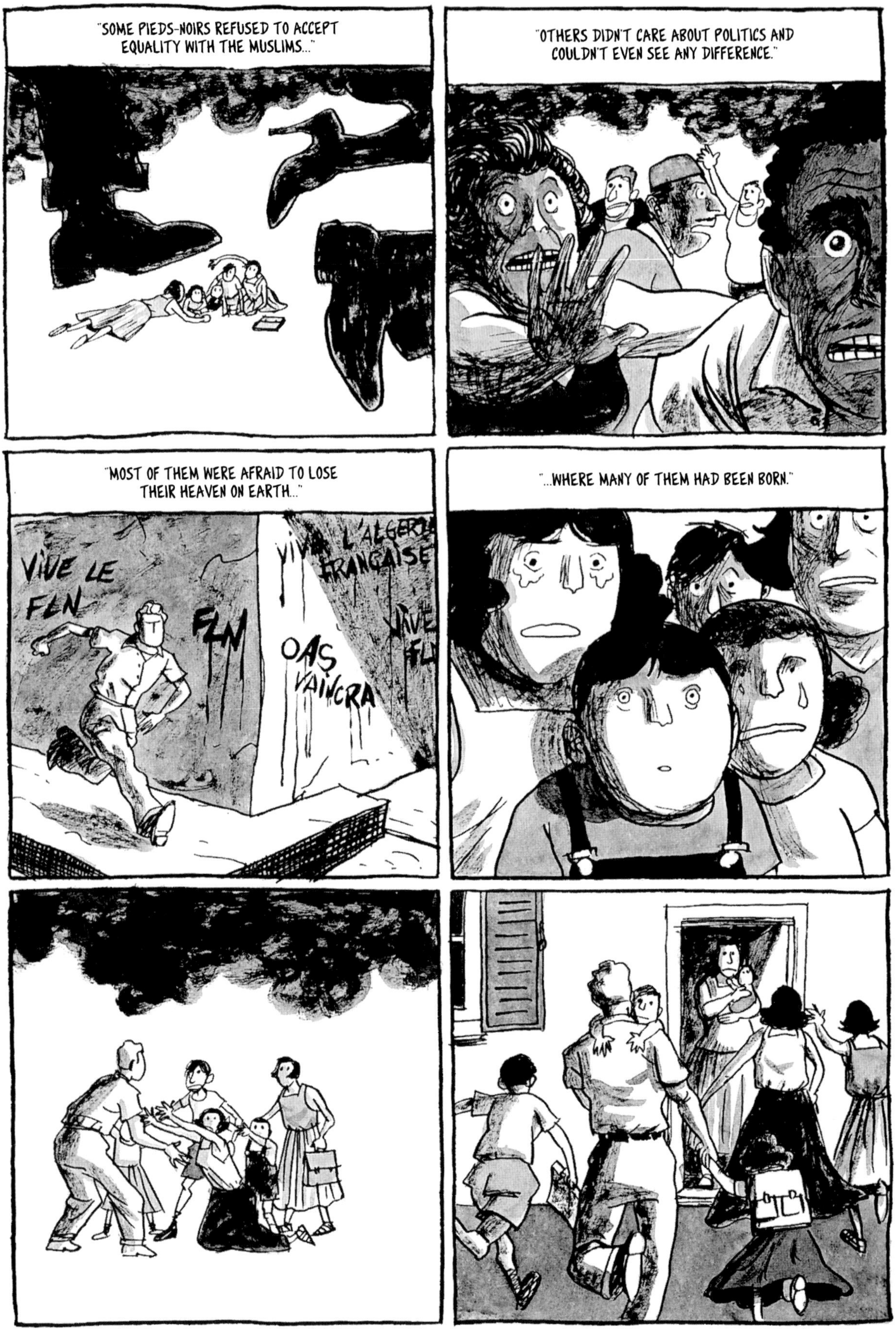
"SOME PIEDS-NOIRS REFUSED TO ACCEPT EQUALITY WITH THE MUSLIMS..."
"OTHERS DIDN'T CARE ABOUT POLITICS AND COULDN'T EVEN SEE ANY DIFFERENCE."
"MOST OF THEM WERE AFRAID TO LOSE THEIR HEAVEN ON EARTH..."
VIVE LE FLN
FLN
FRANÇAISE
OAS VAINCRA
"...WHERE MANY OF THEM HAD BEEN BORN."

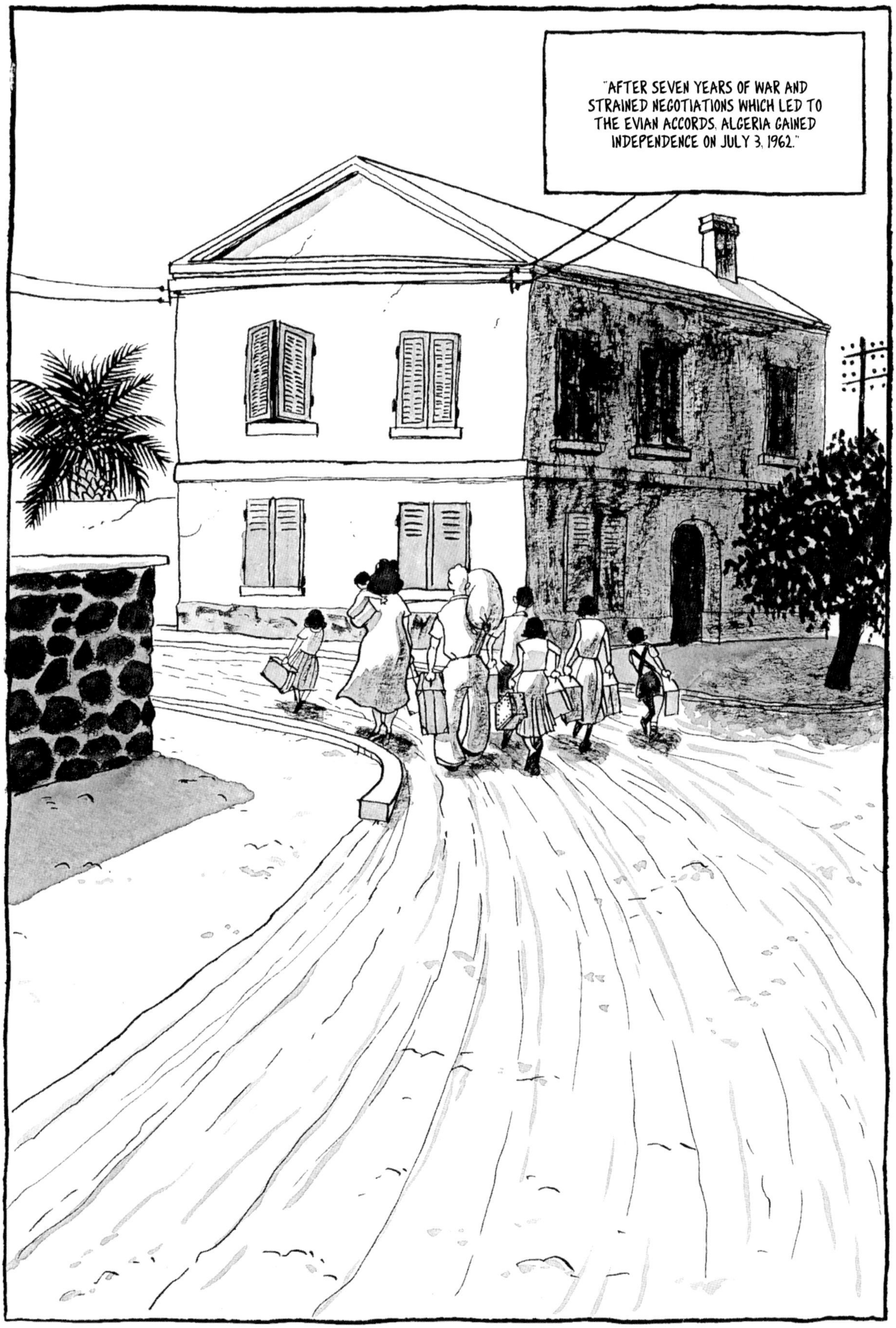
"AFTER SEVEN YEARS OF WAR AND STRAINED NEGOTIATIONS WHICH LED TO THE EVIAN ACCORDS, ALGERIA GAINED INDEPENDENCE ON JULY 3, 1962."

"CRAMMED INTO A SHIP THAT HAD SEEN HAPPIER VOYAGES, CARMEN AND MOST OF
THE OTHERS REGRETTED NOT TAKING THE PLANE."

"AT LEAST THE PARTING WOULD
HAVE BEEN OVER INSTANTLY. THEY
WOULDN'T HAVE SEEN ALGERIA SLOWLY
DRIFTING AWAY, BECOMING NOTHING
MORE THAN A LINE ON THE HORIZON."

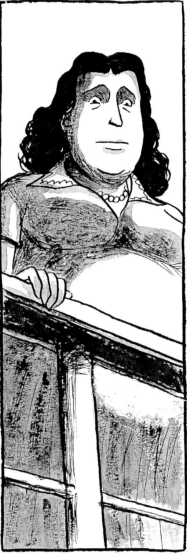

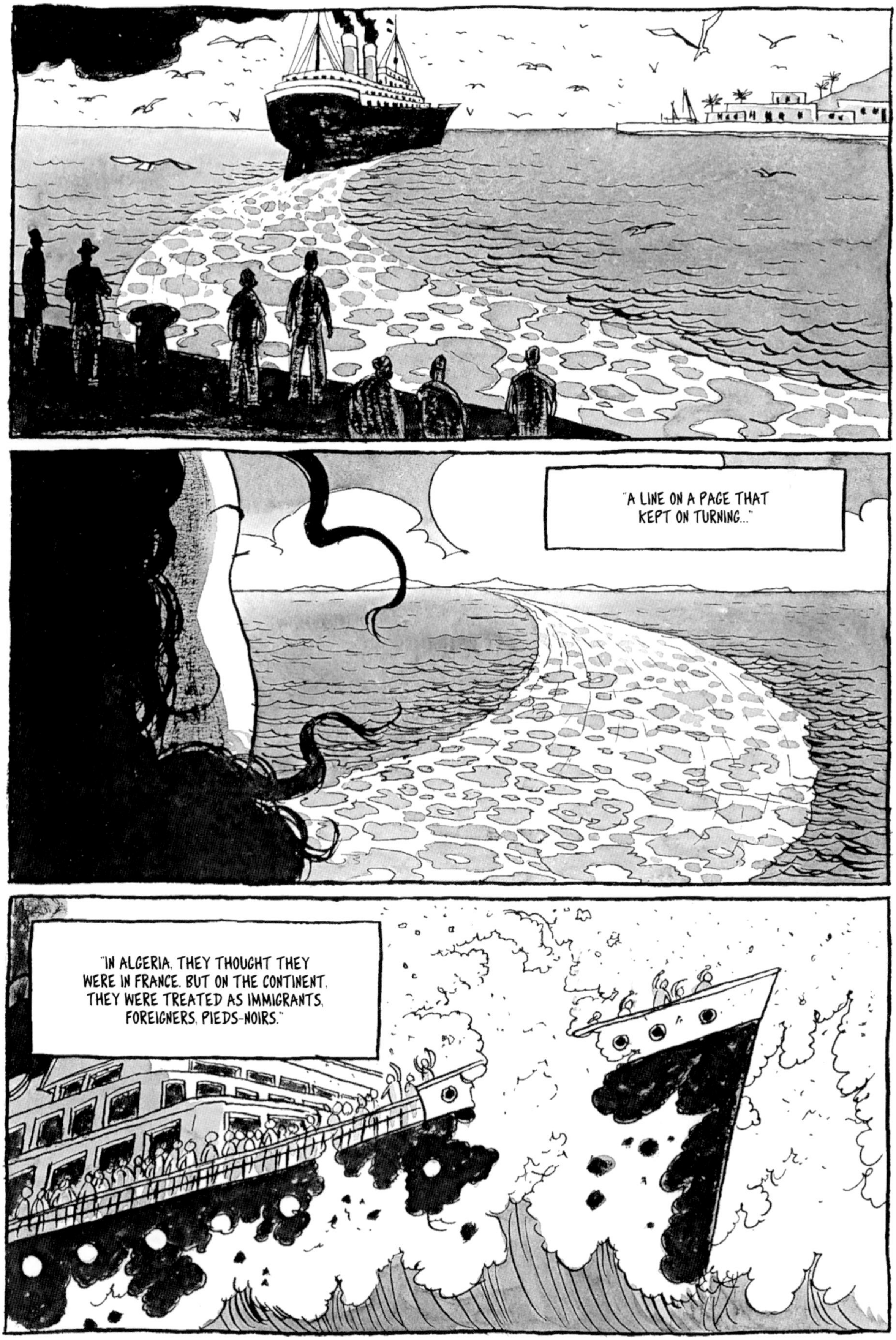
"A LINE ON A PAGE THAT KEPT ON TURNING..."
"IN ALGERIA, THEY THOUGHT THEY WERE IN FRANCE. BUT ON THE CONTINENT, THEY WERE TREATED AS IMMIGRANTS, FOREIGNERS, PIEDS-NOIRS."

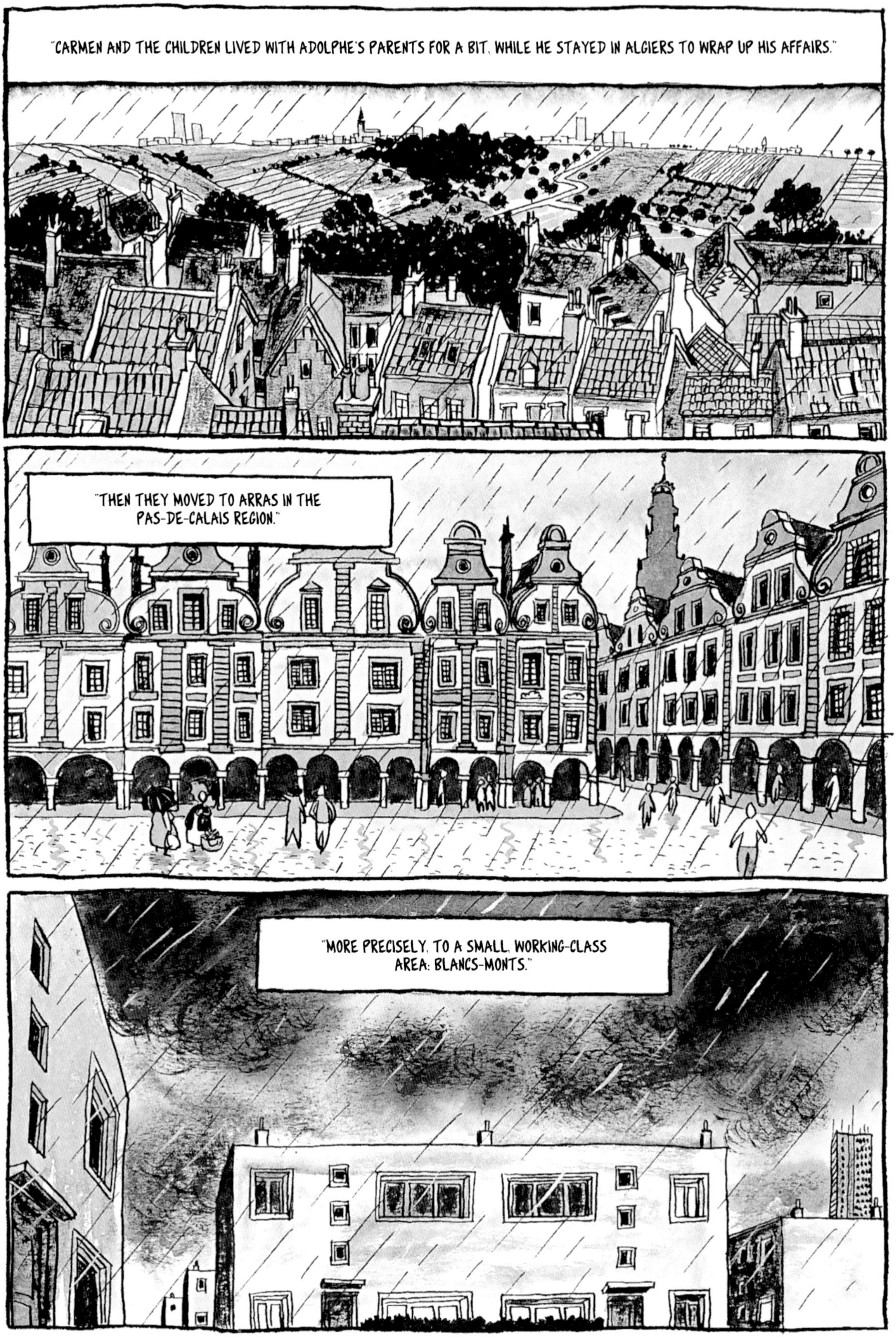
"CARMEN AND THE CHILDREN LIVED WITH ADOLPHE'S PARENTS FOR A BIT, WHILE HE STAYED IN ALGIERS TO WRAP UP HIS AFFAIRS."
"THEN THEY MOVED TO ARRAS IN THE PAS-DE-CALAIS REGION."
"MORE PRECISELY, TO A SMALL, WORKING-CLASS AREA: BLANCS-MONTS."

"CARMEN WAS DEPRESSED, WAITING FOR THE HUSBAND SHE IMAGINED DYING IN ALGIERS."

"SHE HAD ONE LAST BABY GIRL IN AUGUST, RIGHT BEFORE ADOLPHE FINALLY RETURNED."

"HE TRIED HIS HAND AT SEVERAL JOBS FOR A CHANGE... FIRST AS A PLUMBER..."

"THEN CENTRAL-HEATING REPAIRS AND CONSTRUCTION WORK..."

"BEFORE RETURNING TO THE BANQUE DE FRANCE. THEN HE BOUGHT..."

"...A BLUE FORD ESCORT SPORTS CAR."

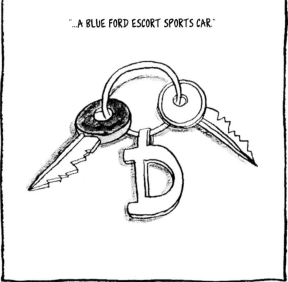

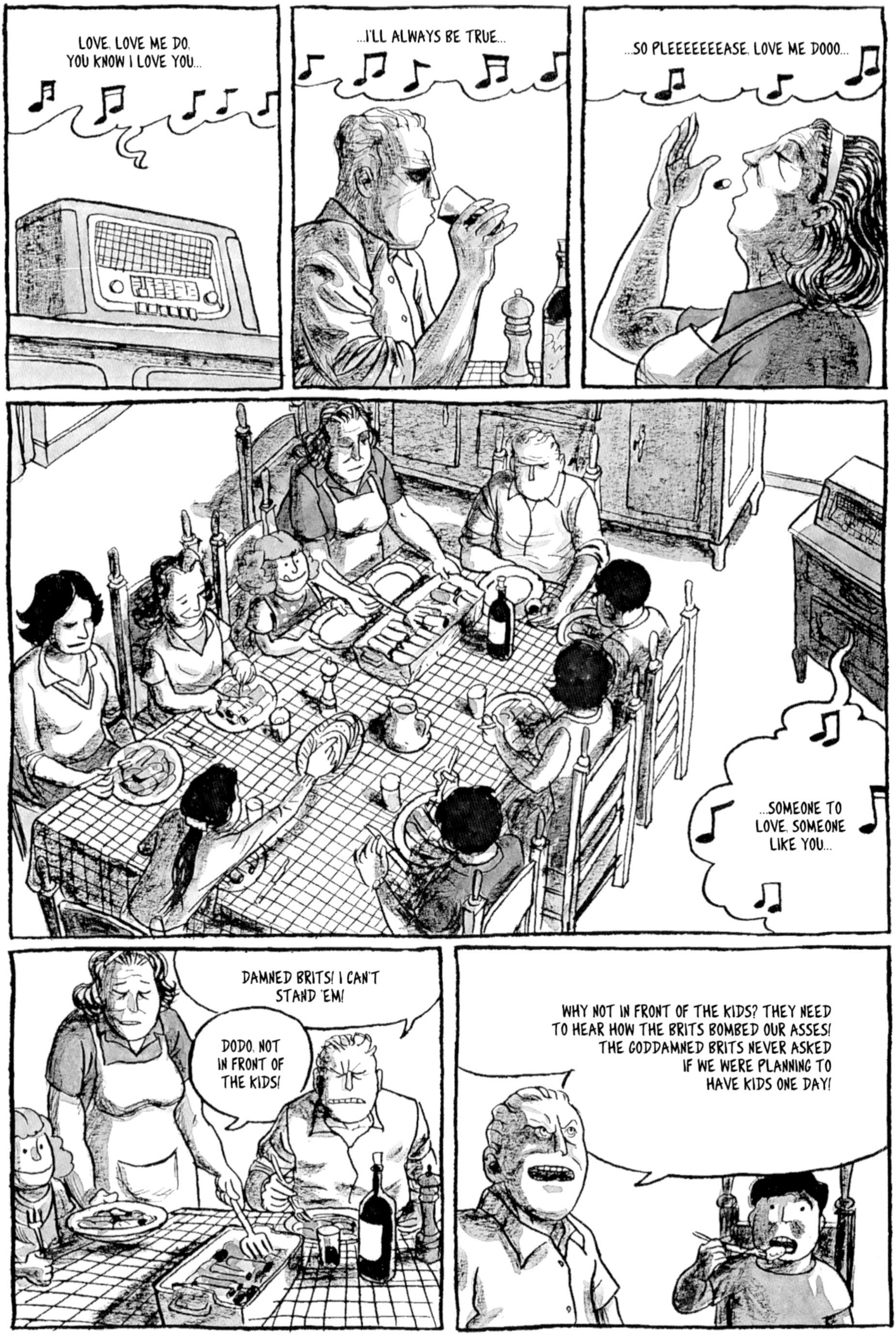
LOVE, LOVE ME DO, YOU KNOW I LOVE YOU...
...I'LL ALWAYS BE TRUE...
...SO PLEEEEEEEASE, LOVE ME DOOO...
...SOMEONE TO LOVE, SOMEONE LIKE YOU...
DAMNED BRITS! I CAN'T STAND 'EM!
DODO, NOT IN FRONT OF THE KIDS!
WHY NOT IN FRONT OF THE KIDS? THEY NEED TO HEAR HOW THE BRITS BOMBED OUR ASSES! THE GODDAMNED BRITS NEVER ASKED IF WE WERE PLANNING TO HAVE KIDS ONE DAY!

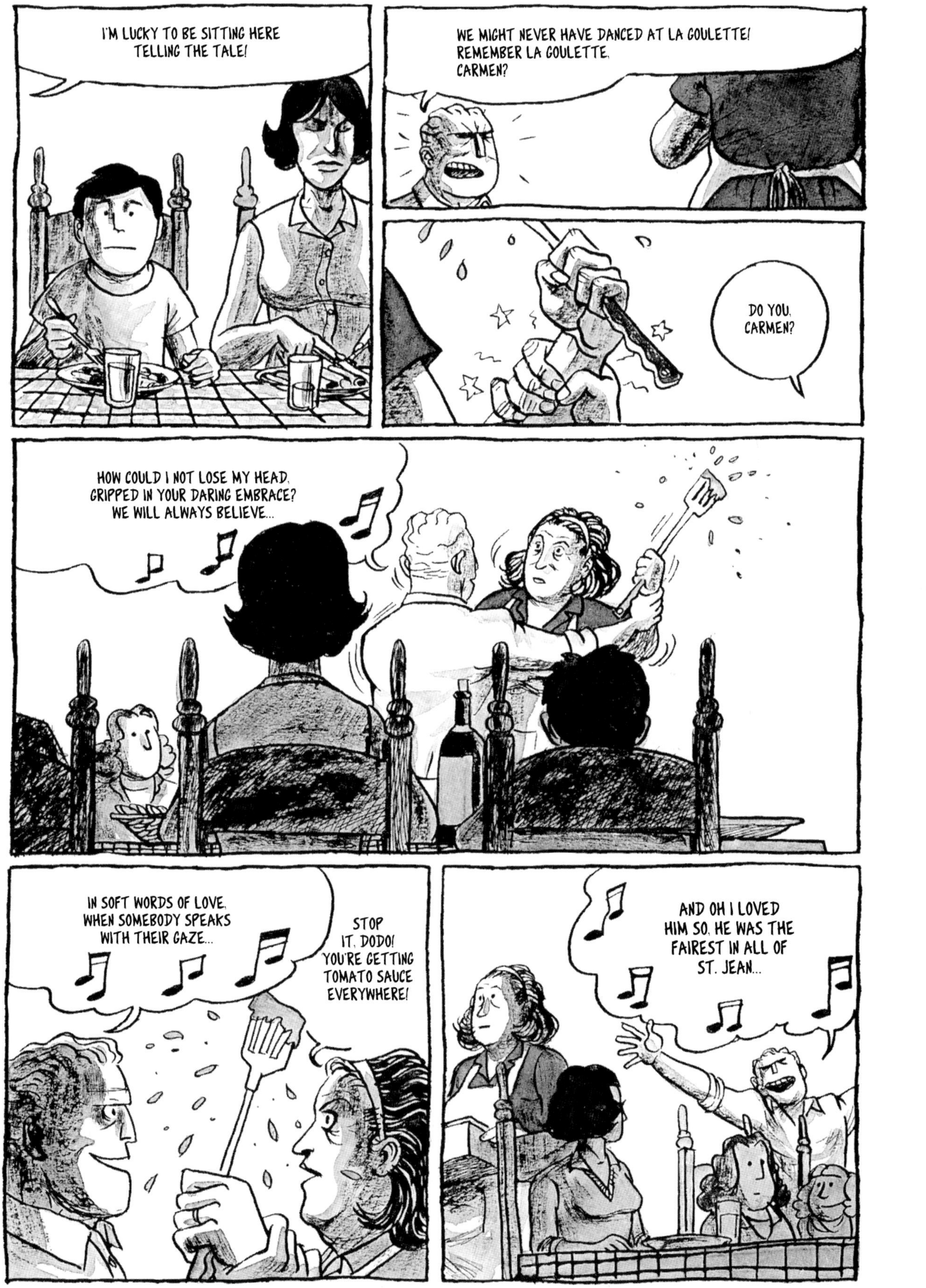
I'M LUCKY TO BE SITTING HERE TELLING THE TALE!
WE MIGHT NEVER HAVE DANCED AT LA GOULETTE! REMEMBER LA GOULETTE, CARMEN?
DO YOU, CARMEN?
HOW COULD I NOT LOSE MY HEAD, GRIPPED IN YOUR DARING EMBRACE? WE WILL ALWAYS BELIEVE...
IN SOFT WORDS OF LOVE, WHEN SOMEBODY SPEAKS WITH THEIR GAZE...
STOP IT, DODO! YOU'RE GETTING TOMATO SAUCE EVERYWHERE!
AND OH I LOVED HIM SO, HE WAS THE FAIREST IN ALL OF ST. JEAN...

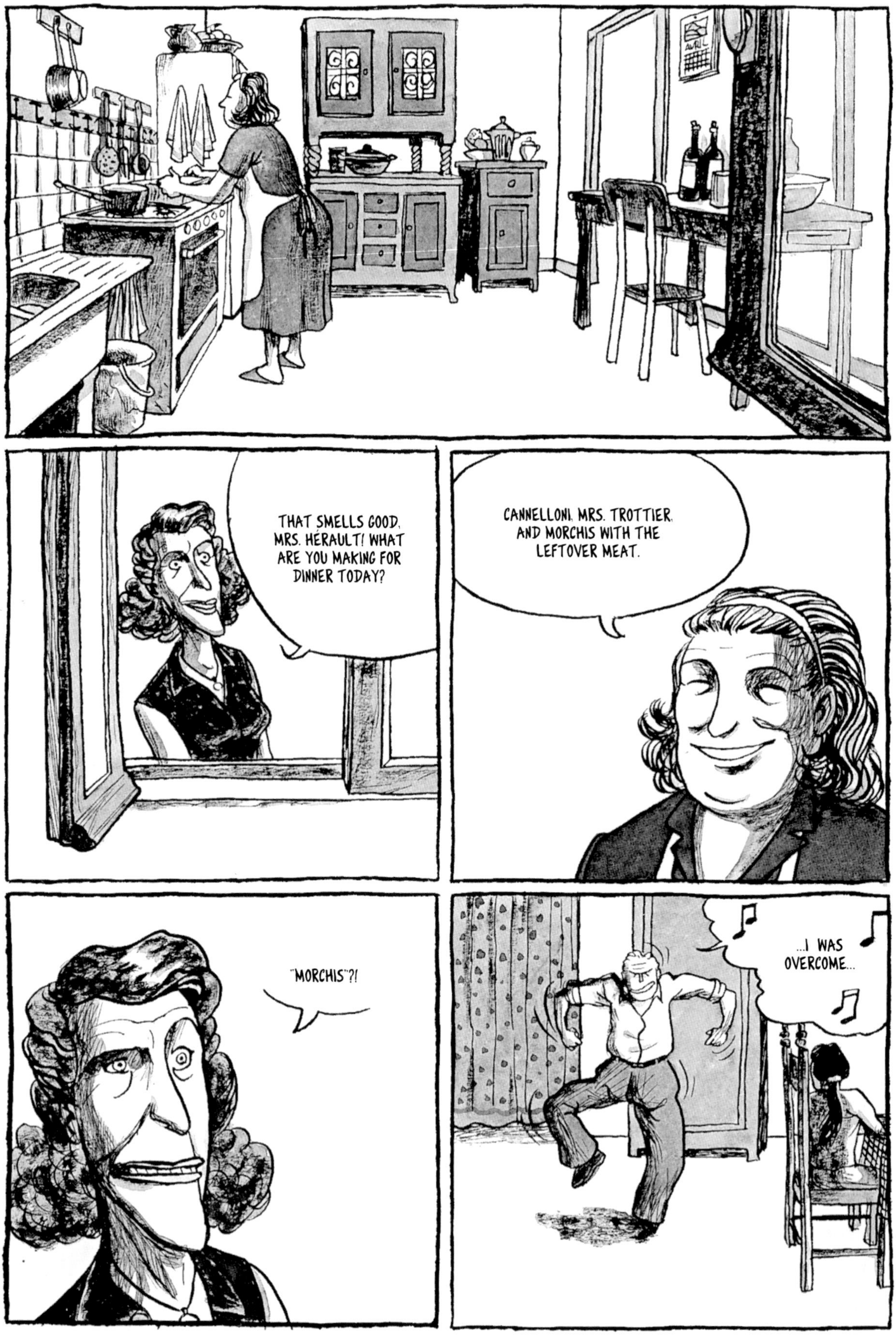
AVRIL
THAT SMELLS GOOD, MRS. HÉRAULT! WHAT ARE YOU MAKING FOR DINNER TODAY?
CANNELLONI, MRS. TROTTIER, AND MORCHIS WITH THE LEFTOVER MEAT.
"MORCHIS"?!
...I WAS OVERCOME...

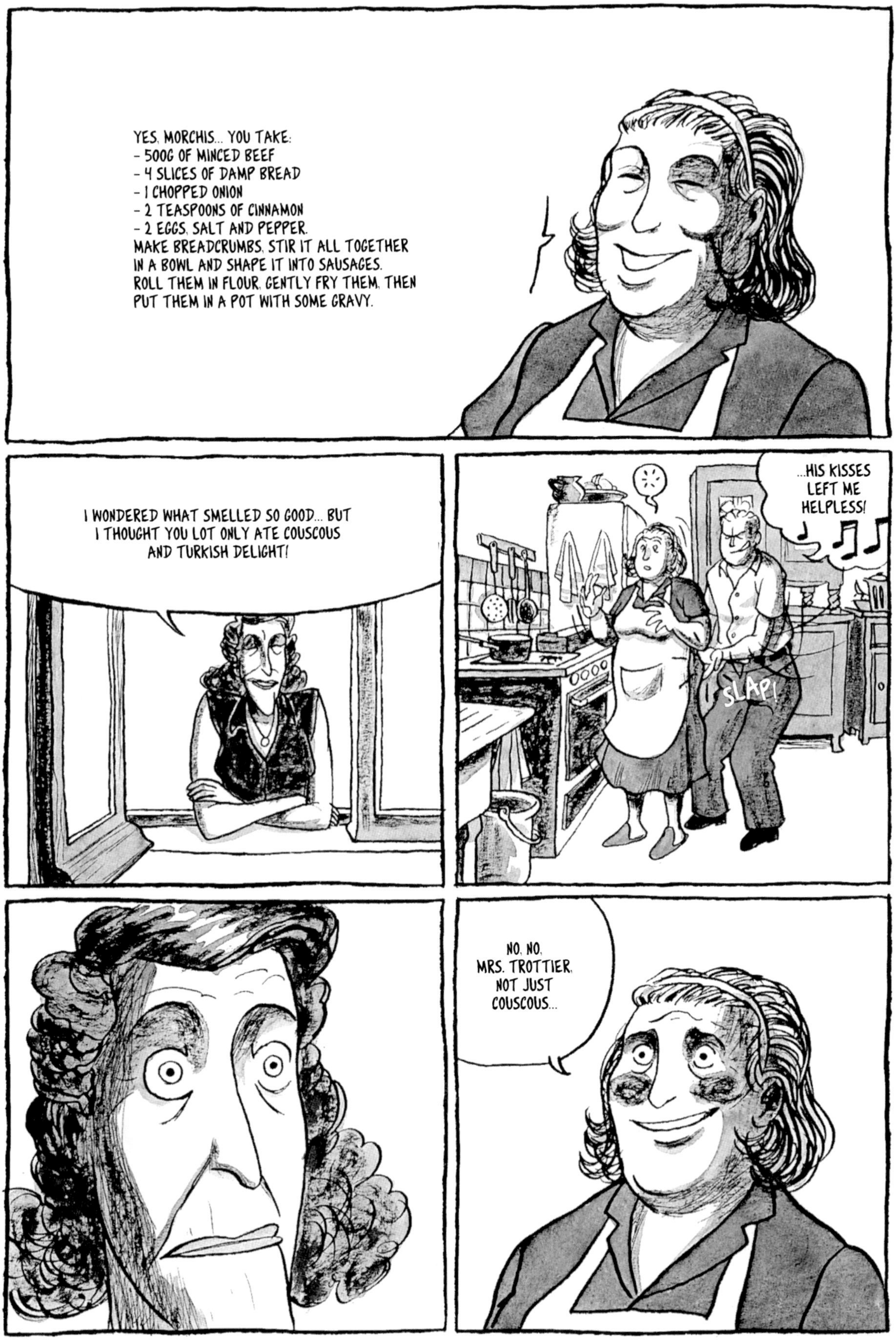
YES, MORCHIS... YOU TAKE:
- 500G OF MINCED BEEF
- 4 SLICES OF DAMP BREAD
- 1 CHOPPED ONION
- 2 TEASPOONS OF CINNAMON
- 2 EGGS, SALT AND PEPPER.
MAKE BREADCRUMBS, STIR IT ALL TOGETHER IN A BOWL AND SHAPE IT INTO SAUSAGES. ROLL THEM IN FLOUR, GENTLY FRY THEM, THEN PUT THEM IN A POT WITH SOME GRAVY.
I WONDERED WHAT SMELLED SO GOOD... BUT I THOUGHT YOU LOT ONLY ATE COUSCOUS AND TURKISH DELIGHT!
...HIS KISSES LEFT ME HELPLESS!
SLAP!
NO, NO, MRS. TROTTIER, NOT JUST COUSCOUS...

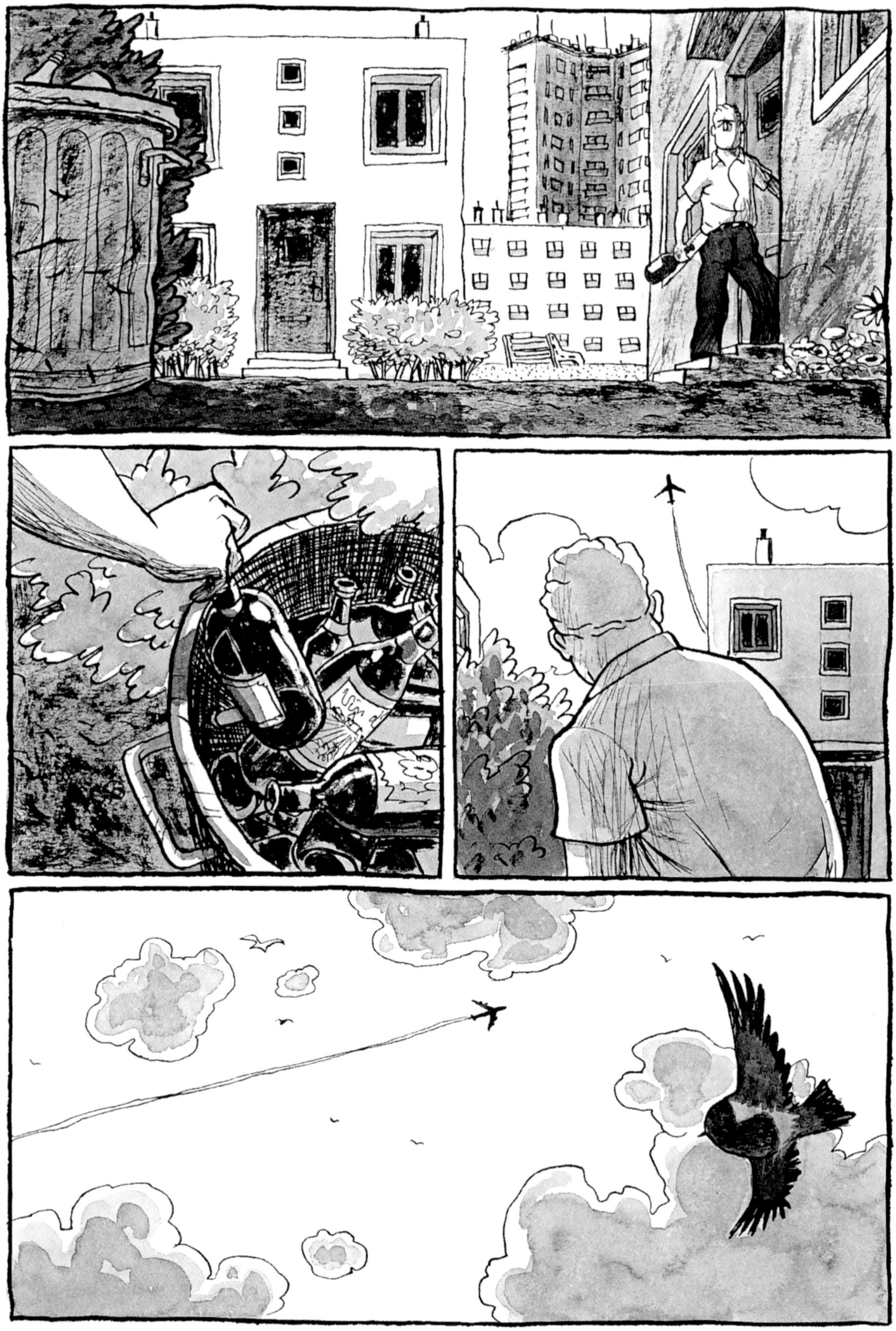

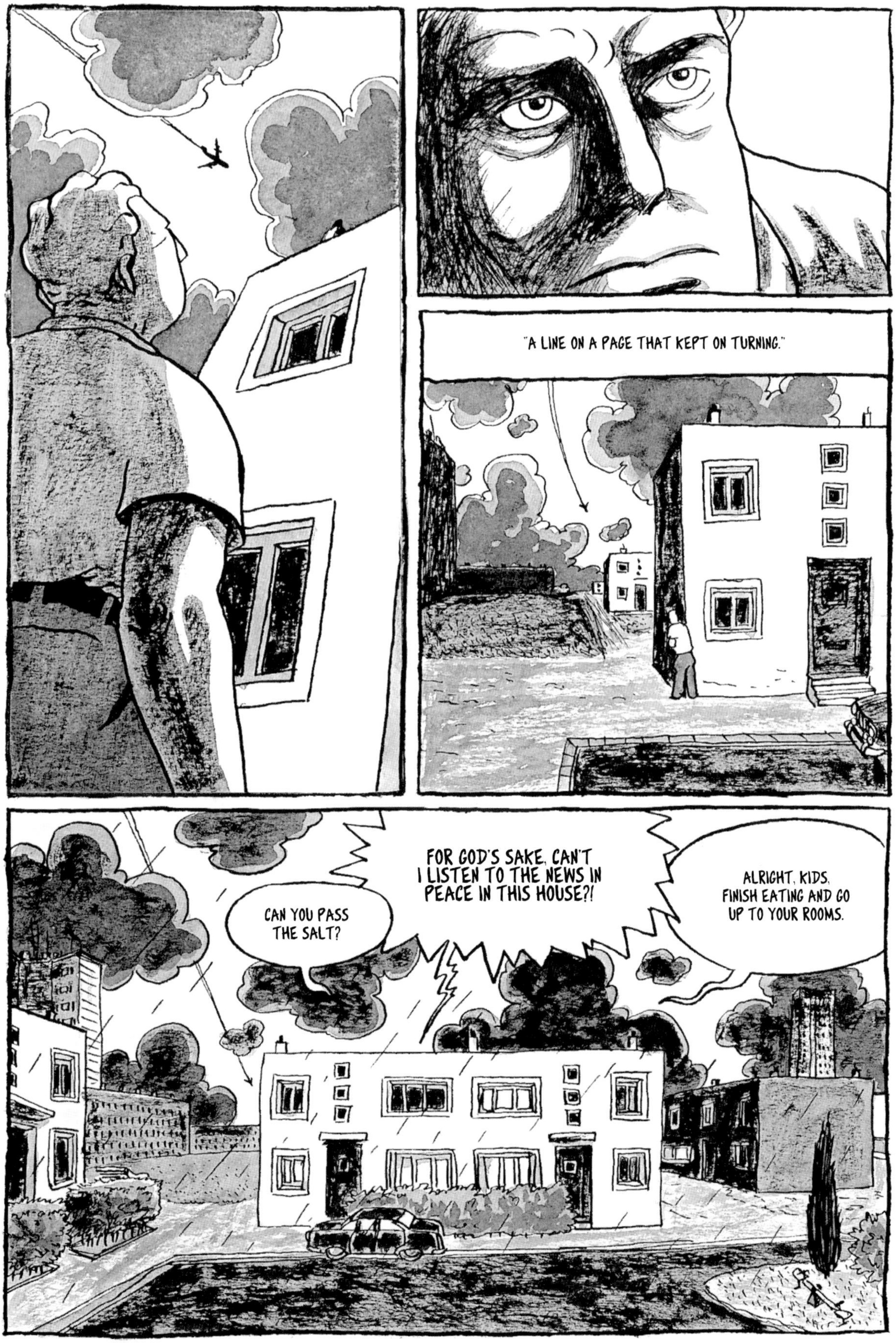
"A LINE ON A PAGE THAT KEPT ON TURNING."
CAN YOU PASS THE SALT?
FOR GOD'S SAKE, CAN'T I LISTEN TO THE NEWS IN PEACE IN THIS HOUSE?!
ALRIGHT, KIDS, FINISH EATING AND GO UP TO YOUR ROOMS.

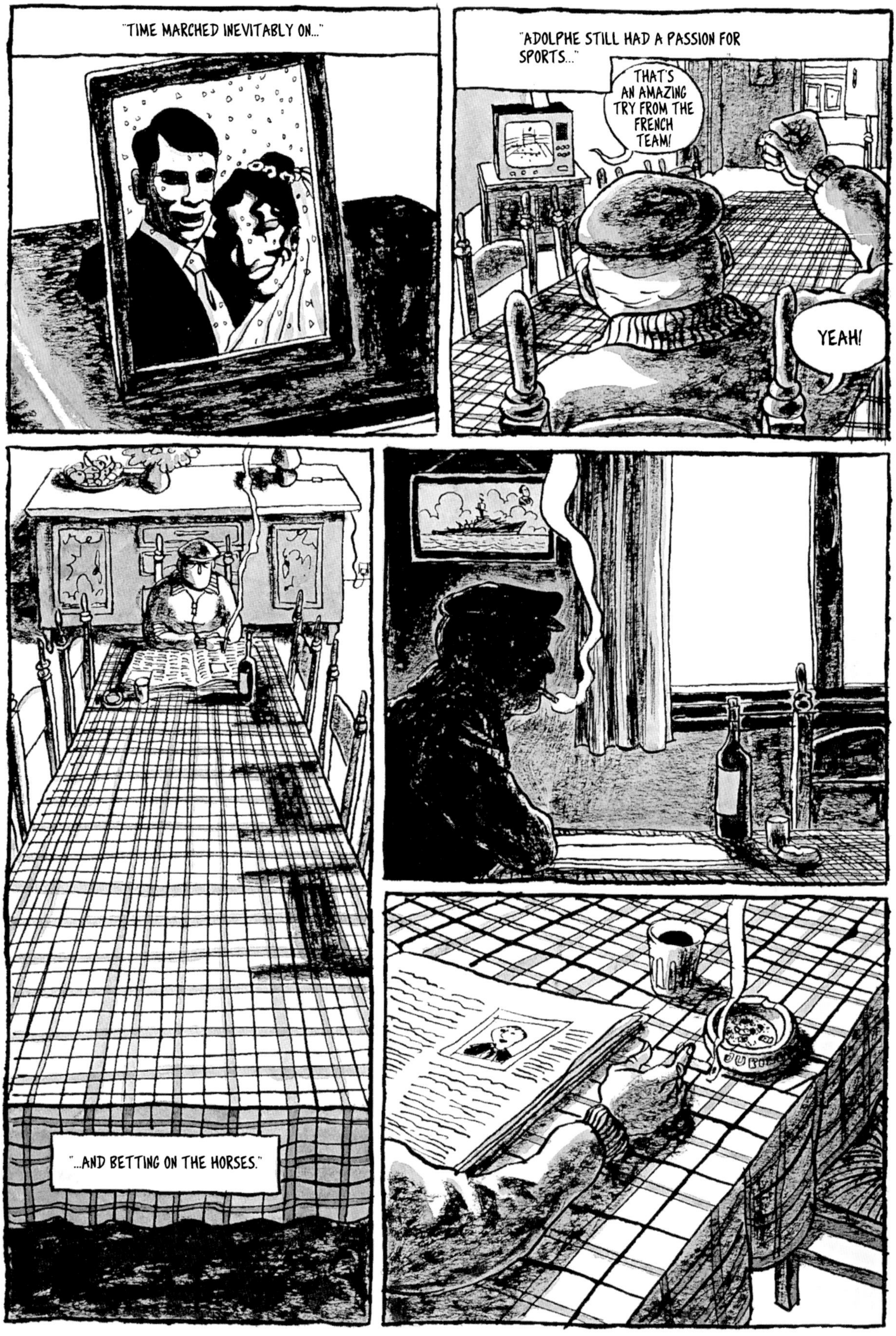
"TIME MARCHED INEVITABLY ON..."
"ADOLPHE STILL HAD A PASSION FOR SPORTS..."
THAT'S AN AMAZING TRY FROM THE FRENCH TEAM!
YEAH!
"...AND BETTING ON THE HORSES."

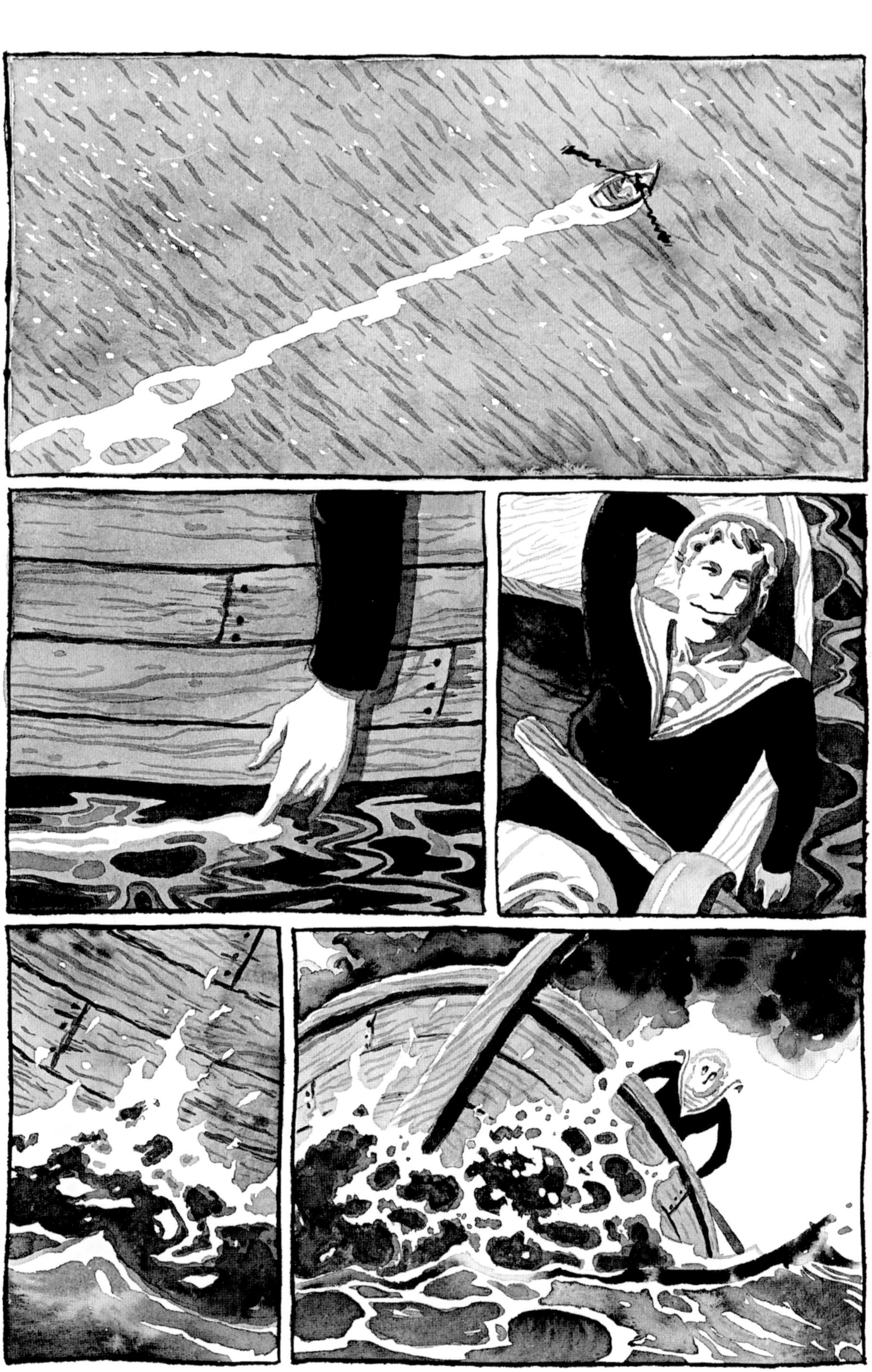

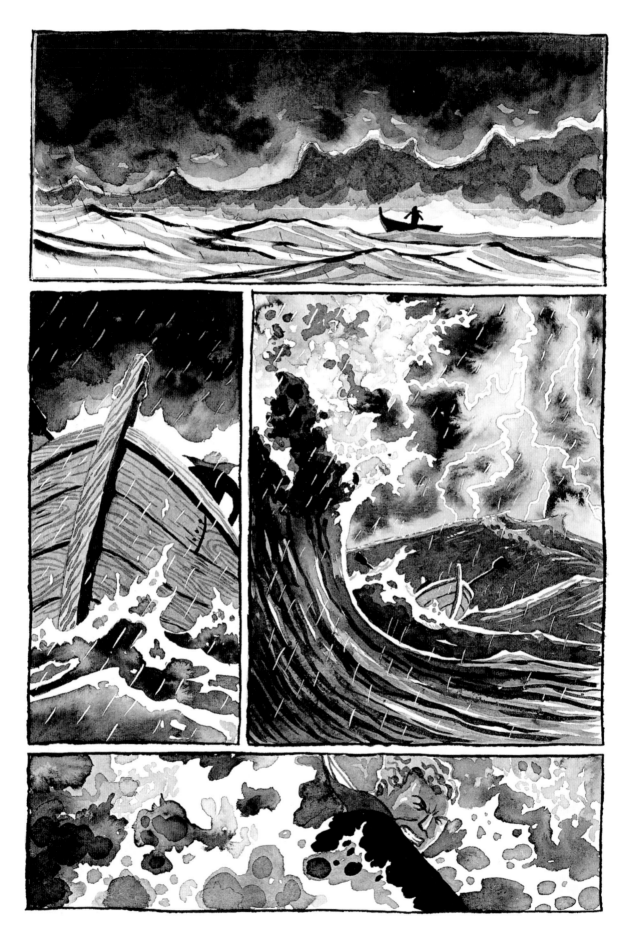

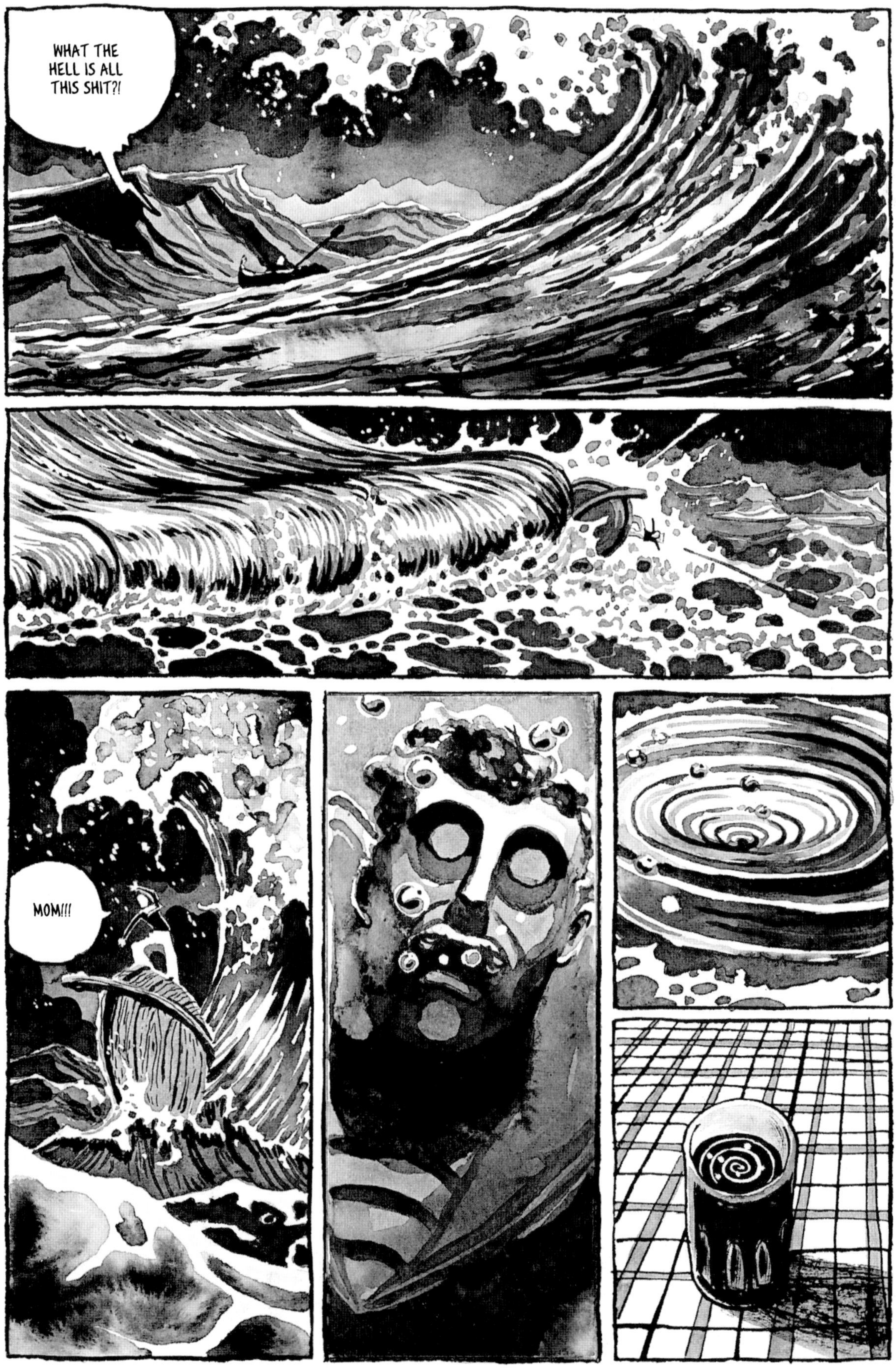
WHAT THE HELL IS ALL THIS SHIT?!
MOM!!!

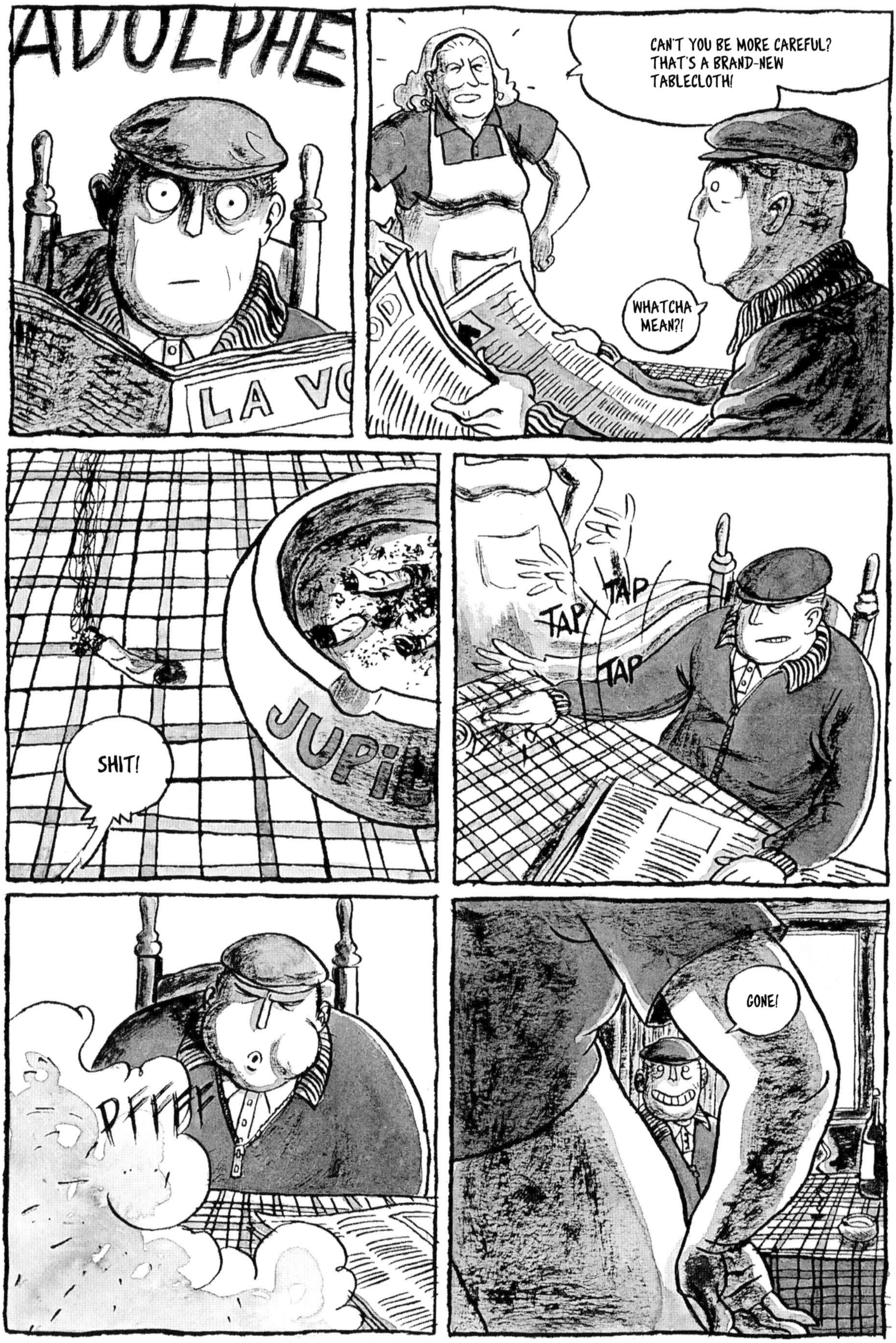
ADOLPHE
LA VO
CAN'T YOU BE MORE CAREFUL? THAT'S A BRAND-NEW TABLECLOTH!
WHATCHA MEAN?!
SHIT!
JUPI
TAP
TAP
TAP
PFFFF
GONE!

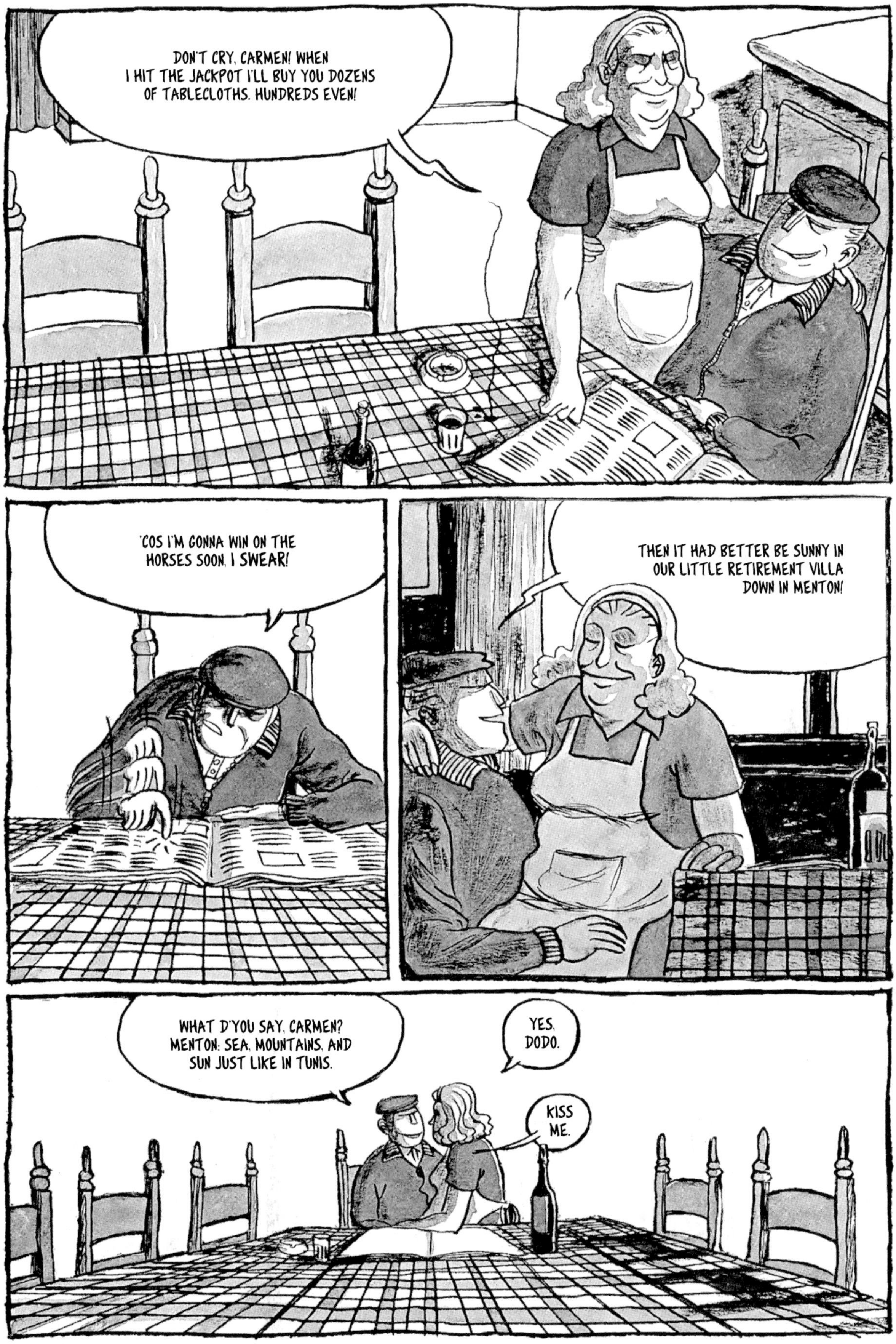
DON'T CRY, CARMEN! WHEN I HIT THE JACKPOT I'LL BUY YOU DOZENS OF TABLECLOTHS. HUNDREDS EVEN!
'COS I'M GONNA WIN ON THE HORSES SOON, I SWEAR!
THEN IT HAD BETTER BE SUNNY IN OUR LITTLE RETIREMENT VILLA DOWN IN MENTON!
WHAT D'YOU SAY, CARMEN? MENTON: SEA, MOUNTAINS, AND SUN JUST LIKE IN TUNIS.
YES, DODO.
KISS ME.

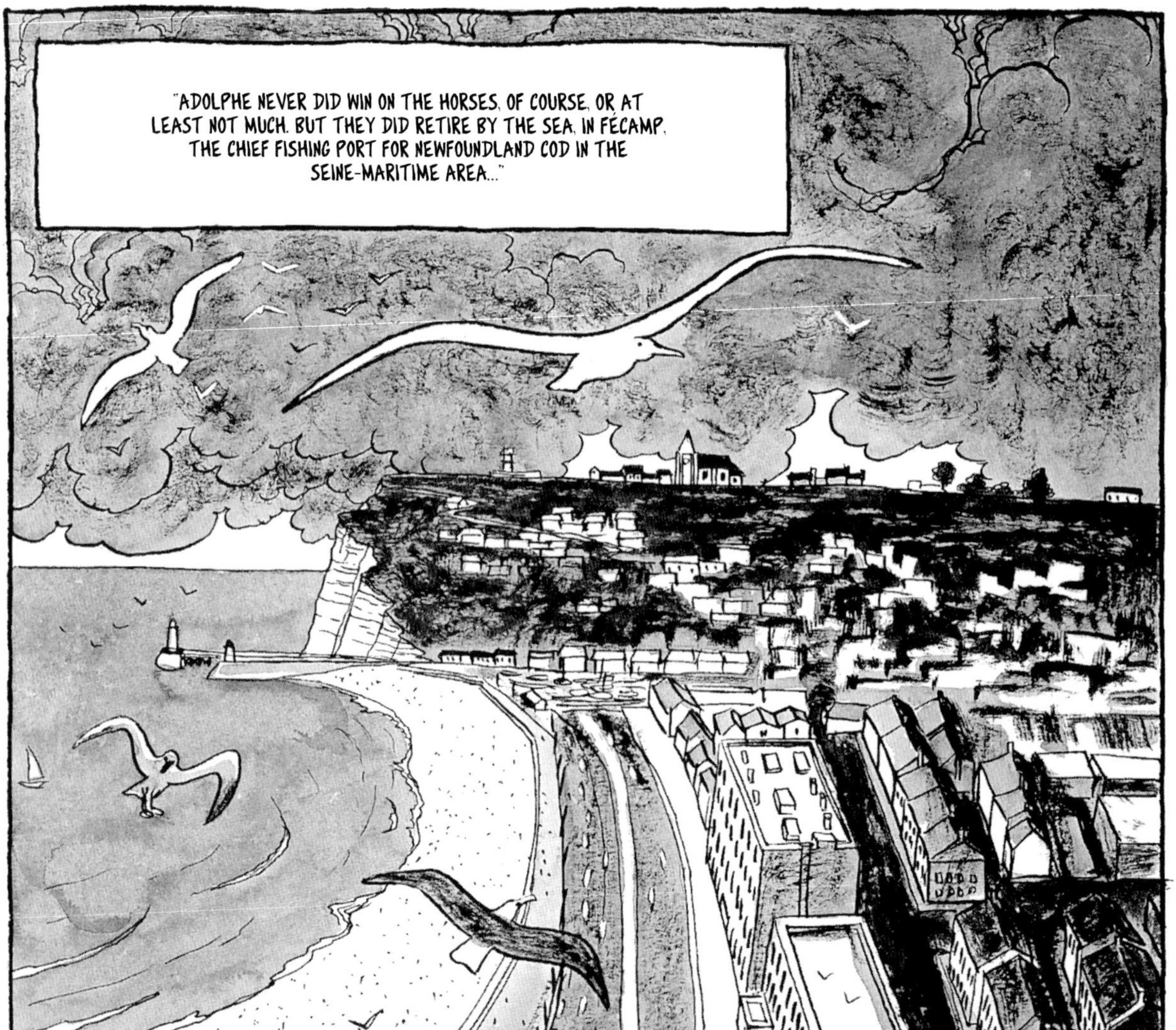
"ADOLPHE NEVER DID WIN ON THE HORSES, OF COURSE, OR AT LEAST NOT MUCH. BUT THEY DID RETIRE BY THE SEA, IN FÉCAMP, THE CHIEF FISHING PORT FOR NEWFOUNDLAND COD IN THE SEINE-MARITIME AREA..."

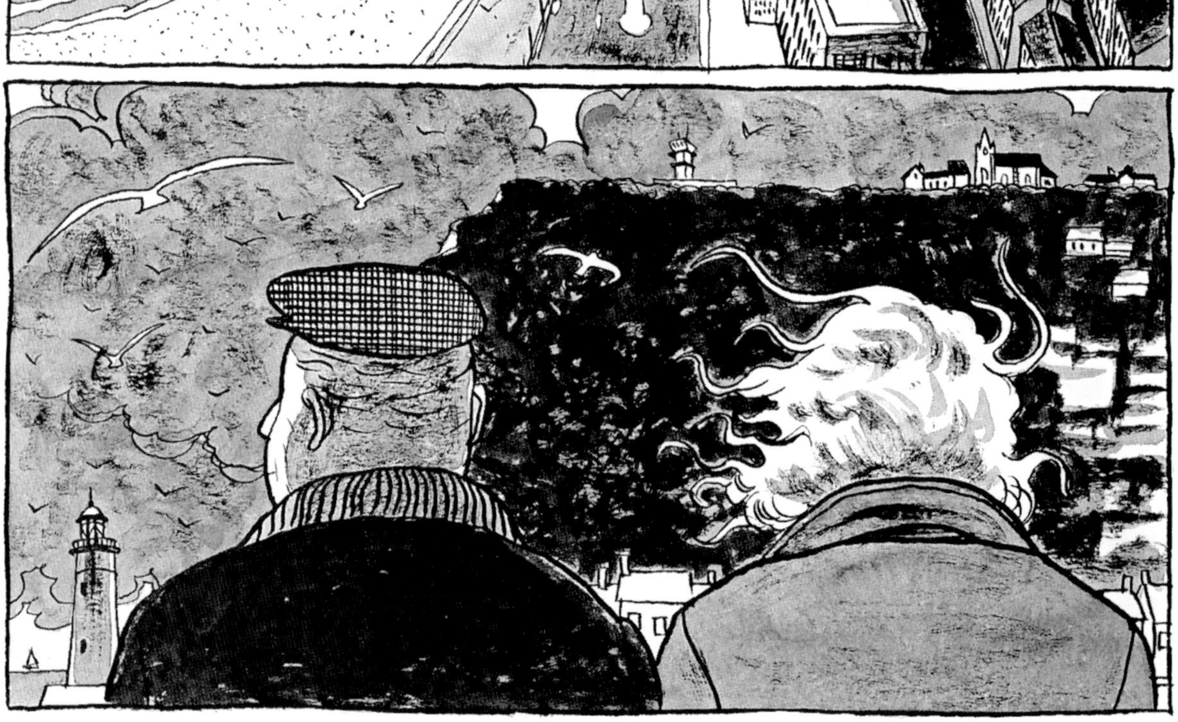

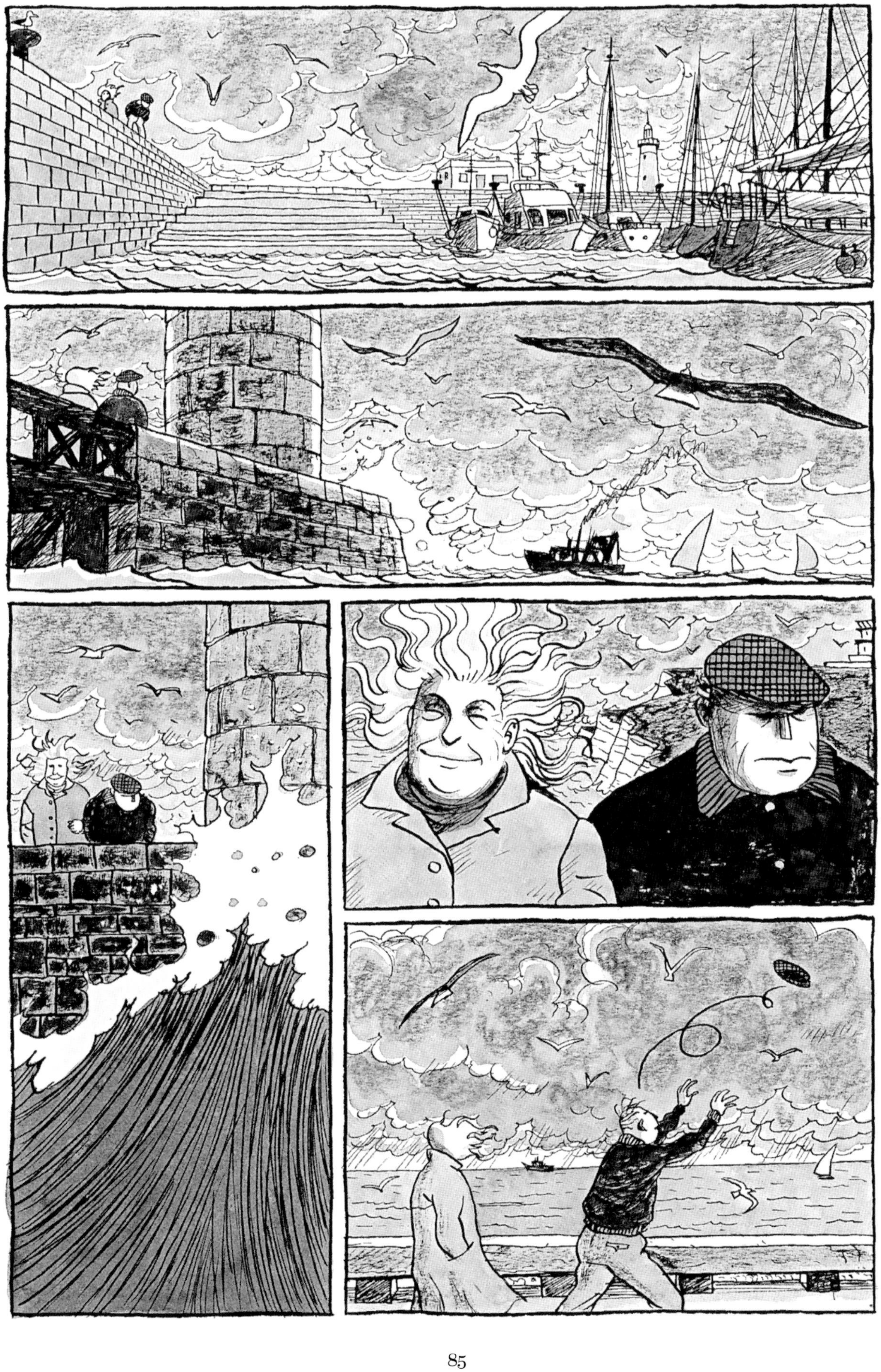

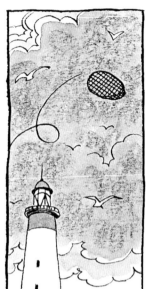

IT'S TOO GODDAMN COLD OUT HERE! I'M NEVER COMING BACK!!!

"SO ADOLPHE STAYED AT HOME, ONLY VISITING HIS CHILDREN OCCASIONALLY, BECAUSE CARMEN AND DODO WERE USUALLY THE HUB OF THE ENTIRE FAMILY."

"DODO WAS MY GRANDPA."

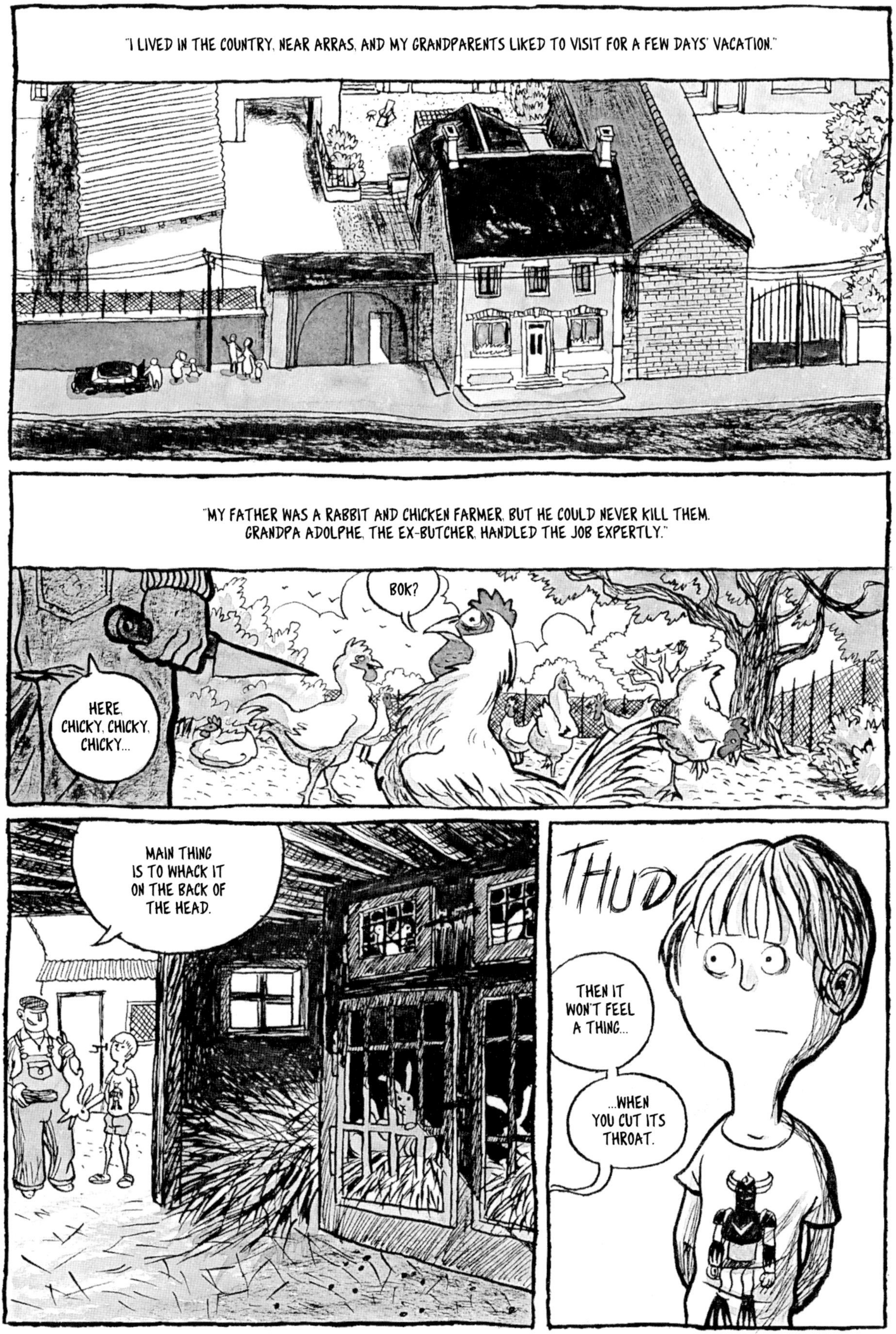
"I LIVED IN THE COUNTRY, NEAR ARRAS, AND MY GRANDPARENTS LIKED TO VISIT FOR A FEW DAYS' VACATION."
"MY FATHER WAS A RABBIT AND CHICKEN FARMER, BUT HE COULD NEVER KILL THEM. GRANDPA ADOLPHE, THE EX-BUTCHER, HANDLED THE JOB EXPERTLY."
HERE, CHICKY, CHICKY, CHICKY...
BOK?
MAIN THING IS TO WHACK IT ON THE BACK OF THE HEAD.
THUD
THEN IT WON'T FEEL A THING...
...WHEN YOU CUT ITS THROAT.

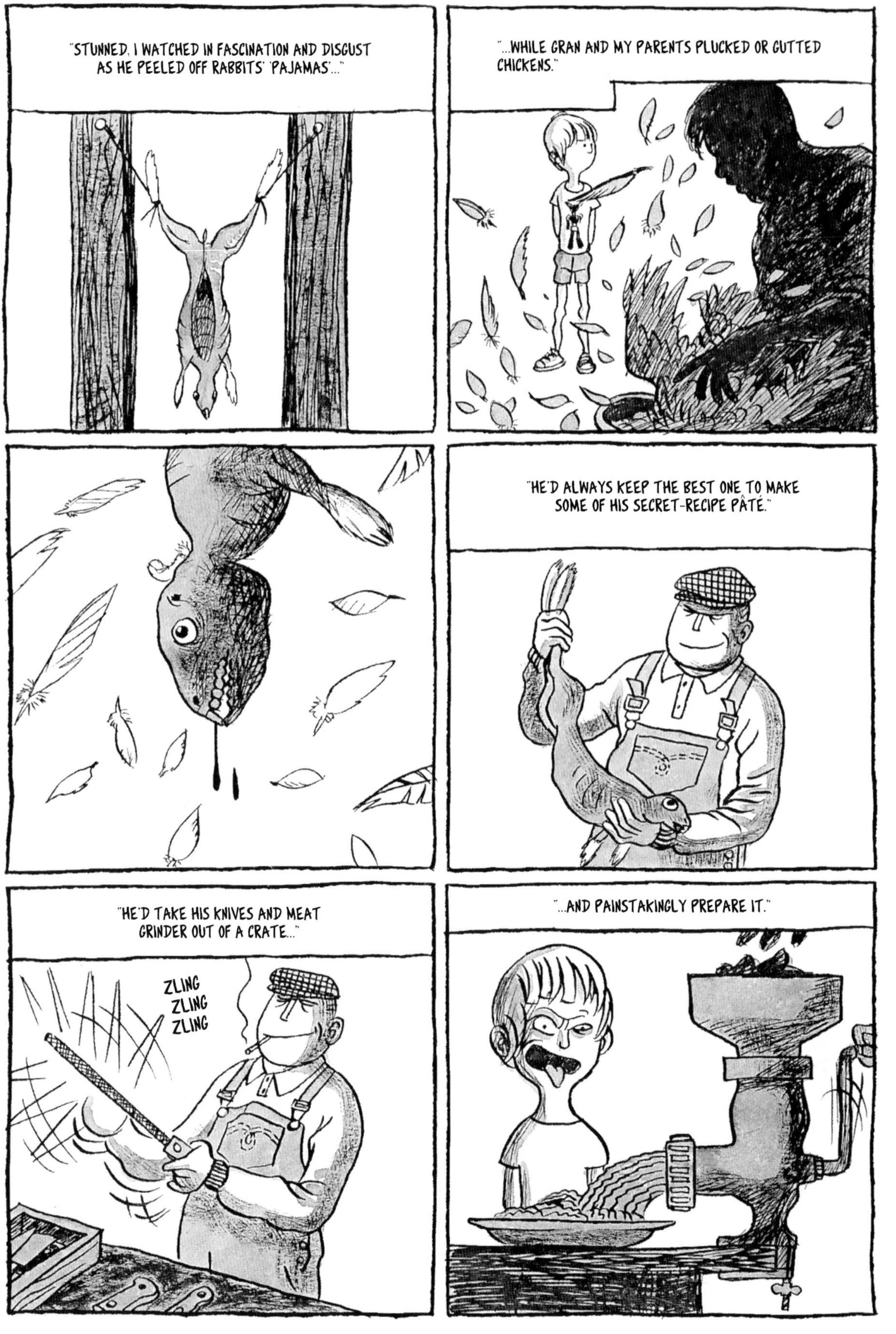
"STUNNED, I WATCHED IN FASCINATION AND DISGUST AS HE PEELED OFF RABBITS' 'PAJAMAS'..."
"...WHILE GRAN AND MY PARENTS PLUCKED OR GUTTED CHICKENS."
"HE'D ALWAYS KEEP THE BEST ONE TO MAKE SOME OF HIS SECRET-RECIPE PÂTÉ."
"HE'D TAKE HIS KNIVES AND MEAT GRINDER OUT OF A CRATE..."
ZLING
ZLING
ZLING
"...AND PAINSTAKINGLY PREPARE IT."

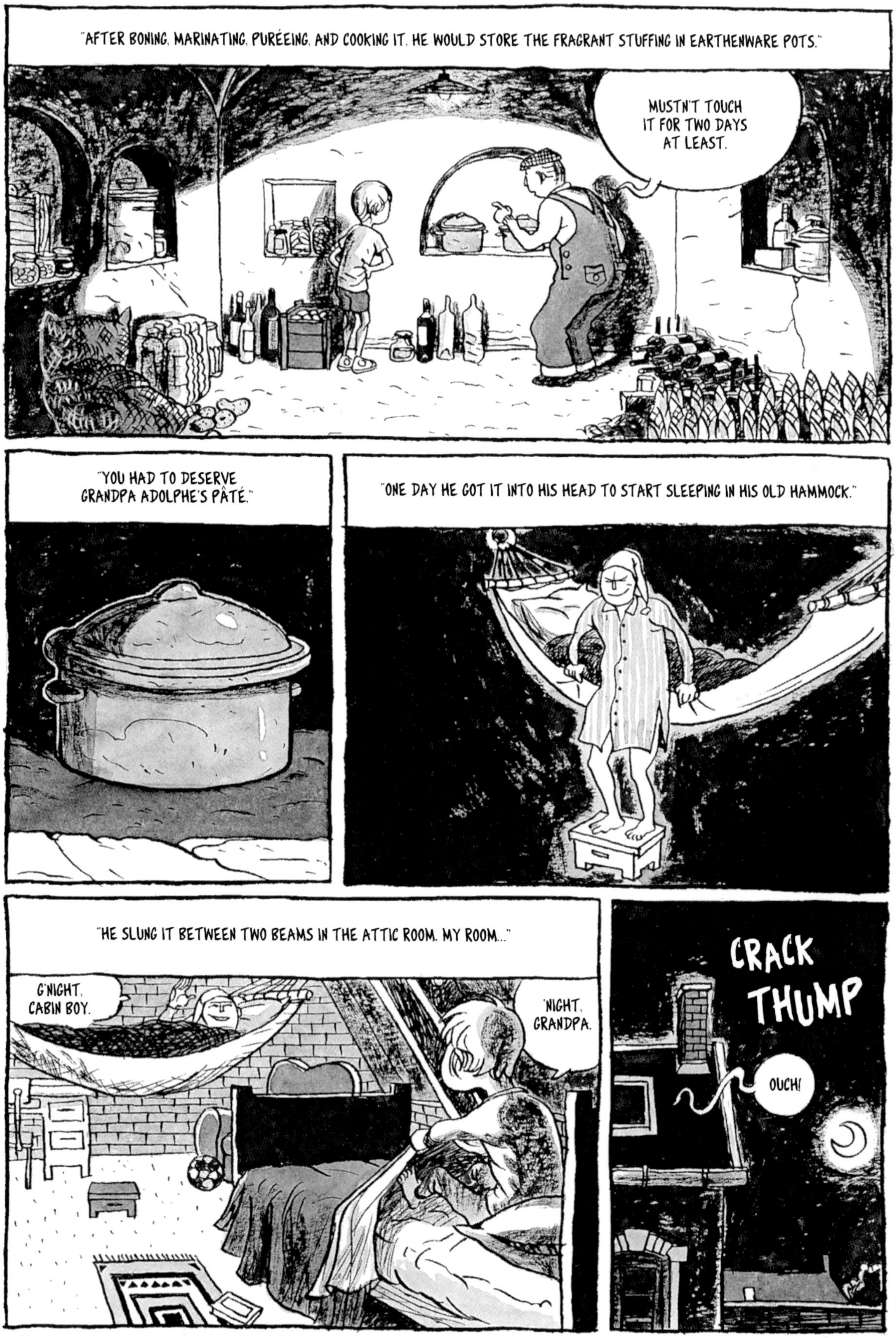
"AFTER BONING, MARINATING, PURÉEING, AND COOKING IT, HE WOULD STORE THE FRAGRANT STUFFING IN EARTHENWARE POTS."
MUSTN'T TOUCH IT FOR TWO DAYS AT LEAST.
"YOU HAD TO DESERVE GRANDPA ADOLPHE'S PÂTÉ."
"ONE DAY HE GOT IT INTO HIS HEAD TO START SLEEPING IN HIS OLD HAMMOCK."
"HE SLUNG IT BETWEEN TWO BEAMS IN THE ATTIC ROOM. MY ROOM..."
G'NIGHT, CABIN BOY.
'NIGHT, GRANDPA.
CRACK
THUMP
OUCH!

"I LOVED TO WATCH HIM SHAVE IN THE MORNING, THEN USE AN ALUM BLOCK TO STOP RAZOR BURN."

WE USED TO PLAY WATER POLO WITH SHARKS ON OUR ASSES, KID!

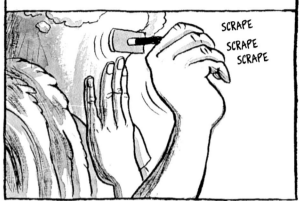

"REPEATED TIME AND TIME AGAIN, LIKE MAKING THE RABBIT PÂTÉ. HIS MOVEMENTS WERE MASTERFULLY ELEGANT AND PART OF A RITUAL THAT CAPTIVATED ME AS A LITTLE BOY. SO, WHEN HE'D FINISHED..."

SCRAPE
SCRAPE
SCRAPE

CLICK

SCRiiiTCH

"...I'D PLAY AT BEING A GROWN-UP."

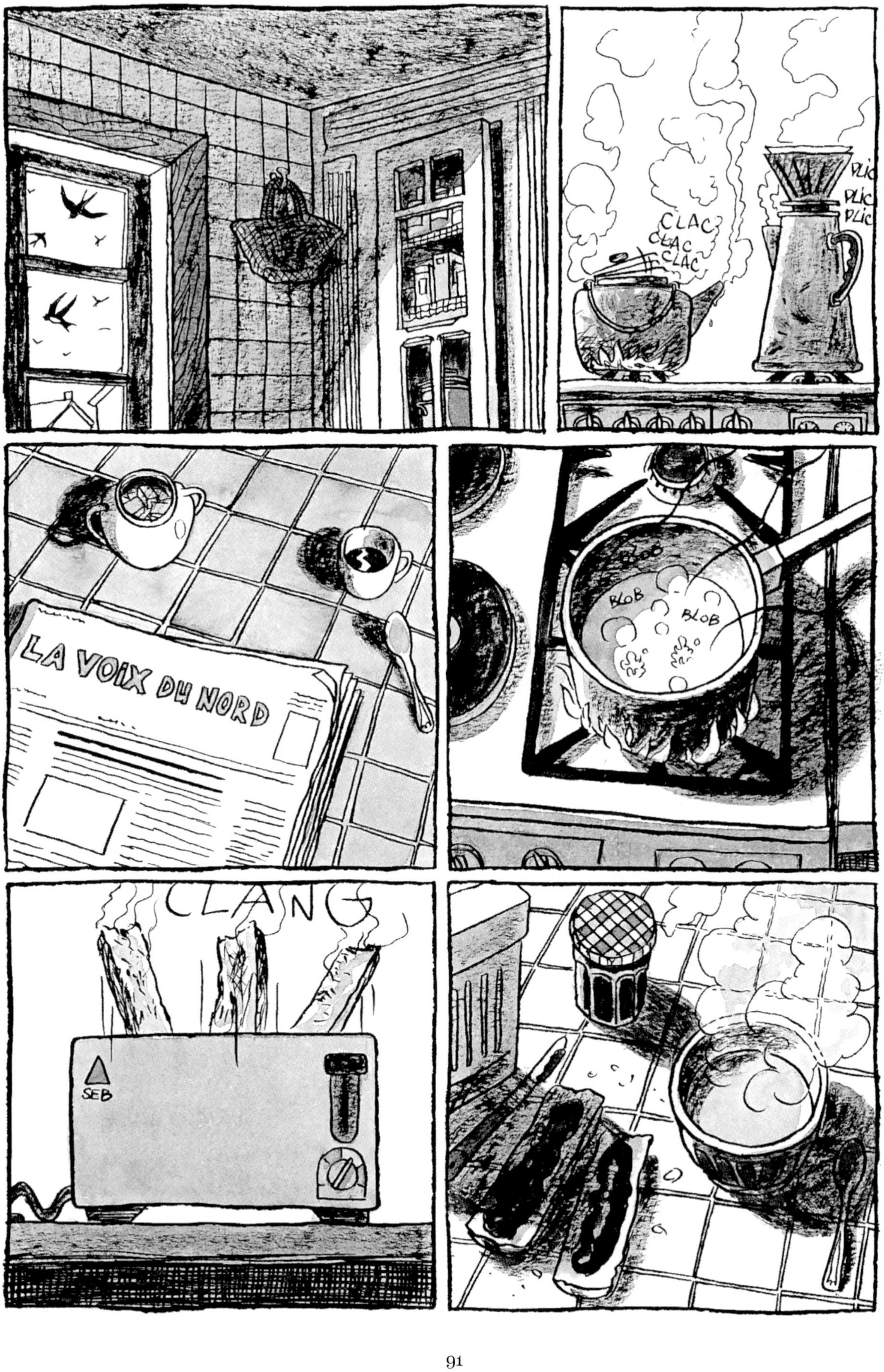
CLAC
CLAC
CLAC
PLIC
PLIC
PLIC
LA VOIX DU NORD
BLOB
BLOB
BLOB
CLANG
SEB

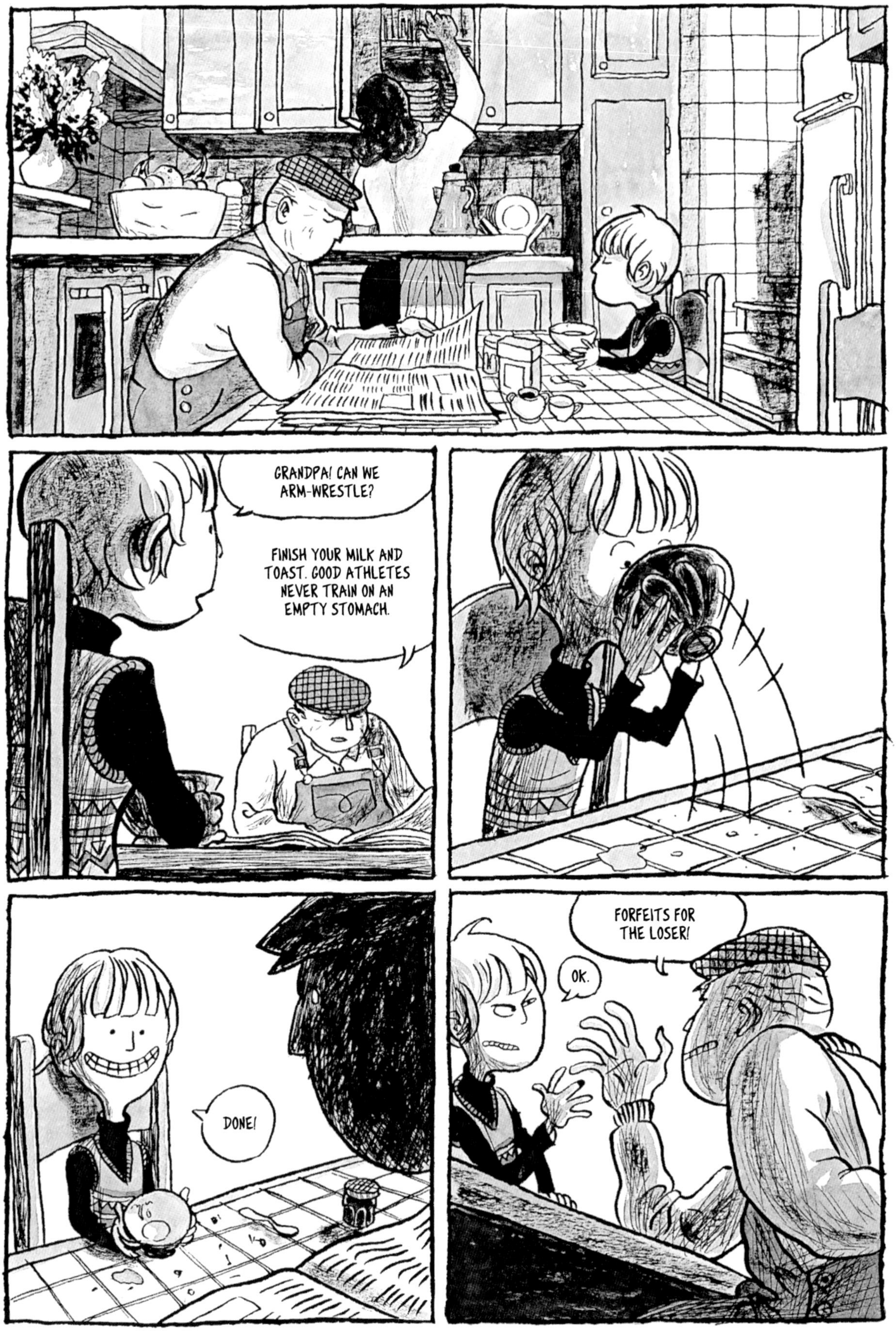
GRANDPA! CAN WE ARM-WRESTLE?
FINISH YOUR MILK AND TOAST. GOOD ATHLETES NEVER TRAIN ON AN EMPTY STOMACH.
DONE!
FORFEITS FOR THE LOSER!
OK.

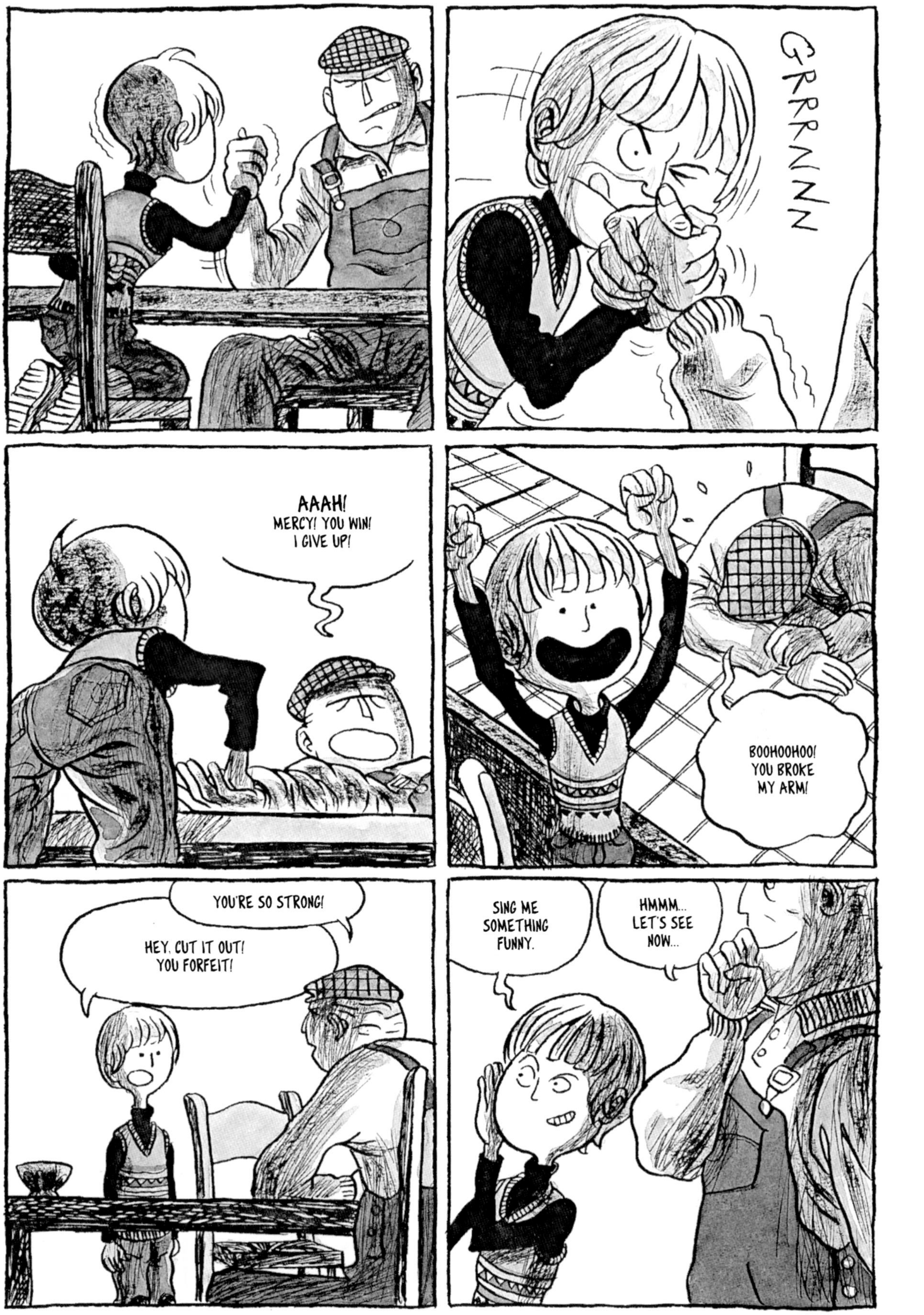
GRRRNNN
AAAH!
MERCY! YOU WIN!
I GIVE UP!
BOOHOOHOO!
YOU BROKE
MY ARM!
YOU'RE SO STRONG!
HEY, CUT IT OUT!
YOU FORFEIT!
SING ME
SOMETHING
FUNNY.
HMMM...
LET'S SEE
NOW...

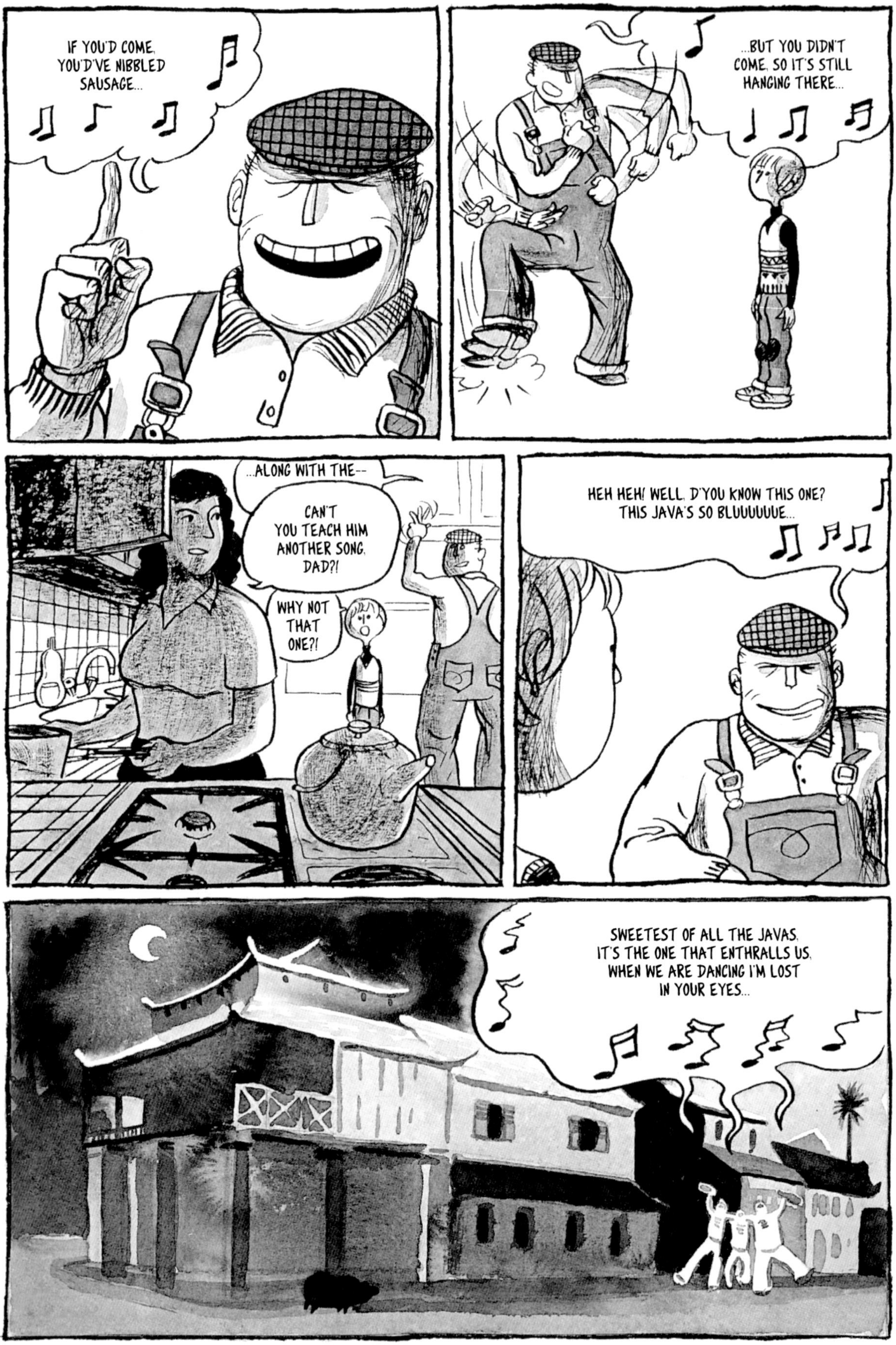
IF YOU'D COME, YOU'D'VE NIBBLED SAUSAGE...
...BUT YOU DIDN'T COME, SO IT'S STILL HANGING THERE...
...ALONG WITH THE--
CAN'T YOU TEACH HIM ANOTHER SONG, DAD?!
WHY NOT THAT ONE?!
HEH HEH! WELL, D'YOU KNOW THIS ONE? THIS JAVA'S SO BLUUUUUUE...
SWEETEST OF ALL THE JAVAS, IT'S THE ONE THAT ENTHRALLS US, WHEN WE ARE DANCING I'M LOST IN YOUR EYES...

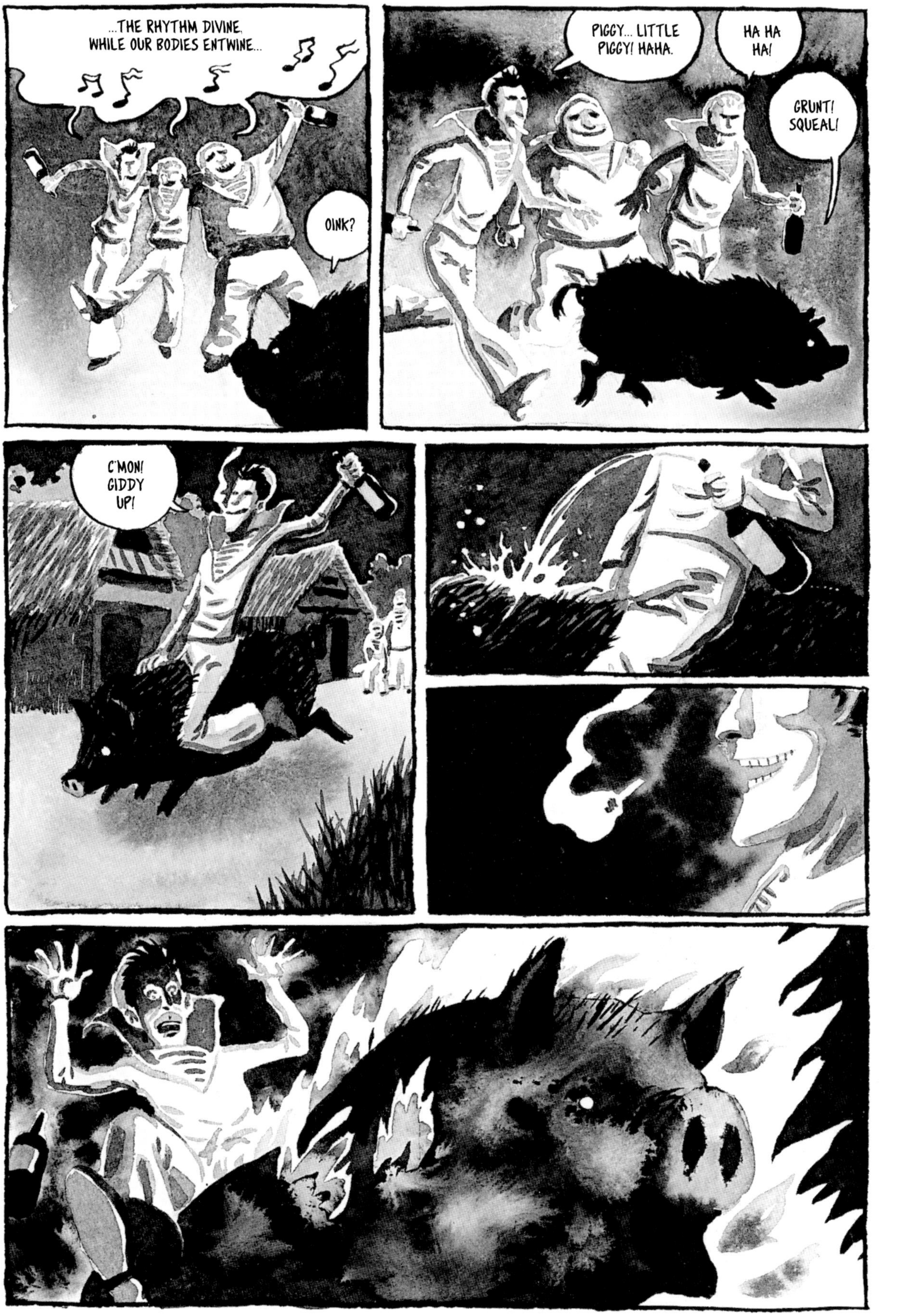
...THE RHYTHM DIVINE, WHILE OUR BODIES ENTWINE...
OINK?
PIGGY... LITTLE PIGGY! HAHA.
HA HA HA!
GRUNT! SQUEAL!
C'MON! GIDDY UP!

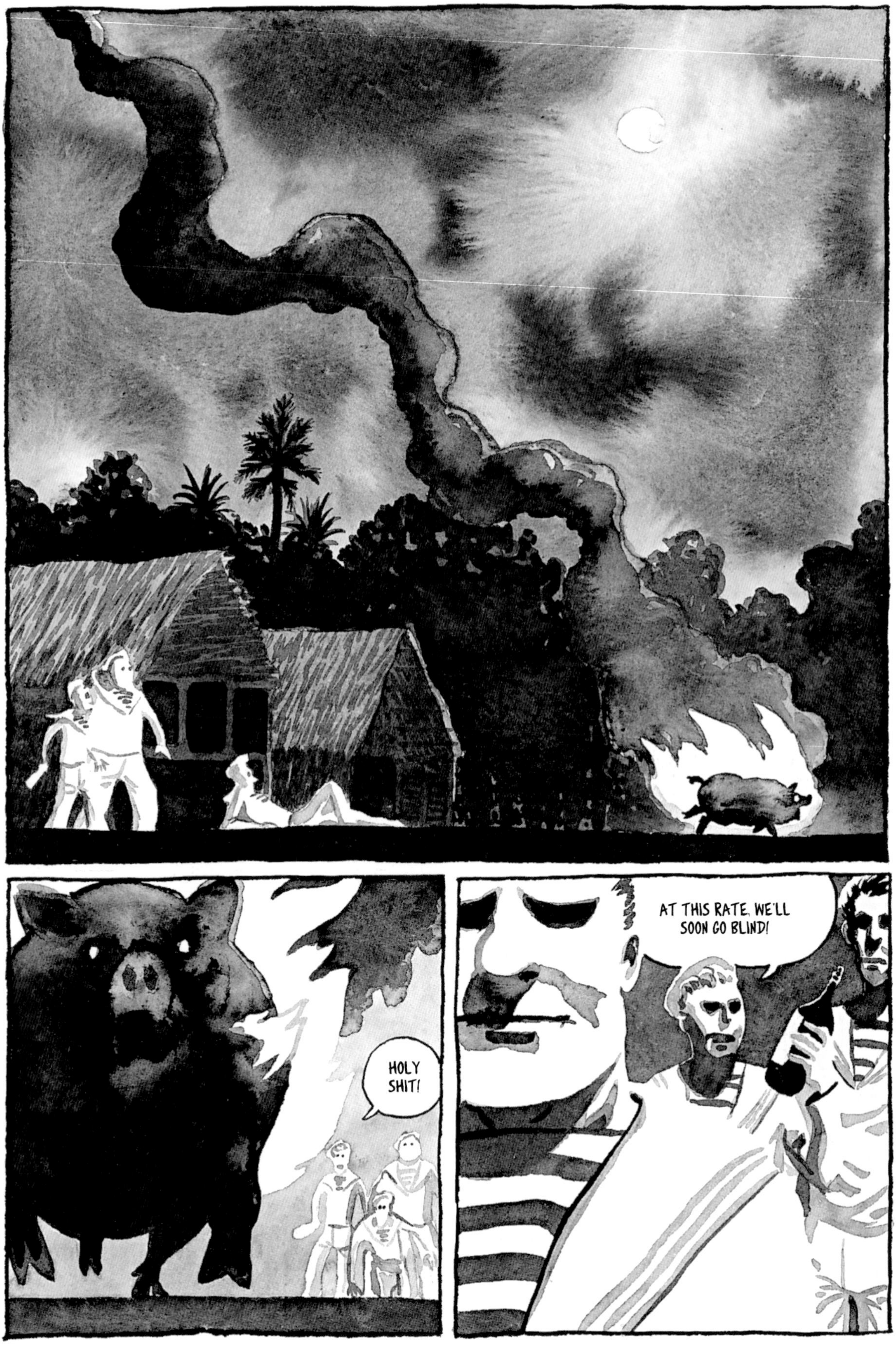
HOLY SHIT!
AT THIS RATE, WE'LL SOON GO BLIND!

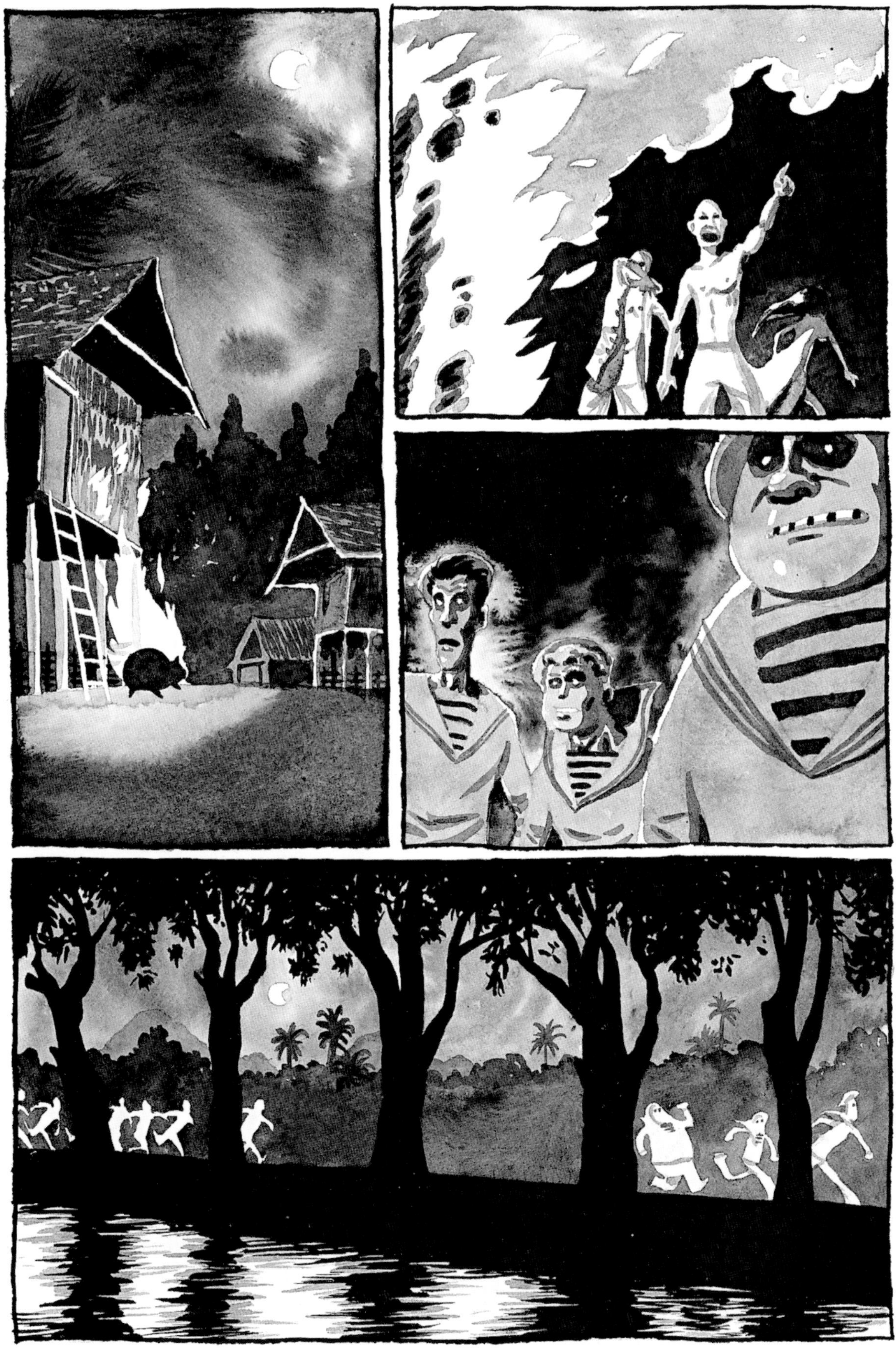

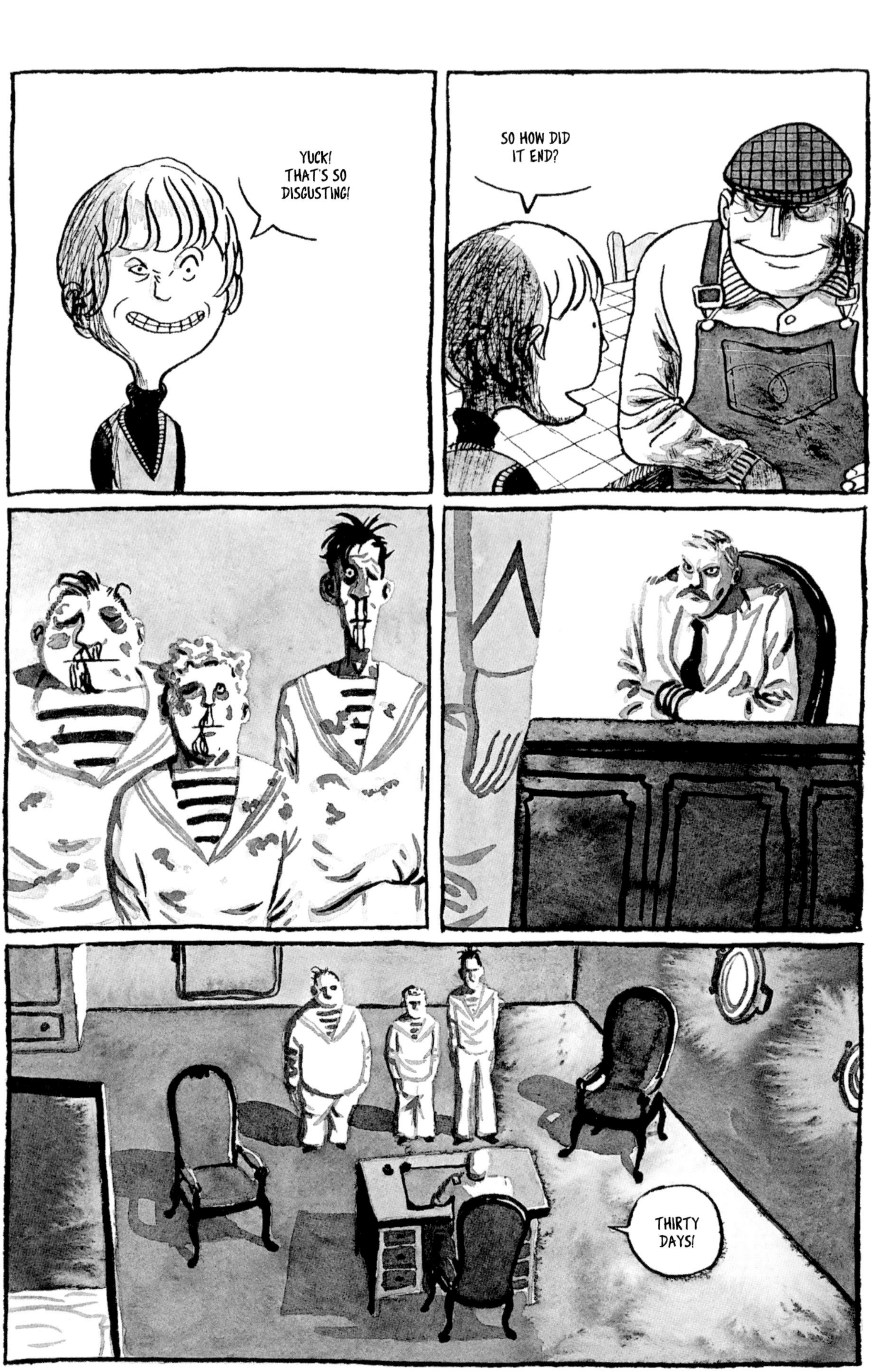
YUCK! THAT'S SO DISGUSTING!
SO HOW DID IT END?
THIRTY DAYS!

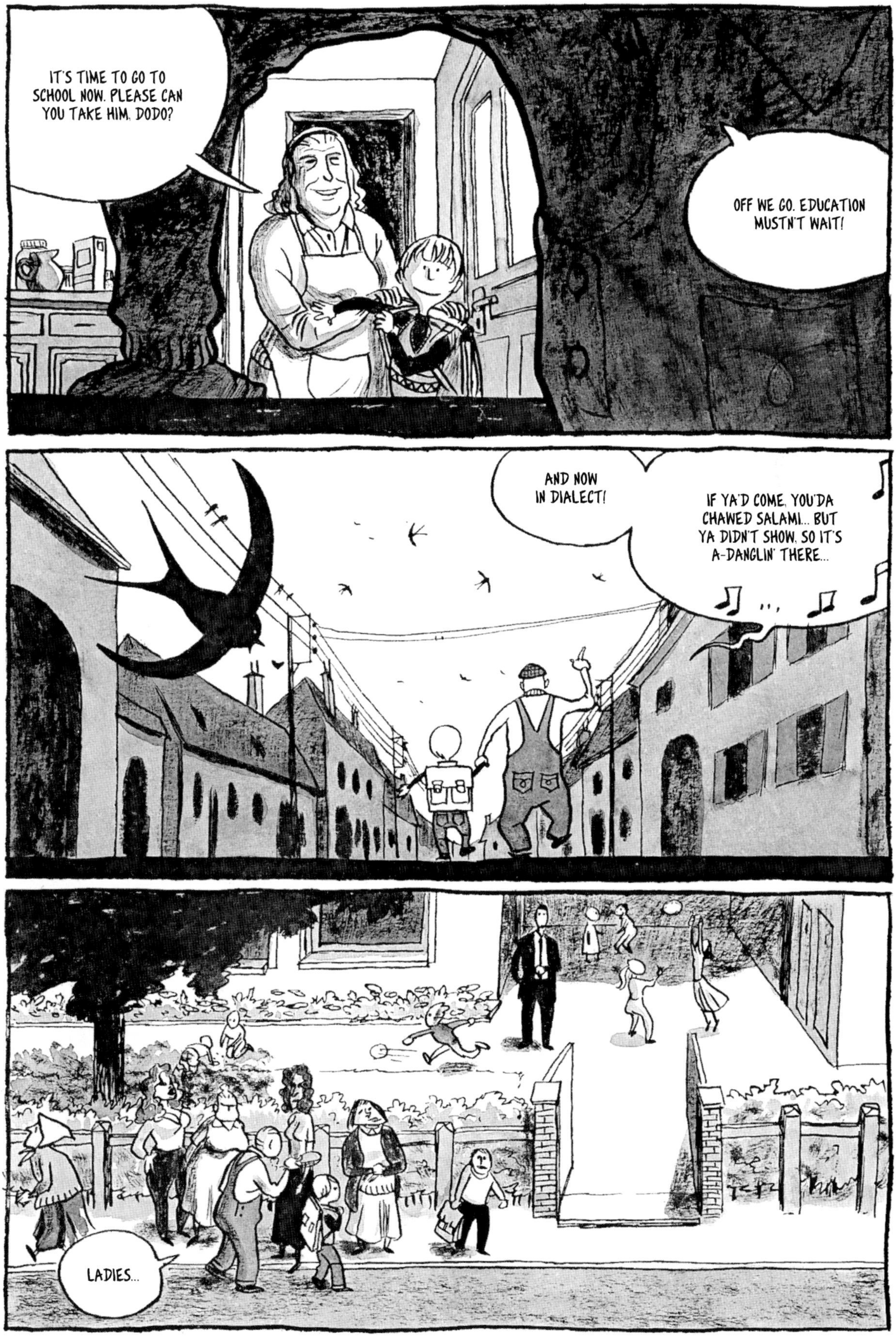
IT'S TIME TO GO TO SCHOOL NOW. PLEASE CAN YOU TAKE HIM, DODO?
OFF WE GO. EDUCATION MUSTN'T WAIT!
AND NOW IN DIALECT!
IF YA'D COME, YOU'DA CHAWED SALAMI... BUT YA DIDN'T SHOW, SO IT'S A-DANGLIN' THERE...
LADIES...

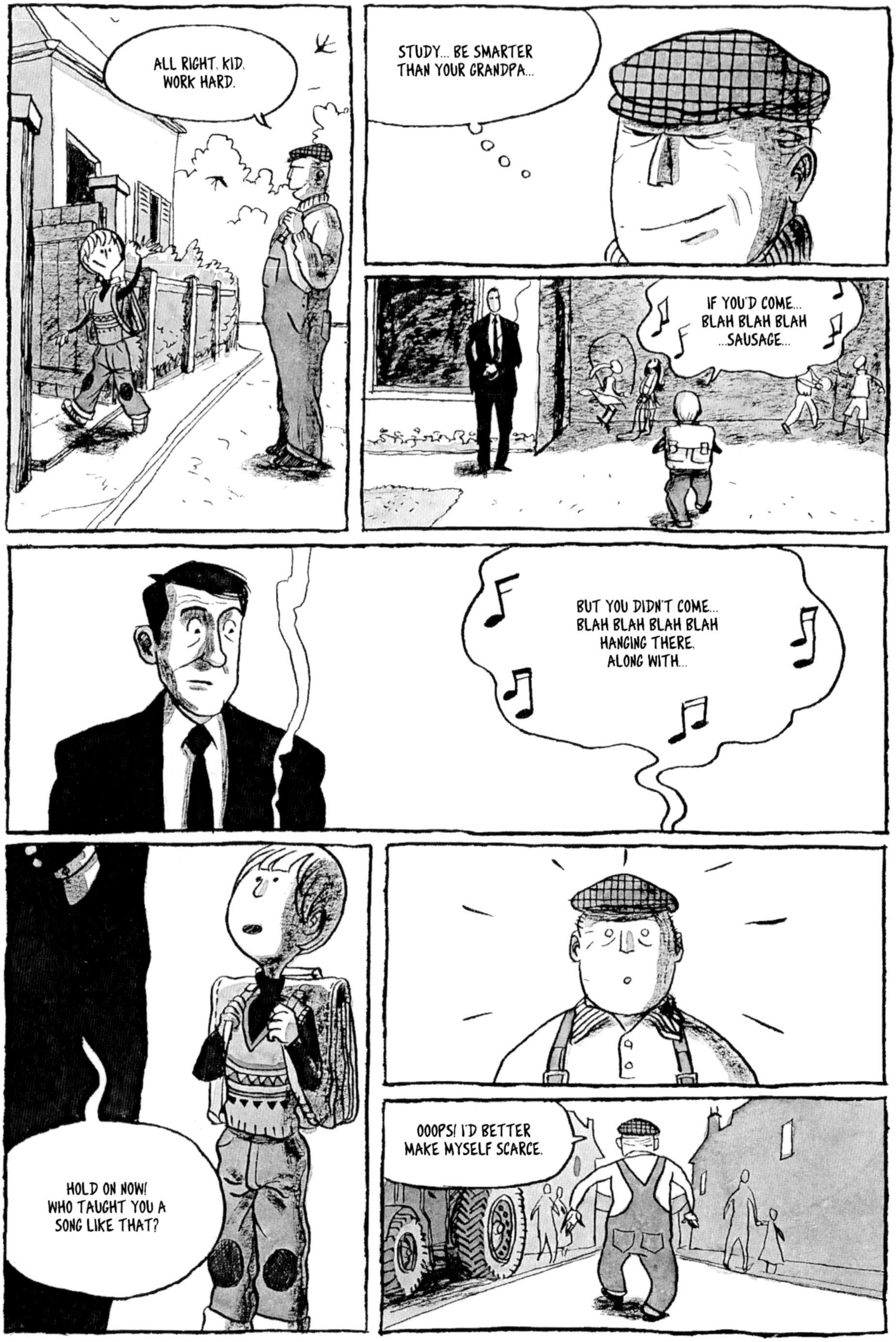
ALL RIGHT, KID, WORK HARD.
STUDY... BE SMARTER THAN YOUR GRANDPA...
IF YOU'D COME... BLAH BLAH BLAH ...SAUSAGE...
BUT YOU DIDN'T COME... BLAH BLAH BLAH BLAH HANGING THERE, ALONG WITH...
HOLD ON NOW! WHO TAUGHT YOU A SONG LIKE THAT?
OOOPS! I'D BETTER MAKE MYSELF SCARCE.

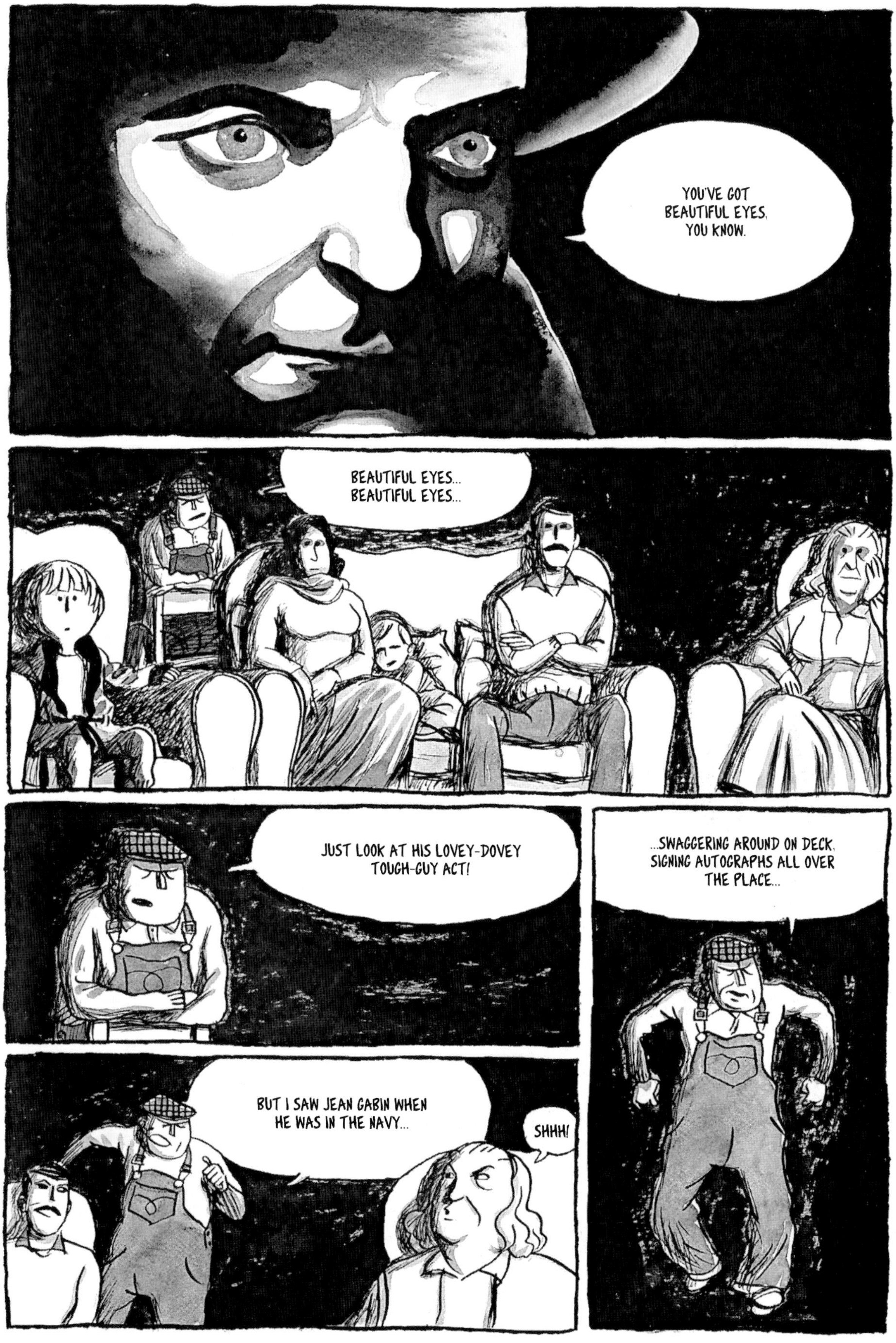
YOU'VE GOT BEAUTIFUL EYES, YOU KNOW.
BEAUTIFUL EYES... BEAUTIFUL EYES...
JUST LOOK AT HIS LOVEY-DOVEY TOUGH-GUY ACT!
BUT I SAW JEAN GABIN WHEN HE WAS IN THE NAVY...
SHHH!
...SWAGGERING AROUND ON DECK, SIGNING AUTOGRAPHS ALL OVER THE PLACE...

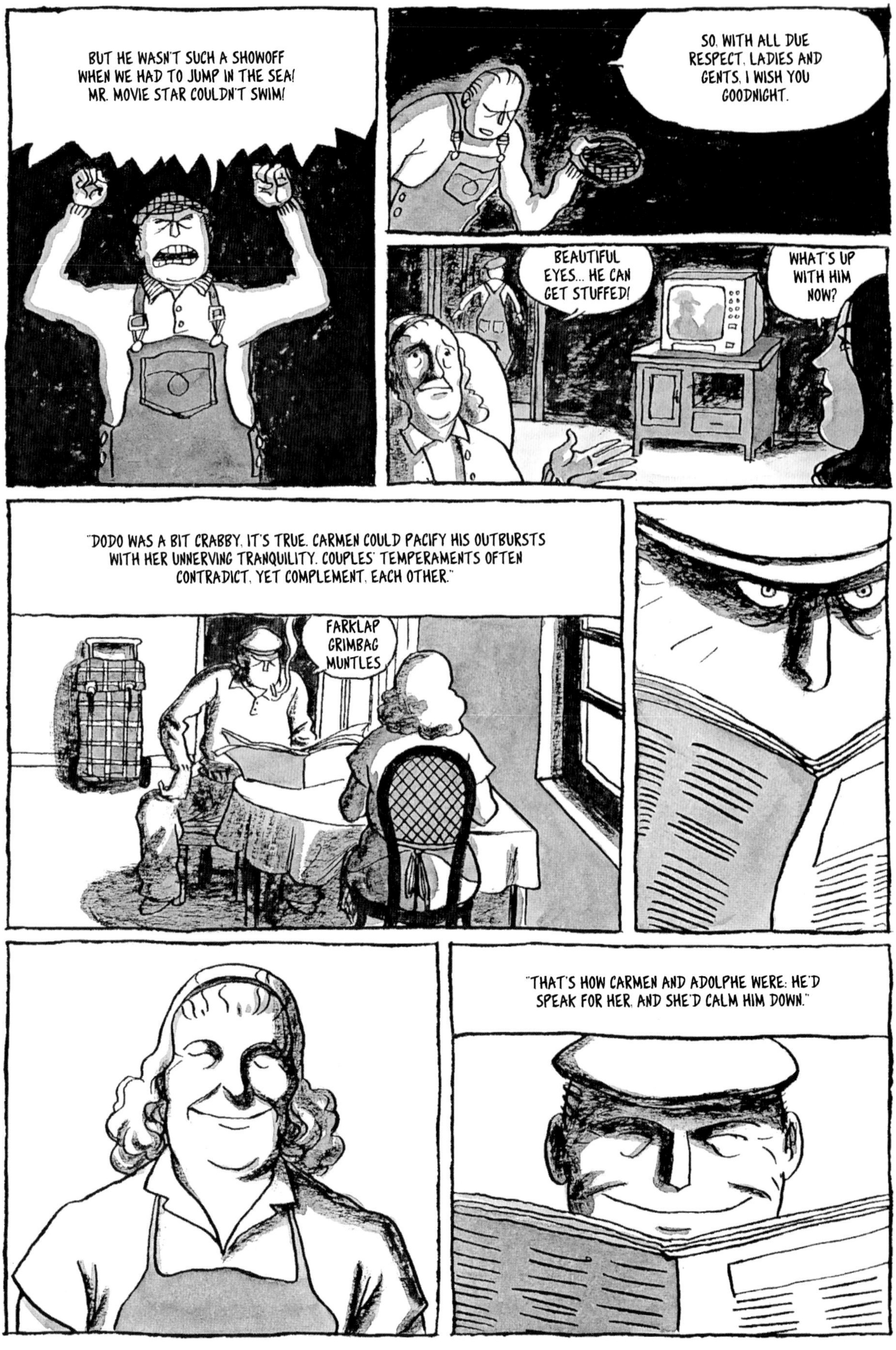
BUT HE WASN'T SUCH A SHOWOFF WHEN WE HAD TO JUMP IN THE SEA! MR. MOVIE STAR COULDN'T SWIM!
SO, WITH ALL DUE RESPECT, LADIES AND GENTS, I WISH YOU GOODNIGHT.
BEAUTIFUL EYES... HE CAN GET STUFFED!
WHAT'S UP WITH HIM NOW?
"DODO WAS A BIT CRABBY, IT'S TRUE. CARMEN COULD PACIFY HIS OUTBURSTS WITH HER UNNERVING TRANQUILITY. COUPLES' TEMPERAMENTS OFTEN CONTRADICT, YET COMPLEMENT, EACH OTHER."
FARKLAP GRIMBAG MUNTLES
"THAT'S HOW CARMEN AND ADOLPHE WERE: HE'D SPEAK FOR HER, AND SHE'D CALM HIM DOWN."

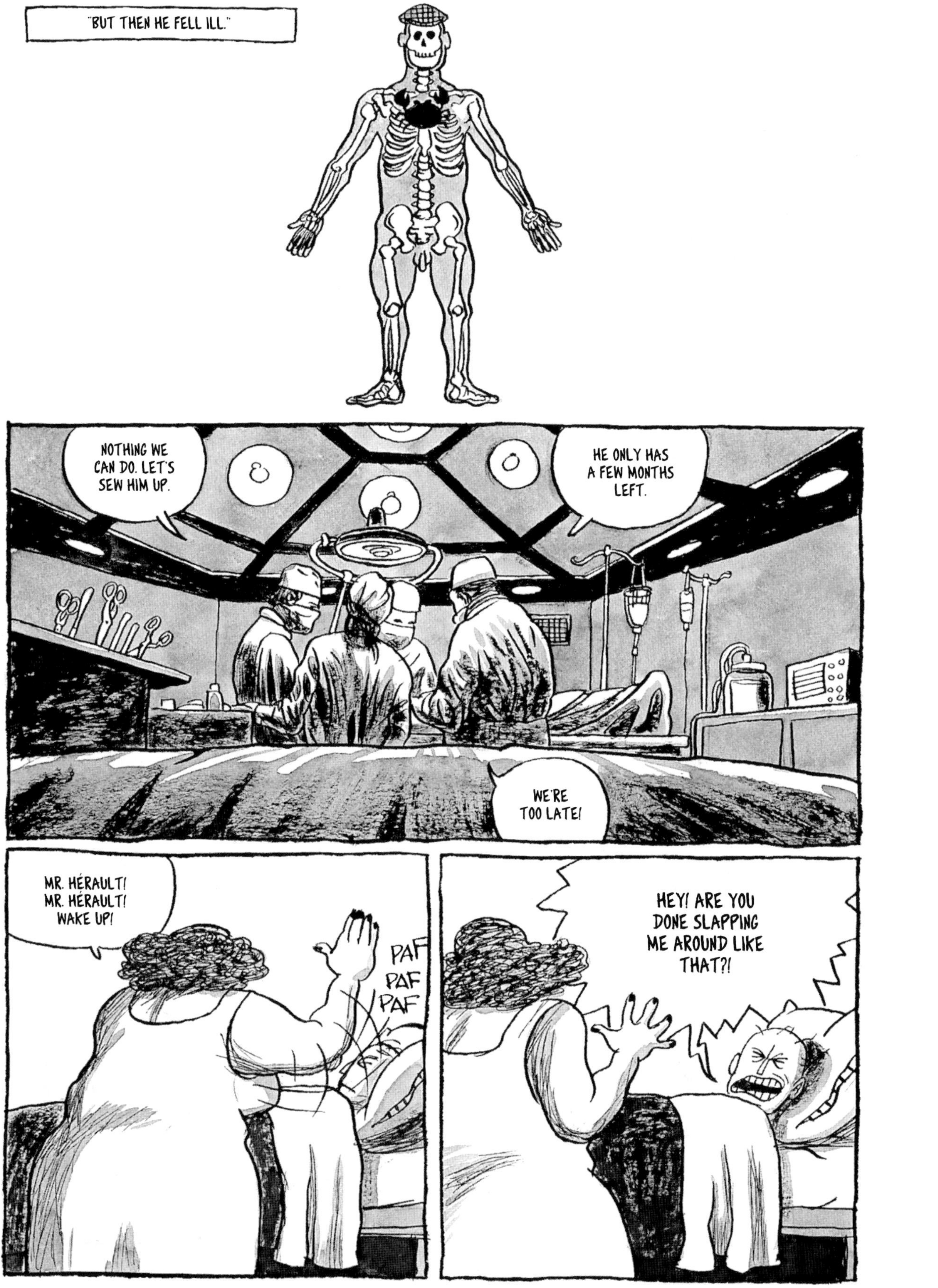
"BUT THEN HE FELL ILL."
NOTHING WE CAN DO. LET'S SEW HIM UP.
HE ONLY HAS A FEW MONTHS LEFT.
WE'RE TOO LATE!
MR. HÉRAULT! MR. HÉRAULT! WAKE UP!
PAF
PAF
PAF
HEY! ARE YOU DONE SLAPPING ME AROUND LIKE THAT?!

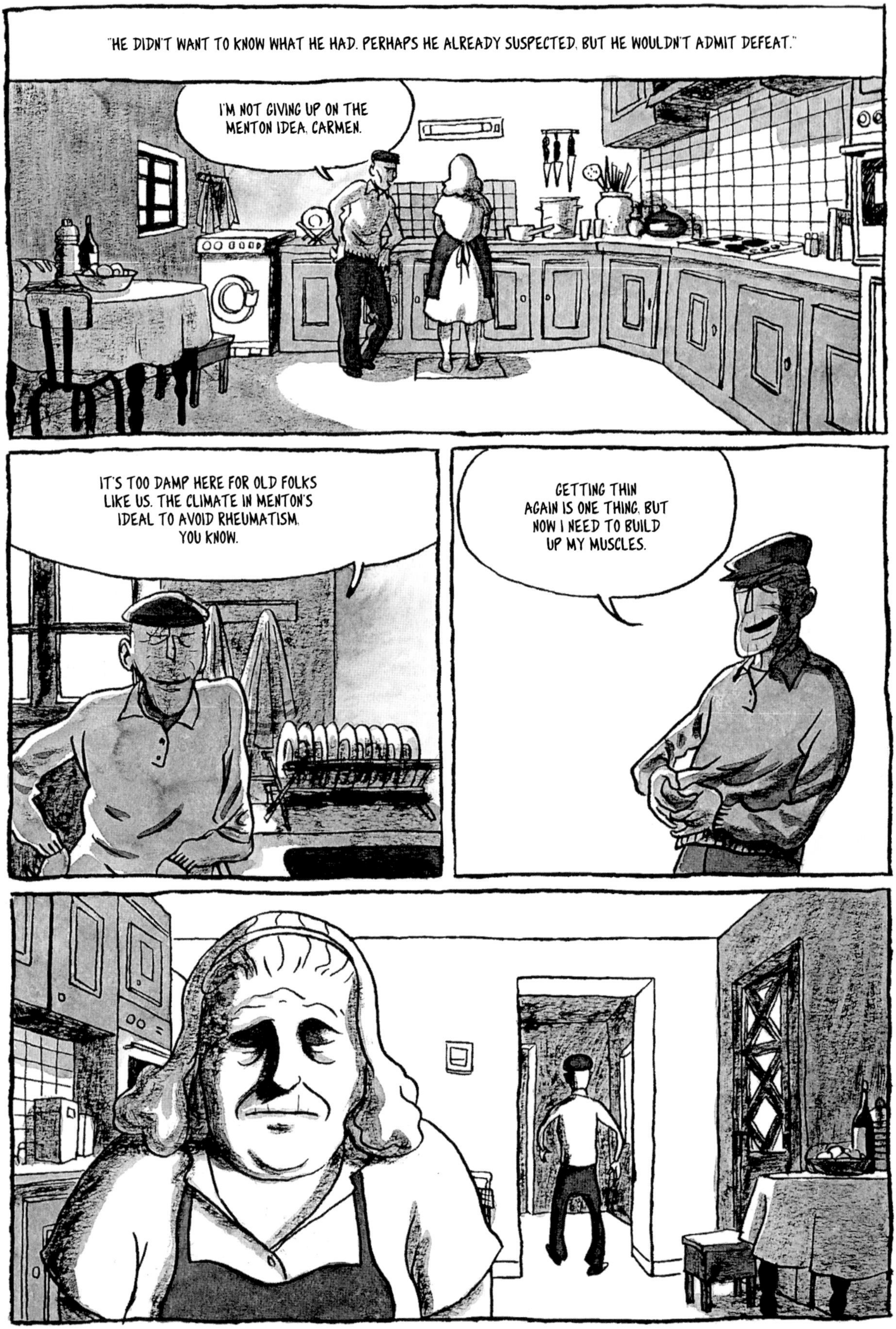
"HE DIDN'T WANT TO KNOW WHAT HE HAD. PERHAPS HE ALREADY SUSPECTED, BUT HE WOULDN'T ADMIT DEFEAT."
I'M NOT GIVING UP ON THE MENTON IDEA, CARMEN.
IT'S TOO DAMP HERE FOR OLD FOLKS LIKE US. THE CLIMATE IN MENTON'S IDEAL TO AVOID RHEUMATISM, YOU KNOW.
GETTING THIN AGAIN IS ONE THING, BUT NOW I NEED TO BUILD UP MY MUSCLES.

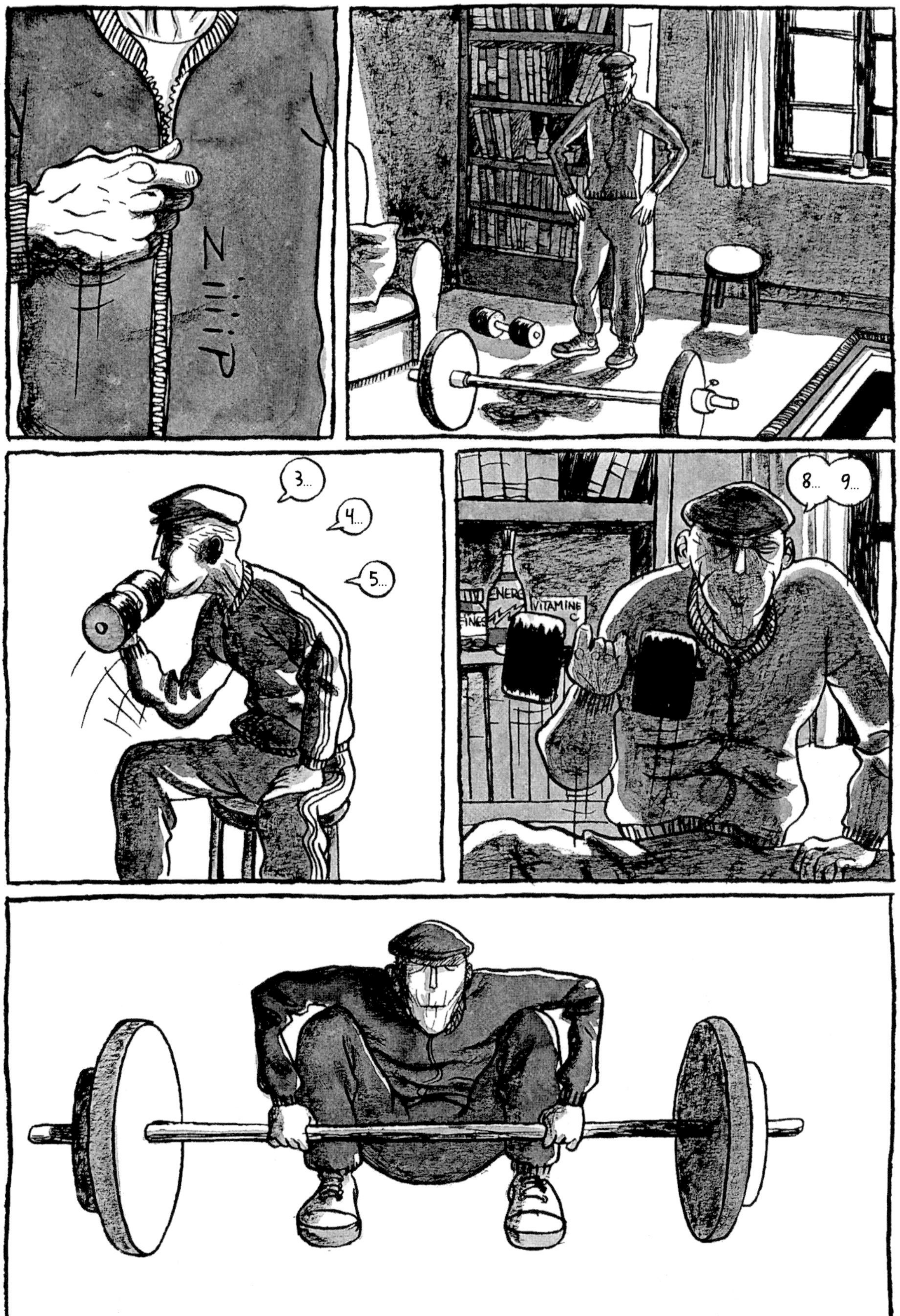
ZIIIIP
3...
4...
5...
8...
9...
ENERG
VITAMINE C

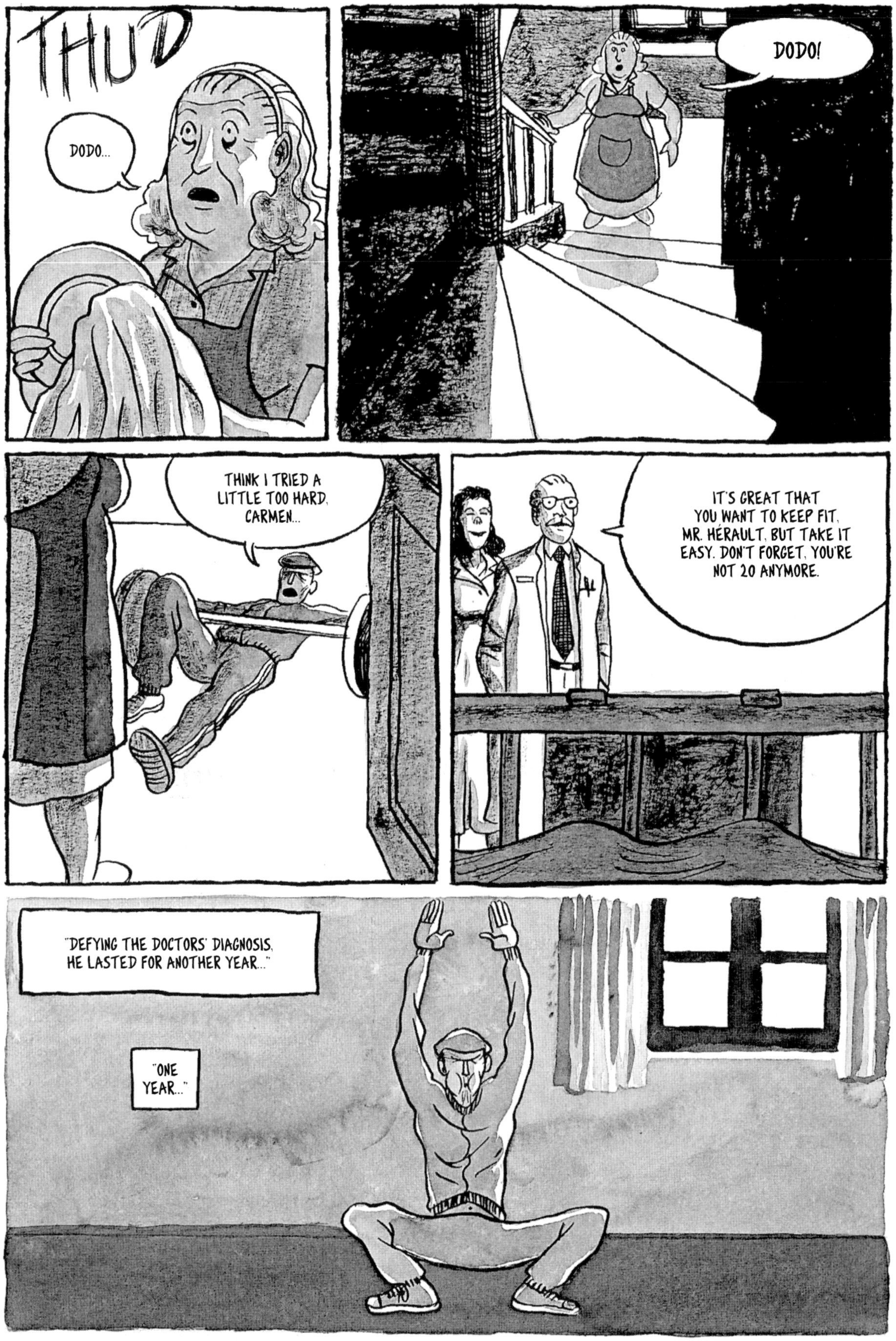
THUD
DODO...
DODO!
THINK I TRIED A LITTLE TOO HARD, CARMEN...
IT'S GREAT THAT YOU WANT TO KEEP FIT, MR. HÉRAULT, BUT TAKE IT EASY. DON'T FORGET, YOU'RE NOT 20 ANYMORE.
"DEFYING THE DOCTORS' DIAGNOSIS, HE LASTED FOR ANOTHER YEAR..."
"ONE YEAR..."

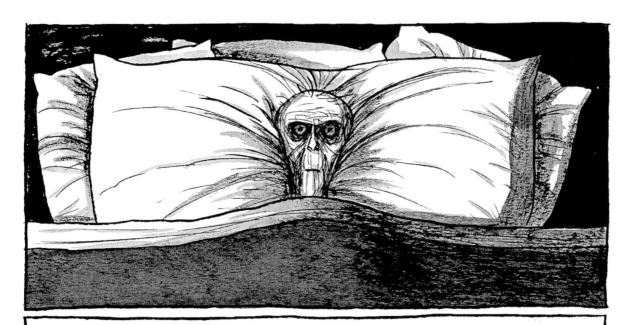

"I WAS 15 WHEN I SAW HIM ON HIS DEATHBED, AND TO THIS DAY I REGRET THAT IT WAS MY LAST MEMORY OF HIM..."

"HE DIDN'T LOOK AT ME OR SPEAK."

"HE WAS NO LONGER THE GRANDPA WHO PLAYED WATER POLO SURROUNDED BY SHARKS OR TAUGHT ME TO WALK LIKE A MAN."

I'M GONNA KICK THE BUCKET... THAT'S IT, THIS IS THE BIG ONE...

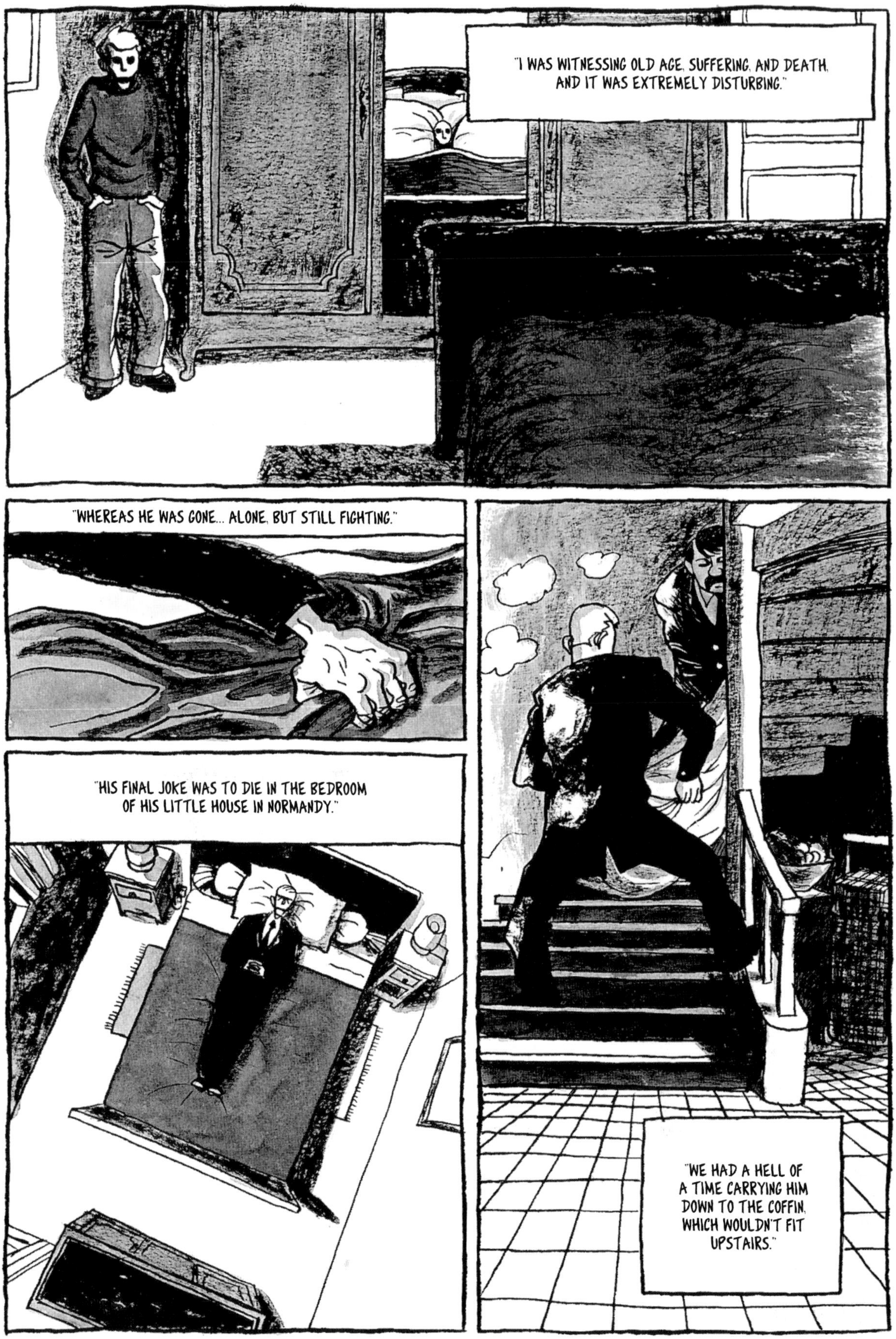
"I WAS WITNESSING OLD AGE, SUFFERING, AND DEATH, AND IT WAS EXTREMELY DISTURBING."
"WHEREAS HE WAS GONE... ALONE, BUT STILL FIGHTING."
"HIS FINAL JOKE WAS TO DIE IN THE BEDROOM OF HIS LITTLE HOUSE IN NORMANDY."
"WE HAD A HELL OF A TIME CARRYING HIM DOWN TO THE COFFIN, WHICH WOULDN'T FIT UPSTAIRS."

"SINCE DODO HAD ALWAYS HATED THE LOCAL PRIEST, CARMEN DECIDED NOT TO PUT A CROSS ON HIS COFFIN."

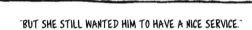
"BUT SHE STILL WANTED HIM TO HAVE A NICE SERVICE."

"ADOLPHE WAS A *CH'TI,* A FRENCH NORTHERNER. HIS EYES WERE THE BLUE THAT HIS HOMELAND LACKED,
HIS HEART HELD THE SUN HE NEVER SAW OUTSIDE, AS ENRICO MACIAS USED TO SING."

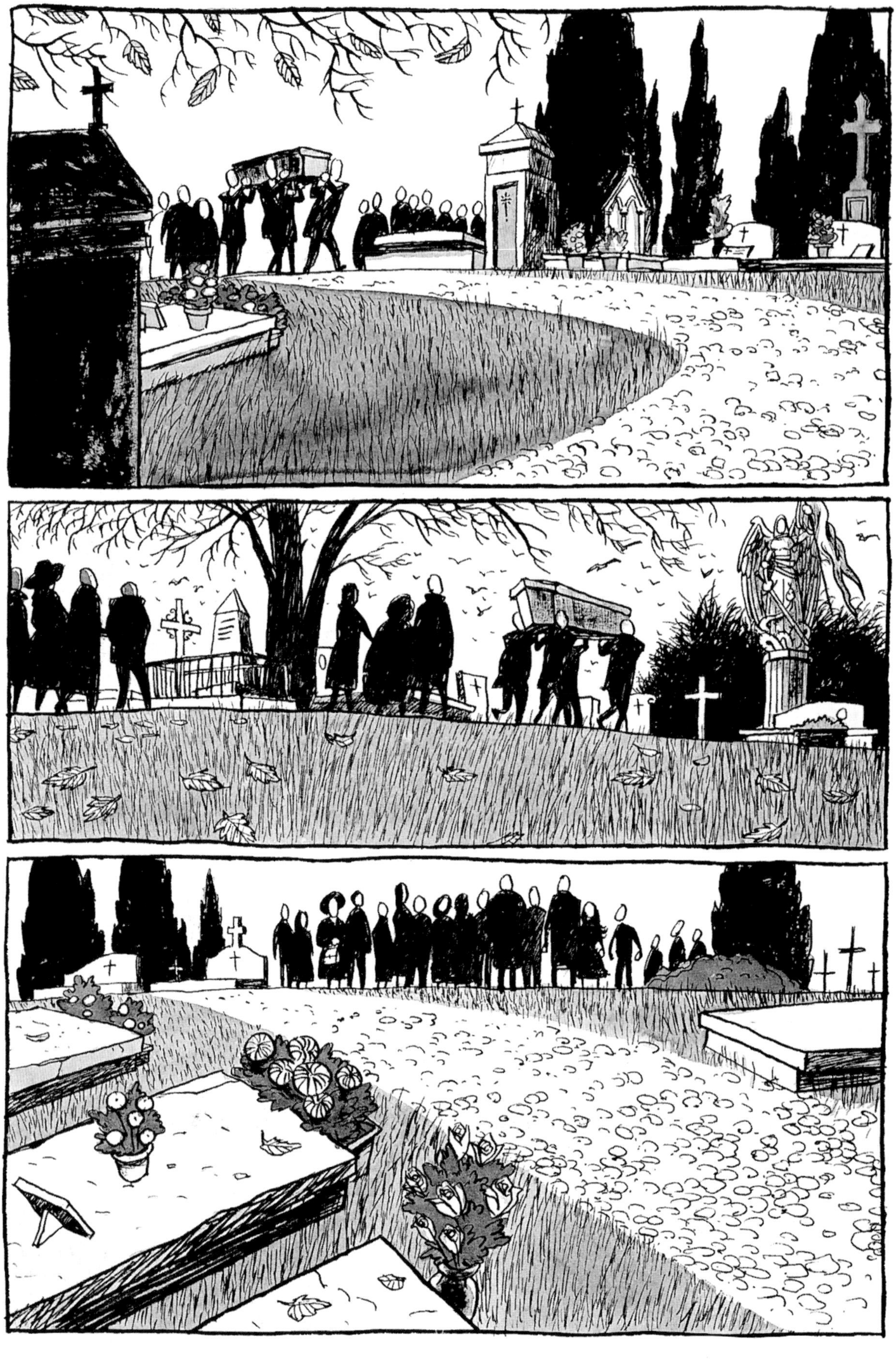

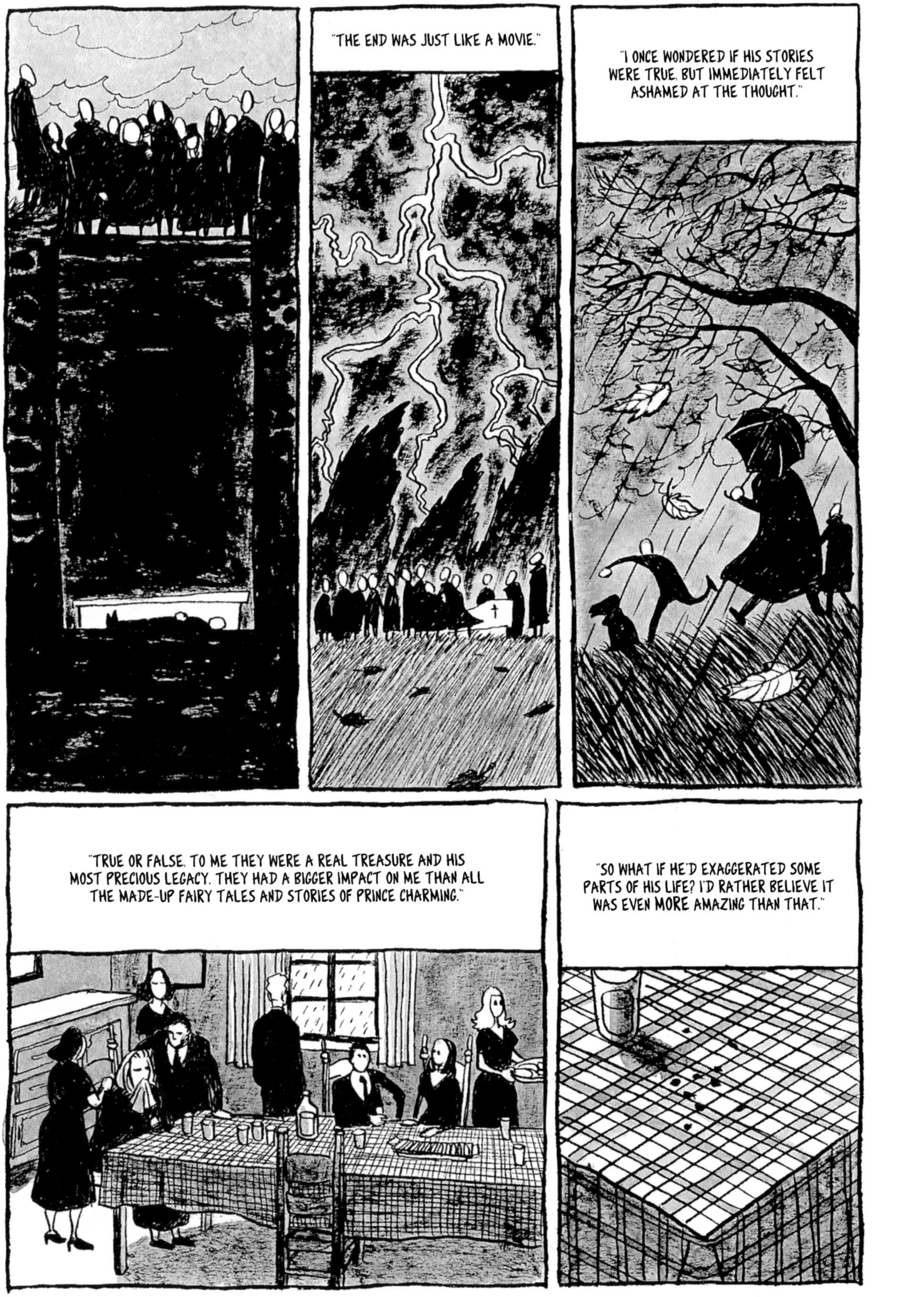
"THE END WAS JUST LIKE A MOVIE."
"I ONCE WONDERED IF HIS STORIES WERE TRUE, BUT IMMEDIATELY FELT ASHAMED AT THE THOUGHT."
"TRUE OR FALSE, TO ME THEY WERE A REAL TREASURE AND HIS MOST PRECIOUS LEGACY. THEY HAD A BIGGER IMPACT ON ME THAN ALL THE MADE-UP FAIRY TALES AND STORIES OF PRINCE CHARMING."
"SO WHAT IF HE'D EXAGGERATED SOME PARTS OF HIS LIFE? I'D RATHER BELIEVE IT WAS EVEN MORE AMAZING THAN THAT."

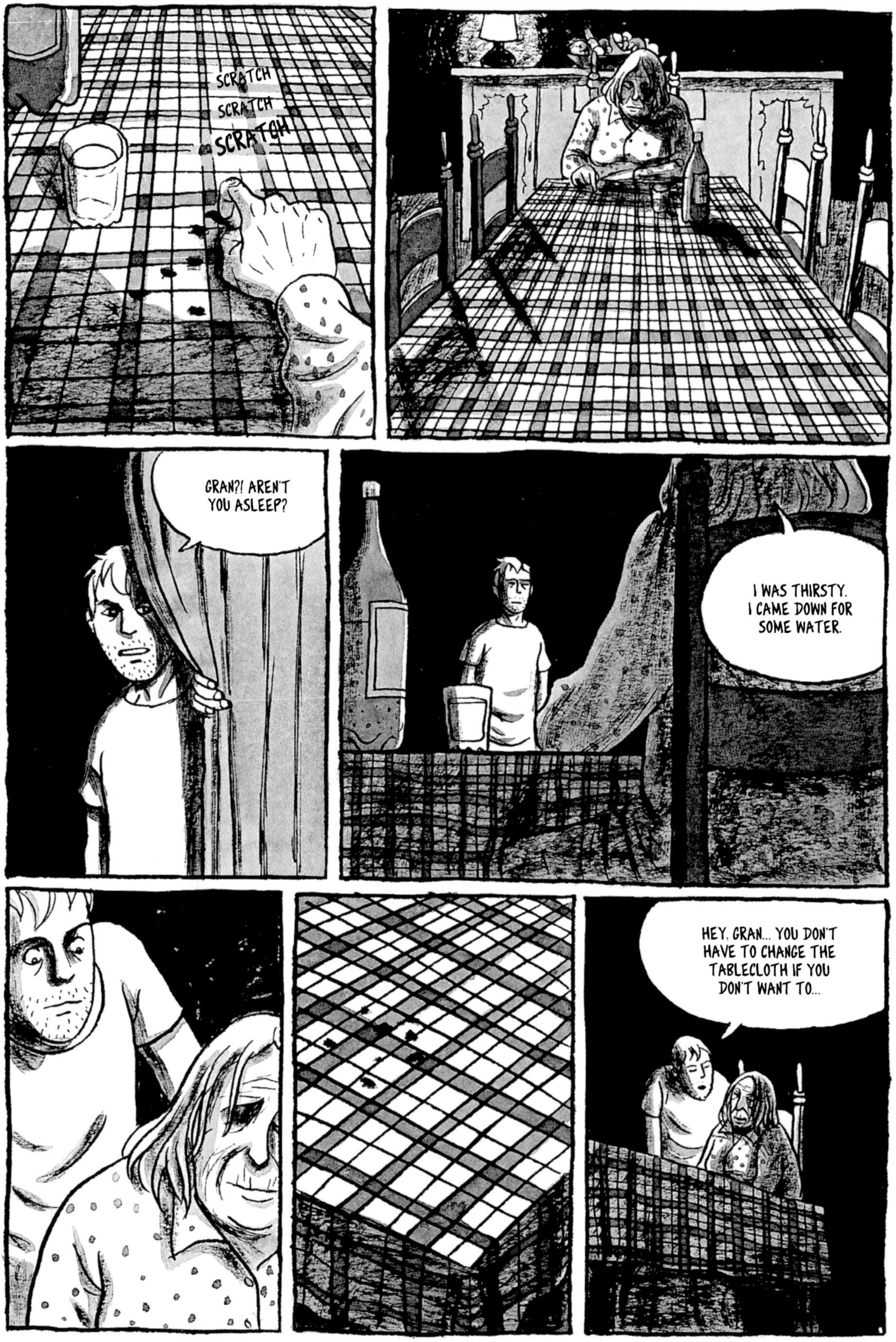
SCRATCH
SCRATCH
SCRATCH
GRAN?! AREN'T YOU ASLEEP?
I WAS THIRSTY. I CAME DOWN FOR SOME WATER.
HEY, GRAN... YOU DON'T HAVE TO CHANGE THE TABLECLOTH IF YOU DON'T WANT TO...

G. Mardon   April, 1999.   THE END.

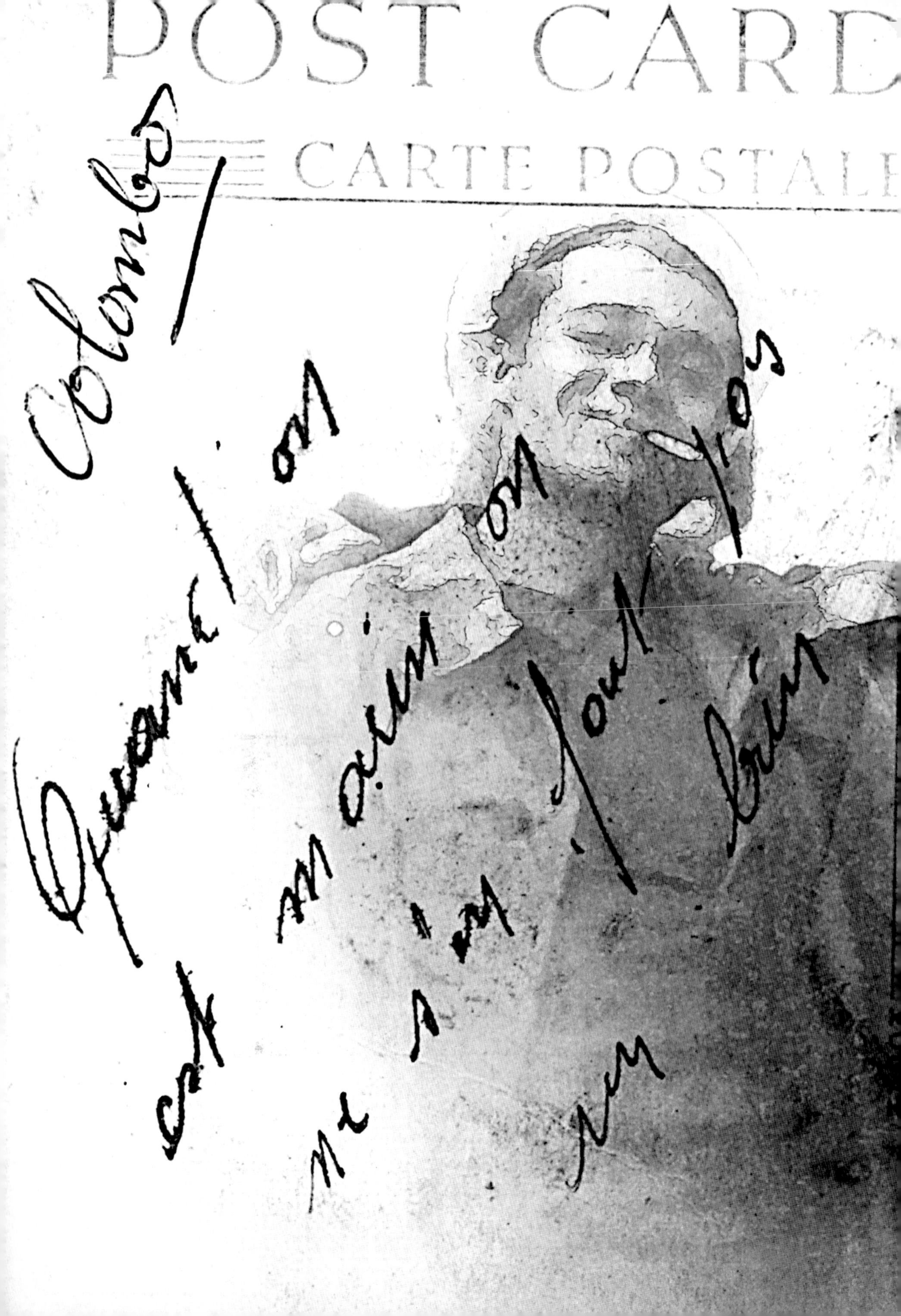
POST CARD
CARTE POSTALE

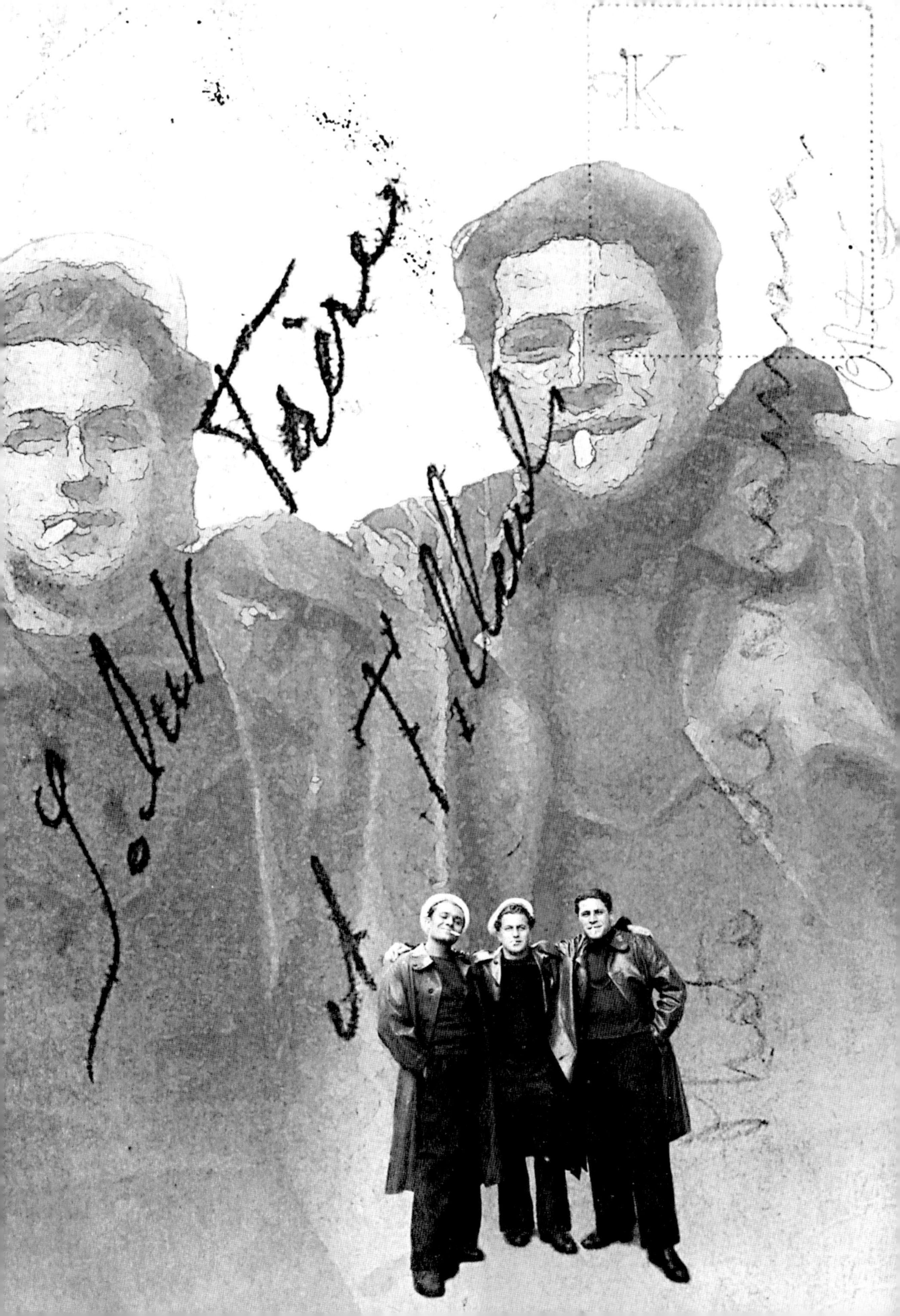